汉英对照

省级非物质文化遗产普及用书

Shandong Provincial Intangible Cultural Heritage Popular Edition
Folklore Volume(Book Two)

下

山东省文化和旅游厅组织编写　　潘帅英　译

济南出版社　汉唐书局

图书在版编目（CIP）数据

山东省级非物质文化遗产普及用书. 民俗卷. 下 ：汉英对照 / 山东省文化和旅游厅编；潘帅英译. —济南：济南出版社，2023.9

ISBN 978-7-5488-5384-8

Ⅰ. ①山… Ⅱ. ①山… ②潘… Ⅲ. ①非物质文化遗产—山东—普及读物—汉、英 ②风俗习惯—介绍—山东—汉、英 Ⅳ. ①G127.52-49 ②K892.452

中国国家版本馆CIP数据核字（2023）第178168号

山东省级非物质文化遗产普及用书　民俗卷（下）

Shandong Provincial Intangible Cultural Heritage Popular Edition

Folklore Volume（Book Two）

出 版 人　谢金岭
图书策划　冀瑞雪
责任编辑　孙育臣
装帧设计　曹晶晶

出版发行　济南出版社
地　　址　山东省济南市二环南路1号（250002）
总 编 室　0531-86131715
印　　刷　山东潍坊新华印务有限责任公司
版　　次　2024年3月第1版
印　　次　2024年3月第1次印刷
开　　本　170mm × 240mm　16开
印　　张　14.75
字　　数　220千字
书　　号　ISBN 978-7-5488-5384-8
定　　价　49.80元

如有印装质量问题 请与出版社出版部联系调换
电话：0531-86131736

Shandong Provincial Intangible Cultural Heritage Popular Edition

Folklore Volume (Book Two)

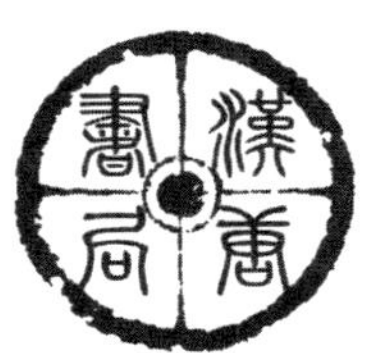
漢唐書局

FOREWORD

President Xi Jinping pointed out: "Culture is a country and nation's soul. Our country will thrive only if our culture thrives, and our nation will be strong only if our culture is strong. Excellent traditional Chinese culture is the most profound soft power of our culture, and the fertile cultural soil in which socialism with Chinese characteristics takes root. We should actively promote creative transformation and innovative development of traditional Chinese culture." Over the long history of five thousand years, Chinese civilization has been going on and on with lasting charms and giving birth to abundant spiritual and cultural wealth. Intangible cultural heritage is an important part of excellent traditional Chinese culture, the representation of lively cultural gene of the Chinese nation, the inheritance of the national history and the condensation of the national spirit, and the vivid expression of the wisdom of the working people since ancient times. We should inherit and carry forward excellent traditional Chinese culture, excavate and preserve intangible cultural heritage of the Chinese nation, research and benefit from excellent cultural heritage in Qilu (i.e. Shandong province), which is the requirements of the era, the necessity of the history, and the expectation of the people.

Shandong province, both the hometown of Confucius and Mencius and the land of ceremonies, has a long history and brilliant civilization as an important part of Chinese civilization. Distinctive and charming intangible cultural heritage has been developing in the vast land of Qilu. The creativity and wisdom of Qilu people are fully implicated in mysterious and fascinating folk literature, folkloric traditions with distinct geographic features, traditional music in various styles, traditional dance with unique charm, traditional arts with endless meanings, charming and graceful operas and Quyi (Chinese folk art forms; including ballad singing, story telling, comic dialogues, clapper talks, cross talks, etc.), dexterous acrobatics and creative handcrafts, which are the important representatives of Qilu culture. Brilliant intangible cultural heritage fully demonstrates the aesthetic feature and peculiar thinking mode of Qilu people and witnesses the cultural development of Shandong province.

Shandong province, affluent in intangible cultural heritage, has taken the lead in protection work. At present, there are 8 projects in the "Representative List of the Intangible Cultural Heritage of Humanity" recognized by UNESCO (United Nations Educational, Scientific and Cultural Organization), 173 by nation, and 751 by province. Besides, there are 51 national inheritors and 296 provincial inheritors, three enterprises named as "Productive Protection and Demonstration Base of National Intangible Cultural Heritage" by the Ministry of Culture, 68 provincial intangible cultural heritage productive protection and demonstration bases, one national and nine provincial experimental areas for cultural and ecological protection. The series books, Shandong Provincial Intangible Cultural Heritage Popular Edition, which are composed of three books giving account of eighty provincial projects on folk literature and two books giving account of fifty provincial projects on folklore. The content of these books is mainly based on various cities' declaring source material data of representative projects for provincial intangible cultural heritage.

Intangible cultural heritage in these books, covering historical origin, basic introduction, expressing patterns, inheritance and development, social value, etc., are introduced by means of story–telling, cultural interpretation, picture with words and multi–perspectives. It is believed that the publication and popularization of these books, which make us have a more vivid, comprehensive and systematic understanding of Shandong provincial intangible cultural heritage, will further enhance the cultural self–confidence and cultural pride of the general public.

Furthermore, we will thoroughly implement the essence of the 20th National Congress of the Communist Party of China, the spirit of the important speeches by the General Secretary Xi Jinping, including speeches during his Shandong inspection visit. And we should take Xi Jinping Thought on Socialism with Chinese Characteristics for the New Era as the guide, promote balanced economic, political, cultural, social, and ecological progress, coordinate implementation of the Four-pronged Comprehensive Strategy, and constantly carry forward the outstanding traditional Chinese culture, constantly promote the cultural construction in depth. All we should do is to meet people's eagerness for a better life, to make contributions to enriching their cultural life, protecting their cultural rights and interests, further promoting the construction of a strong economic and cultural province, and realizing the Chinese dream of great rejuvenation of the Chinese nation.

Wang Lei

Director of the Shandong Provincial Department of Culture and Tourism

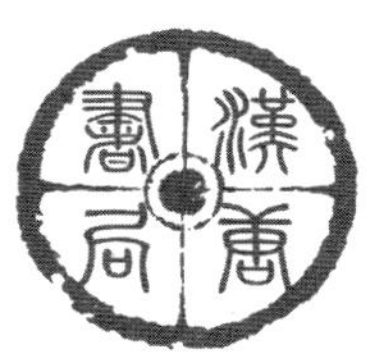
漢唐書局

CONTENTS

目录

Laiyang Bean-flour Bowl Lamp Custom

In 2013, "Laiyang Bean-flour Bowl Lamp Custom" was listed in the third batch of provincial intangible cultural heritage by Shandong Provincial People's Government.

Laiyang Bean-flour Bowl Lamp, usually called Bowl Lamp, is a unique local folklore. This folklore has been popular in more than ten towns and counties within the area under its jurisdiction, in which towns of Wandi, Tangezhuang, Muyudian, Zhaowangzhuang and Tuanwang have been well-known as the representative ones because of their large scale and profound effects.

Lighting lamps on the Lantern Festival can be traced back to the Han Dynasty. Then lantern appreciation activities became more popular in the Tang Dynasty because of the prosperity of the nation and the open-mindedness of the people. The Lantern Festival was paid more attention in the Song Dynasty, which was recorded in *the Reminiscences of the Eastern Capital Bianliang* (*Dongjing Menghua Lu*) written by Meng Yuanlao in the Southern Song Dynasty that people used bean flour to make dough figurines of flowers, birds, fish and insects for sacrifices and tributes. Ever since the Ming Dynasty, lantern appreciation activities lasted ten days continuously from the day of the Lantern Festival. It's recorded in *County Annals of Cheng Cheng* written by Mali in the Ming Dynasty that buckwheat-flour bowl lamps were steamed on the fifteenth day of the first lunar month and then were lighted with peanut oil to be eaten the next morning. What mentioned here was the exact lamps made of bean flour.

There are more than twenty kinds of various Laiyang bean-flour bowl lamps, such common ones are those of the twelve Zodiacal animals, the twelve months, the "Kanchanglao" (an elder man on watch of the yard), five blessings (longevity, wealth, health, love of virtue, and natural death), the Kitchen God, poultry and animals, each of which contains special connotations. For instance, knead the dough into a figurine of a dog and put it at the main entrance, which symbolizes guarding the house and worshiping for safety; knead the dough into a figurine of sacred worm (snake) and put it on the windowsill, which symbolizes being invincible to all poisons; knead the dough into a figurine of a horse and put it in the stable, which symbolizes blessing health and strength for horses; lighting bowl lamps of pigs means that pigs will be full of fat in the sty still. In addition, the auspicious connotation of luck, wealth, longevity, and happiness can be represented by relevant animals or plants. For example, the implied meaning of bat dough figurine is Fortune; the homo-phonic meaning of the magpie lamp is for jubilation and the rooster one for luck; the lotus lamp, with a connotation of lotus seeds, is made to pray for more sons.

The most famous bean-flour bowl lamp is that of twelve months, which can divine ups and downs of the coming twelve months by the size of the sparks let off from the lamps. When the light turned off, the remaining oil could foresee drought or flood of the twelve months in the coming year. It's recorded in *Laiyang County Annals* during the Qing Dynasty, "Then bean-flour bowl lamps are to be made and steamed to divine whether there will be drought or flood in the next twelve months". That was to say, there were bowl lamps made from bean flour in Laiyang under the reign of Emperor Kang Xi during the Qing Dynasty.

There was a story about bowl lamps widely spread in Laiyang. The story went like this. It was said that Jiang Ziya granted titles to all gods and found that he was the only one left out, so he granted himself the Lantern God on the night of the Lantern Festival. Jiang Ziya would go to solve problems on that night when he found wherever there was light in the house. No matter of wishes or sues, he would tackle with it one by one. If the time was up, he would continue to solve it on the Lantern Festival at the same time the next year.

The custom of making bean–flour bowl lamps evolved from the folklore of lantern display at the lantern fair and lighting fireworks on the Lantern Festival. Nowadays, lanterns and fireworks have leaped out of the ravine of Laiyang and entered the site of some government–organized special activities. As farmers' hope in the heart, bean–flour bowl lamps have been still surviving all the households in Laiyang for their unique simplicity.

Laiyang Bean–flour Bowl Lamp Custom is divided into two parts: "Kneading Lamp" and "Sending Lamp".

The first step is "Kneading Lamp": Pinch the dough into a figurine of a bowl with a light wick. Laiyang bean–flour bowl lamp is mainly made of soybean flour. Before making the lamp, mix the bean flour with edible oil and knead it into a dough. The bean flour mixed with oil then becomes very stringy, and the bean–flour bowl lamp can be made with delicate details and craftsmanship. It can glitter a golden halo after being lighted, and thus it is also called "golden lamp".

Among Laiyang bean–flour bowl lamps, the ordinary ones are used for ancestral worship and their original color doesn't change while the colored ones are often made for family genealogy and festivity. The colored dough is pinched by mixing the vegetable soups directly into the bean flour repeatedly until the color of the vegetable becomes the original color of the dough, which mainly includes the color of bright red, bottle green and yellow embellished by other colors with a style of great fortune and prestige as a whole, as if the ancient Egyptians decorated their finished sculptures with colored drawings.

To make bean–flour bowl lamps, the first step is to rough the pinched dough into an embryonic miniature of all kinds of lamps. Then, the processed work is made by means of combs, scissors, mung beans, matchsticks, bamboo strips, coins and other instruments to refine such parts like the head of a pig, the scales of a dragon, the eyes of a hedgehog, etc. The whole process of pinching is random, basically blended with design and creation into a variety of vivid creatures. Last but not the least, a lovely bean–flour bowl lamp is finished with a match stick entangled with a sliver of cotton as the wick inserted in the bowl lamp.

Laiyang bean–flour bowl lamps not only imply blessings but also reflect people's livelihood. For instance, the poor families usually make the lamps of tiger or heavenly hound, etc. Tiger means power while heavenly hound holds a shoe–shaped gold ingot in his mouth with the implication of getting a fortune. Farmers who often suffered from insect pests usually make the lamps of golden toads and frogs and put them on the field manure piles with the implication of blessings for no insect pests in the coming year. Some bowl lamps have such profound meanings like being more (put them onto the grain bin) or being clean (put them onto the water vat), etc. Bowl lamps imply differently in different locations or different environment.

In addition to "Kneading Lamp", "Sending Lamp" is also an important part which constitutes Laiyang Bean–flour Bowl Lamp Custom.

"Sending Lamp" is extremely referential, and little sounds can be heard except for the necessary muttering incantations and greetings during the whole process. When it comes to "Sending Lamp", the husband of every family will sit on the warmer end of a brick bed smoking silently, watch his son deliver one lamp upon another over to his wife and walk around the cowshed or the pigsty once in a while; and the hostess of every household will pour oil to light the lamp stick. In fact, it's full of mystery starting from the moment of sending lamps formally, so people will become respectful and obedient unconsciously.

Because the Kitchen God means everything to farmers, the first lamp delivered is generally starting from it; then the "sacred worm" (snake) lamp is put onto the grain container and the "Kanchanglao" (Watchman) lamp is shaped like an elder man shouldering various tools to the courtyard guarding the threshing floor during the harvest season; and then it comes to the "Zodiac" lamps shaped like horses, dogs, pigs, roosters and so on successively. The order of delivering the lamps is basically in accordance with gods, eating, housing, poultry and livestock including the indispensable "Zodiac" animals.

The custom of sending lamps contains special poetic existence. For instance, while sending lamps, people sing ballads like this, "Shed light on the heath, the scorpion will not sting your mom; shed light on the warmer side of a brick bed, the scorpion will not bite your dad; shed light on the window, the scorpion will not sting your kids." When it comes to send the "Kanchanglao" (Watchman) lamp, turn forward and backward three circles around the yard while walking and singing "The watchman runs all over, the grains harvested cannot be eaten; the watchman runs around the yard, the grains harvested cannot be eaten fully".

In a word, the activities involved with the custom of bowl lamps are closely related to people's daily lives and feelings. When it grows dark at night, fathers will lead their kids towards their ancestral grave to deliver lamps with few crying due to the story that the passed away in the family tend to like serenity. Fathers and sons, the two generations, will speak in turn "secret words" to their ancestors under the ground. No matter of best wishes or thanks-giving, or such feelings as anger, complaint, hatred, "to inform" of the passed away is aiming at the simple and pure wishes carried out by God.

Laiyang Bean-flour Bowl Lamp is typical of the cultivation culture abundant in both content and form. It is not only one of the activities for farmers to bless for best wishes but also the essential parts of the folklore culture. Laiyang bean–flour bowl lamps are one of the arts created by Laiyang people according to their own localities, festivals and customs, rooted deeply in the living soil of the laborers and full of bright artistic characteristics and living interest. This custom is popular with ordinary folk people, which is in fact the activity blended with blessings and sacrificial rites originating from the horror and worships of the mankind for the natural power, worries for fortune and best wishes for life. Throughout a series of activities by means of "Kneading Lamp" and "Sending Lamp" , folk mentality and aesthetic interest will be obviously and naturally revealed.

Laiyang Bean–flour Bowl Lamps, the indispensable real materials to study on the history, folklore and aesthetics of the Jiaodong Island, have profound historical and practical value. The valuable content learned from this custom is helpful for us to understand Laiyang culture profoundly and will offer valuable lessons and materials for us to inherit and develop the traditional Laiyang folklore. From this point of view, it's of great significance for us to protect folklore cultural heritage for the purpose of reflecting local cultural features and developing traditional Chinese culture.

Sacrifice to Mount Yi the Eastern Garrison

In 2013, "Sacrifice to Mount Yi the Eastern Garrison" of Linqu County was listed in the third batch of provincial intangible cultural heritage by Shandong Provincial People's Government. In 2014, Zhang Xiaoyou (male) was listed as the representative inheritor of the fourth batch of provincial intangible cultural heritage by Shandong Provincial People's Government.

Mount Yi, located in the Southern Linqu County of Shandong Province, is the birthplace of River Yi, River Wen, River Shu and River Mi, and also the birthplace of "Longshan Culture". Mount Yi was called "the Mountain above the Ocean" at ancient time (see *the History of Ming*) "the Sacred Mountain" (see *Ode to the Capital of Qi State*), and was called the Eastern Mount Tai, the Eastern Garrison (Dongzhen), which means the eastern main peak of the Taiyi mountains. The ancient people once praised it "as lofty and towering as Mount Tai, beautiful scenery absorb people's sights in appearance and in fact it is a gigantic garrison in the east of Qi State". Therefore, there's a saying in history that "Mount Tai ranks the first of the Five Sacred Mountains, and Mount Yi ranks the first of the Five Mountain Garrisons".

It was recorded in *The Records of the Grand Historian: the Book of Offering Sacrifices to the Heaven and the Earth on Mount Tai* that Huangdi climbed the Eastern Mount Tai (i.e. Mount Yi) offering sacrifices to the Heaven and the Earth; Emperor Shun offered sacrifices at Zhaozhou and chose Mount Yi as garrison of strategic importance; Emperor Yu also offered sacrifices on Mount Yi; and Mount Yi had been added sacrifices offering throughout the past Dynasties of Han, Sui, Tang, Song, Yuan, Ming, and Qing. During the Tang Dynasty, Mount Yi was conferred a title as "Peace Master of the East"; when it came to the Song Dynasty, Mount Yi was bestowed a title as "Peace King in the East"; In the Yuan Dynasty, Mount Yi was added a title as "Peace King in the East for Prime Virtue"; In the third year when Emperor Zhu Yuanzhang took his throne (1370), Mount Yi was bestowed a title as "God of Mount Yi the Eastern Garrison" in the form of imperial edict; when it came to the second year in the reign of Emperor Yongzheng in the Qing Dynasty (1724), Mount Yi was bestowed a title as "God of Mount Yi for Defending against Enemies and Safeguarding People" by Emperor Yongzheng the Shizong of the Qing Dynasty.

Emperors and generals conferred titles and offered sacrifices to Mount Yi, and letters of men wrote poems for it. When it came to the end of the Qing Dynasty, stone rubbings of big or small sizes in front of the Eastern Garrison Temple had arrived at more than 360 tablets, which formed the grand Forest of Stone Tablets in the Eastern Garrison, including *Imperial Monument in the Third Year of Qiande Taizu Zhao Kuangyin in the Song Dynasty, Imperial Inscription in the Reign of Jingyou by Renzong in the Song Dynasty, Mongolian-Chinese Bilingual Monument by Tie Muer the Second Emperor in the Dade Second Year of the Yuan Dynasty Conferring a Title to Mount Yi as Peace King in the East, Imperial Monument by Emperor Zhu Yuanzhang in the Hongwu Third Year of the Ming Dynasty Conferring a Title of "God of Mount Yi", Memorial Tablet of Sending Armed Forces to Surpassing Father An'nan and His Son Li Cang in the Yongle Fourth Year of the Ming Dynasty,*

Ghostwritten Memorial Tablet by Yang Ding the Minister of Works in the Period of Chenghua the Ming Dynasty, Imperial Ancestral Temple Stone Tablets of the Eastern Garrison Written by Jinshi Weng Shizi the Minister of Works in Hongzhi Reign of the Ming Dynasty, Handwritten Running-cursive Script Engravings Praising Mount Yi by Jinshi Chen Fengwu in Hongzhi Reign of the Ming Dynasty, Cursive Script Engravings on Sightseeing Waterfalls of Mount Yi by Zhuangyuan Zhao Bingzhong in the Period of Wanli in the Ming Dynasty, Handwritten Imperial Inscription "Beauty with Ingenuity" by Emperor Kangxi of the Qing Dynasty, Handwritten Imperial Inscription "Grand Eastern Garrison Adjacent to Mount Tai" by Emperor Qianlong, etc. The engravings and red inscriptions of these stone tablets were all from the hand writing of celebrities, not only recording and narrating the incense thriving activities of worshiping and making sacrifices to the Eastern Garrison throughout the past feudal dynasties, but also recording circumstances in military, politics and natural disasters at that time and so on, which has important reference value for the study of the history of Song, Yuan, Ming, and Qing Dynasties.

Sacrifice to Mount Yi originated from sacrifice to "the Heaven, the Earth, Rivers and Oceans", which could be traced back to the primitive worship of the ancients. This was a long-term evolutionary process, basically throughout five stages from totem worship, mountain sacrifice, mountain town sacrifice, ceremony of offering sacrifice to the Heaven and the Earth on Mount Tai, to sacrifice to the Heaven, the Earth, Rivers and Oceans. Totem worship and mountain sacrifice were primitively religious. A wealth of Confucian philosophy was fused from mountain town sacrifice to ceremony of offering sacrifice to the Heaven and the Earth on Mount Tai. However, from the mysterious sacrifice to the Heaven and the Earth on Mount Tai to sacrifice to the Heaven, the Earth, Rivers and Oceans, it made the ancients' worship for famous mountains and great rivers towards rationalization and institutionalization. Among sacrifice to the Heaven, the Earth, Rivers and Oceans, sacrifice to the Heaven and the

Earth was the most important part, because Yue (Zhen) was the symbol of the country. "the Five Sacred Mountains" was the representative of the "Heaven" and the symbol of benevolence and dignity while "the Five Mountain Garrisons" was the symbol of the "Earth" and the symbolization of domain and sovereignty.

According to historical recordings, the time for sacrifice to Mount Yi the Eastern Garrison was the second lunar month before Shang and Zhou Dynasties while the God for sacrifice was Tian Emperor (Shun); After Sui and Tang Dynasties, the imperial memorial ceremony for mountains did not offer sacrifices to Tian Emperor but start to offer sacrifices from the Start of Spring based on the perspective of well–being in the east. From the period of Republic of China on, the imperial sacrifice to Mount Yi began to be transferred into folk sacrifice.

The sacrificial activities to Mount Yi the Eastern Garrison are hosted grandly and solemnly by the Administrative Committee of Mount Yi Scenic Area on the eighth day of the lunar April every year. In the hall of the Jade Palace, the statue of Tian Emperor is wrapped in red silks, red candles are alight high above the altar of the sacrifice, and sacrificial offerings of symbolic significance are arranged full over the case of the sacrifice like three domestic animals (i.e. cattle, sheep and pigs), rooster (with a connotation of abundant harvest of all food crops), fish (with a connotation of surplus year after year), apples (with a connotation of peace in four seasons), birthday peaches (with a connotation of living to a hundred or beyond), wheat, corn, soybean, deep beam, sesame (with a connotation of abundant grain harvest), etc. A flagpole is put up in front of the hall, streamers decorated with gold foil fluttered in the wind on the top of the pole. A senior Taoist priest is the person in charge of the sacrificial activity, four Taoist priests in uniform stand before the altar of the sacrifice as the person first or second to offer sacrifice. During the period of the day (from 9 a.m. to 11 a.m.), sacrificial offering will be announced to commence by the master of the ceremony. Then at the grand sacrificial ceremony, smokes are curling up from the burning incense, with the rolling sounds of music and drums (bell, drum, lyre, lute, Sheng, gong, cymbals, etc.). The mater of the ceremony arranges the person in charge of activities to welcome and greet gods, offering wine, worship gods, and recite the prayers. The first movement for sacrifice to Mount Yi the Easter Garrison is "stare towards the east to greet gods in peacefulness", and the prayer reads "the most lofty virtue only exists in woods; the refreshing grasses absorb the gods that bring birth to all beings; Mount Yi, Mount Tai and the Ocean of Huai comes into being; while the common people deserves the credit; thus a large number of altars and sills spring out; praises are supposed to all gods; the smell of sacrificial offerings arrive in advance; then gods and spirits all come along". The second movement is "keep peaceful at sunrise and sunset all the time", and the prayer reads "a waist belt is tied to leather garments tidily; a jade pendant attached to the waist belt looks fresh as the heart of flowers; as for what I am going to do, a sacred swallow seems joyous for it; the emperor orders to prepare for the sacrifice rites; who dare not to do it altogether? Everyone bustles to and fro at his exact post, solemnly and harmoniously". In addition, the following movement is "offer jade coins in sacrificial rites for safety", "offer wines in sacrificial rites for safety", "send off gods for peace and safety", "welcome gods in the east in peacefulness", "wash hands after the first offering for safety altogether", "offer jade coins for safety altogether", "offer sacrifices in the post of the eastern garrison", "offer wines at the last second time (the same for the four positions)", "send off gods for peace and safety" and so on successively. The prayers among these movements mostly are fabulous words of praises and eulogies.

After chanting the movements of the sacrificial rite, the common people participating in the sacrificial rite spontaneously burn paper money in order and bow to Tian Emperor with hands holding together three times as an etiquette. The bowing action is supposed to follow the Taoist rites, and the exact orders are as follows: hold the thumb of the left hand in the right hand, make a bow, place the right hand on the Mat for kneeling, protect the pubic region by the left hand, two knees kneel down on the Mat, the right hand press on the left hand, kowtow, stand up by protecting the pubic region with the left hand, the right hand holds the thumb of the left hand shaped like Yin and Yang.

On the day of the sacrifice, temple fairs are also held at the mountain market temple beside a pavilion named grassy hill (the site of long-distance salute by Taizu Zhaokuangyin of the Song Dynasty) at the east gate of Mount Yi, which are echoed with grand sacrificial rites held in the Jade Palace at a distance. There are very lively markets of mountain goods, antiques, jewels and ornaments, flower roots, carvings and grotesque stones, etc, like a feast for the eyes. In addition, on the day of the sacrificial rites, a theatre stage is set up at the mountain pass, on act from 9 a.m. to 4 p.m.

The sacrificial activities to Mount Yi the Eastern Garrison have been deeply popular with the general public all the time. The sacrificial rites to the Eastern Garrison can not be inherited without the efforts of generation after generation. Zhang Xiaoyou, who is in charge of the Temple of Mount Yi the Eastern Garrison and who nicknames himself auspice of the Temple of the Eastern Garrison, works together with his "comrade-in-arms" in safeguarding Mount Yi. "The more beautiful Mount Yi becomes in landscapes, the more valuable historical relics become, and the more pressure we're under. Not to mention the forest coverage of Mount Yi has arrived at 98.6% as a national 4A-class scenic spot crowded with tourists every day with a climax up to more than 20,000, so it's necessary for more frequent look-out, inspection and safeguarding." During the past many years, Zhang Xiaoyou and other mountain watchers have safeguarded Mount Yi like their own sons, so they are quite clear about the location and the content of every stone table, even more clear about which edge of the field every stone table came from.

Thanks to the efforts of mountain watchers of generation after generation, the sacrificial rites to Mount Yi the Eastern Garrison can get better inheritance and development. Just as what Wang Qingzeng the associate research librarian in Linqu County Library of Weifang city, "Imperial sacrifices lasted from the period of the Five Emperors to the Qing Dynasty, then developed into folk sacrifices in the period of the Republic of China, but both of them came from the same cultural source. As the descendants of Chinese nation, We should carry forward the tradition of sacrificial rites to Mount Yi for the sake of cultural roots seeking."

Pilgrimages to Emperor Dongyue and Goddess Bixia

In 2013, "Pilgrimages to Emperor Dongyue and Goddess Bixia" of Tai'an City was listed in the third batch of provincial intangible cultural heritage by Shandong Provincial People's Government.

Pilgrimages to Emperor Dongyue and Goddess Bixia originated from Mount Tai, centered with Mount Tai, and influenced all the other places across the whole country. Mount Tai was regarded by the ancient people as the place of the origin of life and respected by generations of mountain people. The worship of Mount Tai in the earlier period, with the change of socialist policies and the transmission of cultures, gradually developed into offering sacrifices to and paying homage to the Heaven and the Earth by emperors. According to the testifying by Sima Qian in *The Records of the Grand Historian: the Book of Offering Sacrifices to the Heaven and the Earth on Mount Tai*, several ancient emperors followed one by one to Mount Tai for the worship of the Heaven and the Earth. In addition, because of the oriental worship ever since the distant ancient times, Mount Tai evolved into Emperor Dongyue—Emperor of the East Sacred Mountain. A verse in the Han Dynasty went like this, "Climb Mount Tai, worship the God ... drive the Flood Dragon, and step on the floating clouds ..." (*Mount Tai Lens Mirror*), which described Emperor of the East Sacred Mountain to the point.

Along with emperors of dynasties offering sacrifices to the Heaven and the Earth on Mount Tai, the influence of God Mount Tai started to be immersed into every layer of the society. Besides the emperors and ministers, the ordinary people from the whole country rushed to Mount Tai for worship and pilgrimage. Emperor Xuan Zong in the Tang Dynasty conferred titles of nobility on Mount Tai as "King to the Heaven". During this period, those who went to Mount Tai for offering sacrifices to the Heaven and the Earth included not only emperors, but all the other people from the imperial family frequently went to Mount Tai for worship, and the pilgrimage to God Mount Tai was enlarged further. Emperor Zhenzong of the Song Dynasty conferred titles of nobility on God Mount Tai as "Merciful Sacred King to the Heaven", "Merciful Sacred Emperor to the Heaven" and set March 28th in the lunar calendar for the date to celebrate its birthday. After Dynasties of the Tang and Song, the influence of the pilgrimage to God Mount Tai became increasingly deepened, large activities were held regularly, and evolved into temple fairs. Emperor Yuan Kublai Khan canonized God Mount Tai as "Merciful Sacred Emperor the Great to the Heaven" in twenty-eight year of Zhiyuan (in 1291). Thanks to the recommendation and worship of emperors, the status of God Mount Tai become more prominent. In the Hongzhi sixteenth-year of the Ming Dynasty (in 1503), it's recorded in *The Filial Piety Imperial Tablet System Rebuilt Temple of the East Sacred Mount Memorial*, "Temples of the East Sacred Mountain were set up all over the country, and that set up on Mount Tai was built for peculiar worship and thus was paid special attention by all dynasties. Therefore, the regulations of the temple was superior to those of the others, and incense burning was especially thriving." The contemporary famous writer Wang Zengqi recorded in *Mount Tai Piece Stone*, "Emperors of all dynasties canonized God Mount Tai several times, and the common people called it Emperor of the East Sacred Mountain. There was almost one temple of the East Sacred Mountain throughout the country, which is called Mount Tai Temple. The Mount Tai Temple of our county is quite near my home..." From the ancient governments' attention to Mount Tai and the common people's worship for it along with the works of ancient and contemporary scholars, we can see people's reverence and worship for Mount Tai and Emperor of Mount Tai.

Goddess Bixia (Sovereign of the Clouds of Dawn) was also called "Mount Tai the Jade Girl" and "Mount Tai the Granny" or "Mount Tai the Empress" among the people. According to the recording written by Zhang Erqi in the Qing Dynasty, there was sculptures of a golden boy and a jade girl in front of the palace of Benevolent Emperor in the Han Dynasty. With time passing by, the palace fell down; the sculptures fell down, too, because the sculpture of the golden boy was eroded by winds and rains and the sculpture of the jade girl fell down into the pool which was thus called the Pool of Mount Tai the Jade Girl. It's said that Emperor Zhen Zong of the Song Dynasty considered that the goddess showed her spirits because the sculpture of the Jade Girl floated out of the water unexpectedly when he washed his hands in the Pool of Mount Tai the Jade Girl. Therefore, he ordered to dredge this pool, have the sculpture re-carved in white jade, set up a temple and rename it as the Ancestral Temple Showing the Truth, and assign the messengers to perform sacrificial activities and worship her as "Daughter of the Holy Emperor" and canonize her as "Fairy Princess Bixia Yuanjun" . This is the origin of the name Goddess Bixia.

In the Ming Dynasty, the Ancestral Temple Showing the Truth was renamed as the Palace of the Spirit. Ever since Dynasties of the Song and Yuan, the influence of Goddess Bixia even surpassed God Mount Tai, so the temple fair of Mount Tai the Empress thrived. March 15th was the birthday of Mount Tai the Empress every year, and the number of people who rushed to the temple fair even exceeded that to March 28th temple fair. In the Emperor Wanli twenty-second year of the Ming Dynasty(in 1594), Wang Xijue wrote in *Dongyue Bixia Palace Museum*, "Walking along the route of kingdom of Qi and Lu, Buddha recited amitabha in mind for fasting thousands of *li* afar, although they wore a pair of straw sandals with calluses on their feet for the rest of life. When asked by others what they're going to do, they answered 'to ask Bixia to do some favour in some matters'. When asked why they asked her to do favour, they answered, 'Yuanjun can bring benefit to all living creatures as they wish.'" Goddess Bixia described in the folklore had vast magic powers. It's believed that this goddess can shelter all the beings, solve the puzzle for adherents, and bless all the living creatures. There are three temples named the upper temple, the middle temple and the lower temple, and lots of "the Goddess Temple" set up in other places. Goddess Bixia is deeply loved and esteemed by the civilians, and the incense lit up for her has never been stopped and interrupted after a thousand years.

The main approaches to express belief in God Mount Tai are worships and pilgrimages. Persons to pilgrimage are called "pilgrims" or "the officers who bring incenses". Those who bring incenses altogether in an organized group are called "the community of pilgrimage". Generally speaking, the community of pilgrimage consists of the pilgrims of a village or several villages, the number of the pilgrims is somehow not fixed, and the organizer, called the head of the incense, the head of the society or the head of the goodness, was usually held by the highly respected local person.

The community of pilgrimage consists of a set of complete organization and etiquette system. It's generally necessary to agree on the date for the incense burning and prepare for such incense etiquette like God's robe, bells and drums, and flags, etc. There are ceremonies to be held when we start off for pilgrimage, one of which is to pray for a safe journey, and the other of which is to convey the message to Emperor of the East Sacred Mountain or Empress of Mount Tai in advance. The regular pilgrimage is to burn a pillar of incense, while "acting clubs" occurred at greater ceremonies of a pilgrimage, which means that Emperor of the East Sacred Mountain or Empress of Mount Tai carried in a royal carriage paraded along the streets burning the incenses to inform people that the ranks of those for pilgrimage is about to start off. During the journey of pilgrimage, those in the ranks of incense society all beat gongs and drums, march ahead with music, lift their own flags, drum up and set off firecrackers while passing by a village; when they arrive at Mount Tai, they worship the Temple of Mount Tai and then sacrifice to the Ancestral Temple of Goddess Bixia, which is described in great detail in literary works like *A Tale of Lucky Marriage to Awaken the World*.

There are many stone tablets recording pilgrimages in Mount Tai, more than thirty stone tablets in front of the northern gate to Red Gate Palace, which record such content like that about pilgrims praying for gods and goddesses, overdoing the dead for the feathered Taoist, burning incenses and redeeming a vow, etc. Famous inscriptions like *Inscription of Beidou* (*Big Dipper*) *Saint Opportunity Title* read at the very beginning, "Pray for (Qifu) longevity (Yansheng) and practice fasting (Xiuzhai), comply with well-being and hope for everything going well; congratulate for longevity wishes showed in Huazhou, and put it in priority among the three congratulatory wishes for longevity, happiness and many descendants." "Qifu" means praying for good fortunes blessed by gods; "Yansheng" means sacrificial rituals to pray for longevity; "Xiuzhai" means gathering monks and Taoists and serving them fasting. There are more than 360 stone monuments for pilgrimage saved to today on Mount Tai, and those who set up such stone monuments come from more than twenty provinces and cities all over the country including Fujian province to the south and Heilongjiang province to the north.

Besides worships and pilgrimages, beliefs in Emperor Dongyue and Goddess Bixia by people in Tai'an evolve into activities closer to life, which are temple fairs. Temple fairs in Mount Tai develop continuously and are added into such new activities as trade and entertainment to serve worshipers from far and near. Thanks to the constant expansion of the influence of Goddess Bixia, the time of the temple fair in

Mount Tai the East Mountain has been extended and the sacrificial rites of worshiping Goddess Bixia have been increased.

The temple fair we saw so far included various trade activities, tourist sightseeing and cultural entertainment in addition to normal religious activities. From the peculiarly charming folk music to the breathtaking amusement competition, from the mountain worship ceremony to the grand ceremony of offering sacrifices to the Heaven and the Earth on Mount Tai, peculiar local cultural features fill every corner of the temple fair in Mount Tai the East Sacred Mountain, which can let the tourists on the temple fair feel colorful and unique cultural atmosphere all the time. There are more and more folklore activities deriving from the pilgrimages to Emperor Dongyue and Goddess Bixia for the purpose of enriching people's daily life and spiritual world.

Jiaodong Jiaozi Cuisine Custom

In 2013, “Jiaodong Jiaozi Cuisine Custom” of Rongcheng City was listed in the third batch of provincial intangible cultural heritage by Shandong Provincial People’s Government.

As the saying goes, “On the mountain, one lives by mountain products. By the sea, one lives by seafood.” There are many traditional Chinese folk customs in Rongcheng with a little “taste of the sea”, among which the most typical example is eating seafood jiaozi on the Spring Festival and other holidays.

Wonton and jiaozi are the most representative foods in the northern food cultural pedigree, and the relationship between them has a long history and is very complicated. Around the Qin and Han Dynasties, there was wonton, and jiaozi was made from it while the wonton wrapper was made into a half-moon. Yan Zhitui from the Northern Qi Dynasty said in *Family Instructions of Yan Clan*, “Modern wonton is moon-shaped and is quite popular at that time.” In recent decades, jiaozi in the Tang Dynasty has been repeatedly found in archaeological investigation, indicating that jiaozi had been widely circulated at that time.

According to what recorded in ancient Chinese literature materials, due to the differences of age, region, production method and fillings inserted, there were different names of jiaozi like "jiao zi" (silver coin) "jiao er" (horn) "pink jiao" (pink angle) "dumpling" "wonton" "dumpling bait" "boiled bun" "boiled dumplings". "Jiao" (角) is the pictographic reference of jiaozi, while "jiao (角)" "jiao" (交) and "jiao" (饺) is homophonic, thus the name of Jiaozi came into being. Around the Ming and Qing Dynasties, eating jiaozi had become a custom throughout northern China. At this time, the appellation of jiaozi is more diversified, in addition to "jiao zi" "dumpling" "dumplings" and other previous titles, there are also "water jiaozi" "water dessert" "water dot" "soup jiaozi" and other names, the names of jiaozi was quite different due to different regions and production methods.

According to some relevant historical records, the custom of eating jiaozi on the Eve or the first day of the Spring Festival began to be popular as early as the Ming Dynasty and flourished in the Qing Dynasty. The meaning of "eating jiaozi at the moment the old year is replaced by the new" (Geng Sui Jiao zi) basically formed in the Ming and Qing Dynasties, and became a national custom.

Jiaozi has been spread around the country, took root in a number of areas and became popular, forming a variety of jiaozi "family clan", seafood jiaozi in Jiaodong peninsular is one of them. Jiaodong peninsular was located against the sea where marine resources were very rich, ancestors in Jiaodong peninsular could choose local materials and mix different seafood with vegetables, pork with fillings to make Jiaodong seafood jiaozi typical of marine flavor.

A variety of seafood, such as Spanish mackerel, yellow croaker, sea intestines, sea cucumber, shrimp, shellfish, etc., can be filled into Jiaozi as stuffings, represented by Spanish mackerel stuffed jiaozi and eagle claw shrimp stuffed jiaozi, and their production processes are not very complicated. To make Spanish mackerel stuffed jiaozi, people need to prepare Spanish mackerel, soy sauce, pure water, pork belly, ginger, scallion, cabbage, chives, peanut oil, salt, vinegar, sesame oil, wheat flour and other ingredients. After it is prepared, the first step is to deal with Spanish mackerel. The fresh Spanish mackerel should be first cleaned, its head removed, its belly taken out, its internal organs removed, then the fish flesh cut from the fish body and the fish bones removed with a kitchen knife. The second step is to make the meat stuffing. The first step is to prepare a bowl of soy sauce with a little water, chopping the stuffing while sparkling the soy sauce on it, which can not only season the meat but also make the meat not to attach to the knife and remove the fishy smell of the fish as well. When people chop the fish, they should pay attention to the delicate degree of meat stuffing, which must be minced into muddy state so that the jiaozi made can taste moderate in softness and hardness. To add adequate amount of water for diluting the Spanish mackerel stuffing, stir it by hand in order to make the meat stuffing more soft and the juice more full for better taste after cooking. The next step is to cut the pork belly into pieces of 1 cm, and remember not to crush them. Because the heavy fat of shredded pork belly will be lost, which will affect the taste and flavor of jiaozi. Then cut the ginger into dots, remove the spring onion leaves and chop them into slices, join all of them into the pork, pour right amount of soy sauce, stir with chopsticks, pickle for a period of time, and the longer the pickle time the better but in no less than twenty minutes. This can not only make the pork belly tasty but also remove the smell of pork. Garnish dishes can be prepared while the stuffing waiting to be pickled. Cut off the head and tail of the whole cabbage (with cabbages stored in the cellar as the first preference), and only choose the juicy middle part. Cut the cabbage into small pieces and pour in some peanut oil to keep the fresh flavor of it. Take right amount of fresh chives (the first cut of spring chives as the best choice), wash them and cut into pieces, and reserve for usage. Then pour the pickled pork into the Spanish mackerel stuffing, add right amount of salt according to your own taste, stir it in a clockwise direction. The longer the stirring time is, the thicker and more delicate the meat stuffing will be. Do not stop stirring it halfway until it has been stirred well. This is the most difficult part of the whole process.When the mixture is pretty good, add the chopped cabbage and chives minces and then stir it in a clockwise direction. After mixing, add a little vinegar and sesame oil to the stuffing and stir it well. The vinegar should be appropriate to avoid tasting astringent. The last step is to make jiaozi. The making of jiaozi wrapper is also exquisite, and it's advised to choose the newly ground wheat flour to knead dough with cold water and into a more "chewy" one appropriate for making jiaozi and then cover it with a basin to make it yeast. Place the fermented dough on the chopping board until it becomes soft and shiny. Then knead the fermented dough into even-sized "dough sheets", flattened them, rolling them with a rolling pin into jiaozi wrappers of 10 cm in diameter and a little thick in the middle and a little thin surrounding all sides; and then wrap the stuffing into it and knead the edges of it into the shape of a gold or silver ingot. While making jiaozi, the whole family sit around table watching TV programs, talking and laughing happily and harmoniously. Jiaozi is supposed to be put on the exact round curtain made from wheat straw from the middle to the outer ring with an implication of the ring of wealth.

The difference in the production steps between eagle claw shrimp jiaozi with Spanish mackerel jiaozi lie mainly in the jiaozi stuffing. To make the eagle claw shrimp jiaozi stuffing, it needs to prepare eagle claw shrimps, chives, cabbage, pork, soy sauce, ginger, minced green onion and other ingredients. First, peel the shrimps. When peeling the shrimps, the person is supposed to peel it with light, fast and accurate hands, and the head and tail of the shrimp should be pinched and the meat should be taken out. It is necessary to avoid waste and not have a trace of shrimp skin, and it must be clean. Second, remove off "the shrimp line", namely take out shrimp intestines. Third, cut the peeled shrimps into pieces of 1 cm with your fingernails. Do not use a knife at this step so as to prevent from the smell of the iron which can affect the flavor of the shrimp. In addition, the shrimp slices should not be too crushed or made into shrimp puree, as the stuffing will not only lose the delicious taste of the shrimps, but also look unattractive. The next step is to prepare for the side dishes. Chives should be put into the basin which can not be covered after being washed and chopped. Otherwise, it will be sulked, so it is advised to put it into the basin for mixing before making. Similarly, the cabbage is washed and chopped into minces. Finally, the shrimp meat and side dishes will be processed in the container, mixing with soy sauce, ginger, and spring onion for simmering, which can make the meat dish more flavorful.

Jiaodong Seafood Jiaozi has become a local cultural symbol, containing strong coastal characteristics and folklore characteristics of Jiaodong peninsular, which is the best reflection of Jiaodong people's homeland feelings.

The Custom of "Stringing the Yellow River"

In 2013, the Custom of "Stringing the Yellow River" of Wendeng City was listed in the third batch of provincial intangible cultural heritage by Shandong Provincial People's Government.

"Stringing the Yellow River", also known as "the Nine Turnings of the Yellow River Lantern", "the Nine Turnings of the Yellow River Array", "the Earth Lantern", "the Lantern for Safety", "the Nine Turnings Array" and "the Maze Array", is a custom with large-scale traditional folk games spread in Wendeng Prefecture. There are many explanations for its origin.

It was said that it originated from Laozi, the ancestor of Taoism, and the "Nine Turnings" is essentially the transformation of the Yin-Yang Tai Chi Diagram of Taoism. Some people said that it was evolved from the pattern of the maze in ancient wars. In addition, there was a more legendary statement that in the last years of the Shang Dynasty, Emperor Zhou was cruel, violent and unscrupulous. He was extremely loyal to his concubine Daji and did not care about the affairs of state. His ministers could not bear the life in accompany with him like a tiger, and the people could not bear heavy taxes and labor. Emperor Wu of the Zhou Dynasty decided to let Jiang Ziya lead the army to attack Emperor Zhou. He defeated Emperor Zhou's troops and horses one by one. Zhao Lang, also known as Gongming, one of the four grand marshals of Taoism, received the request of his good friend Grand Tutor Wen, planned to lead the army and fight the enemy. Zhao Gongming, accomplished in Taoism with strong magic, was a talented person who practiced in the Emei Mountain Luofu Hole holding a magic weapon with twenty four sea beads in his hands, even the immortal and leaders in Jiang Ziya's troops were not his opponent, and successively were defeated. In despair, Jiang Ziya had to ask Lu to assassinate him with magic. "The Three Xiaos" (Zhao Gongming's three sisters: Yunxiao, Qiongxiao, Bixiao), in order to avenge their brother's death, set up "the Nine Curves Yellow River Array" according to the zigzags of the Yellow River. This array was dexterous and flexible with lots of twists and turns and layers of traps, easy to defend but difficult to attack. God Erlang, Jinzha, Muzha, Nezha and other magical and powerful celestial beings were trapped in the battle, unable to escape and in face of danger. In the end, Jiang Ziya broke through the battle with the help of Laozi, the Heavenly Worthy of Primordial Being (Yuanshi Tianzun) and the Immortal Old Man of the South Pole (Nanji Xianweng). "The Three Xiaos" died after the array had been broken through. Later generations developed "the Nine Turnings of the Yellow River Array" into a recreational activity for leisure entertainment and sightseeing. Since then, this large-scale leisure activity had been handed down in Wendeng and become a local custom.

The performance location of "Stringing the Yellow River" was mostly chosen in spacious and open space. There were many kinds of arrays, such as "the Nine Turnings of the Yellow River Array", "Eight Diagrams of the Yellow River Array", "Six Cities of the Yellow River Array" and so on, winding back and forth like a maze. In Qitai Yangko *Small Siew Lamp*, the libretto about the Nine Turnings of the Yellow River Array read, "Call my sister to have a quick look; there is a lamp on the top of the stick. Based on the Eight Diagrams, the Yellow River Array is arranged. The array attracts people to swim in the river but dare not, and makes them easy to get in but hard to get out. This is what called the Nine Turnings of the Yellow River Array, zigzag like a maze with one array after another." "The Nine Turnings of the Yellow River Array" consists of 19 × 19 straw bars as stakes, and an oil lamp is installed at the end of the stakes. The stakes are spaced 1.6 meters or 2.3 meters apart, equidistant and separated by ropes. Three cities on the left and three on the right are separated by ropes, with twelve arrays communicating with each other and 361 lamps on the top of flags hanging in the gateway set up before the array. The traditional activity of "Stringing the Yellow River" must first be inspected by the "Lamp Officer" , and when the auspicious time arrives, he orders the whole audience to light the lamps. Then the "Lamp Officer" will offer incense, burn paper money and make offerings in front of the altar. Then the gun will fire three times and the drum and music will play together. The dragon team, the Yangko team, the seesaw team, the land boat team, the donkey team and the lion team would enter the field from the entrance one by one and circle around in the sea of lamps singing and dancing. If someone does not follow the path or re-enter the string, he will have to go under the rope, which is called "Drilling the Dog Hole" . When the activity comes to its climax, the crowd, the gongs and drums are loud, the lamps are bright, the procession is suddenly from the east to the west, from the south to the north, and the crowd lining up will be constantly flowing, but the atmosphere is warm and the scale is grand and fascinating.

According to the recordings of *Wendeng Cultural and Historial Records*, before 1949, large-scale "Stringing the Yellow River" activities would be held in the territory of such big villages as Lin village, Gejia village, Gao village, Kun Long and Xingjia village, Wendeng barrack, etc. on the evening of the fifteenth day of the first lunar month or on the second day in the second lunar month. However, because the event is expensive and time-consuming, and must be carefully planned by people skilled at organizing and commanding, these villages hold it every few years or even hold it for three years in a row and then suspend it once but never hold it every year. On the fifteenth day of the first lunar month in 1947, a performing show of "Stringing the Yellow River" was held. On that evening, the festive atmosphere reached its climax with tens of thousands of crowds and dozens of performing teams marching back and forth along the Yellow River.

Xing Dehai, 87 years old, from the Beixingjia village, was a man good at both array arrangement and organization. He once experienced "Stringing the Yellow River" twice when he was young. The first time was about from 1936 to 1937 when he was a teenager and that was the first time he performed in the array with his father and brother. The second time was in 1945 on the open land in front of the village land temple; Mr. Xing organized manpower, material resources and personally performed. In the 20th century, because of the construction of a reservoir, Kunlong Xingjia village was divided into three villages: North Xingjia, Middle Xingjia and South Xingjia. On the evening of the 15th day of the first lunar month in 1962, a performing activity of "Stringing the Yellow River" was held. From 1993 to 1994, Xing Dehai sponsored at his own expense two consecutive "Stringing the Yellow River" activities in the village open land, while the enthusiasm of the villagers was also extremely high, donating money and materials to show their support for the activities one after another. On the fifteenth day of the first lunar month in 1995, a large-scale activity of "Stringing the Yellow River" was held in Xingjia village. Many villagers from surrounding villages also enthusiastically sent performance teams to participate. Mr. Xing dressed himself up as a mouse in a sedan chair taking part in the performance. On June 1st, 1996, at the invitation of Wendeng Experimental Primary School, villagers organized a performance of "Stringing the Yellow River" in the school playground. The teachers and students of the whole school, along with some villagers and parents of students, experienced a feast of traditional culture.

The large-scale traditional Yangko folk leisure activity "Stringing the Yellow River" has been containing the ancient Chinese cultural tradition, enriching people's spiritual and cultural life in the past eras lack of cultural activities, which is a kind of traditional skills for us worthy to inherit forever.

Cricket Fighting Custom in Ningjin County

In 2013, "Cricket Fighting in Ningjin County" was listed in the third batch of provincial intangible cultural heritage by Shandong Provincial People's Government.

Ningjin, a county belonging to Dezhou City of Shandong, is located in the northwest of the province. Cricket fighting in China has a long history and is a typical folk custom. Since the ancient time, it has existed in every corner of China, and has been especially popular in Ningjin. While crickets are widely distributed in China, the kinds that are used for fighting usually can only be found in the middle and lower reaches of the Yangtze River and the Yellow River. Fighting crickets in Ningjin are typical of those in the middle and lower reaches of the Yellow River, and the county is acclaimed as "No. 1 County of China in Cricket Fighting".

Ningjin County's agricultural products include cereals such as wheat, corn, beans, cotton, vegetables, fruits and so on. Its soil is rich in calcium, iron, manganese, inorganic salt, and minerals. The diverse food products and fertile soil create an ideal environment for crickets. Ningjin crickets are strong in body and good at fighting.

Cricket fighting started in the Tang and Song Dynasties and reached its peak in the Ming and Qing periods. It was mainly popular in courts and among aristocrats. For the common people, they enjoyed listening to the voice of crickets and often put crickets in cages for enjoyment. According to *Memoirs of the Kaiyuan and Tianbao* (two periods while the Tang Emperor Li Longji was in reign) written by Wang Renyu of the Five Dynasties period, "When autumn comes, imperial concubines caught crickets and put them in small golden cages. At night, they put the cages beside pillows to listen to their voice. Such a custom gradually became popular among the folks." This book proved that crickets could be found both in courts and houses of the common people.

In the process of playing and observing crickets, people gradually found that male ones were bellicose, and cricket fighting became increasingly popular. Many princes and court ministers were indulged in the game, not caring about government affairs. The notorious Prime Minister Jia Sidao in the Southern Song Dynasty regarded cricket fighting as "Military Priority", and according to *History of the Song Dynasty: The Legend of Jia Sidao*, "He was still enjoying cricket fighting when the Mongolian soldiers surrounded Xiangyang (a strategic city) and the court was in great danger. He even turned a deaf ear to ..." This proved the extent to which some people were addicted to the game.

Cricket fighting was most popular in the Ming and Qing Dynasties. Emperor Xuanzong of the Ming Dynasty was so addicted to the game that he often forced the common people to present him strong crickets as tributes, and those who did not obey his order could even be killed. He was therefore called "the Cricket Emperor". There was a saying at that time, "The cricket cries, cries, cries, the emperor needs, needs, needs." The story "The Cricket" in *Strange Tales of a Lonely Studio* was based on the story of this emperor. At that time, there were even casinos for the game. According to *Ningjin County Annals* written during the period of Emperor Qianlong in the Qing Dynasty, "People enjoy keeping crickets. Cricket fighting is immensely popular and becomes a fashion." This showed the great popularity of the game in Ningjin area.

Ningjin crickets were so famous in the north that crickets presented to emperors as tributes often came from this place. There were many legends about Ningjin crickets. It was said that at the end of the Northern Song Dynasty, Huizong and Qinzong (the eighth and ninth emperors of the dynasty) were so addicted to cricket fighting that they played the game day and night in the court with aristocrats and ministers, ignoring government affairs. At last, both emperors were captured by the State of Jin and were carted off to Youzhou (nowadays Beijing). Many valuable items were also taken away, and when the team reached Ningjin, a delicate porcelain jar suddenly broke and seven colorful insects jumped out, flapping their wings and singing loudly. Emperor Qinzong were very depressed and told the insects to escape and return back to pay tribute to emperors when the country would be rejuvenated. Eight hundred years later, Ningjin crickets dominated the market. What a coincidence.

There was another story about "Ningjin crickets tease the Empress Dowager Cixi". During the Tongzhi period (1862—1874) in the Qing Dynasty, the Empress Dowager loved cricket fighting so much and knowing that Ningjin was famous for high-quality crickets, she sent men to look for best crickets in the place. The two men were eager to finish their task to please the empress, and when they came to Ningjin, they caught crickets everywhere and treated the locals badly. To avenge themselves on the two men, the locals gave them female crickets that looked strong. The two men took them as valuables, returned to Beijing, and presented the crickets to the empress. At first she was very happy, but soon she found that the crickets could not fight. She was exasperated, believing that the two men were insinuating that she, a female, was governing the country. Then she sent the two men to prison.

There are many kinds of fighting crickets in Ningjin. According to the skin color, they can be divided into eight categories (green, black, purple, yellow, red, white, three-color, and two-color) including 200 varieties, among which green ones make up 70% of the total. According to the teeth color, there are seven categories including red teeth, yellow teeth, purple teeth, colorful teeth, ink-color teeth, heteromorphic teeth, and black-head silver-wing ones, among which red and yellow teeth make up more than 80%, followed by purple and colorful teeth. The green ones with red teeth are most famous for fighting and they have won many chairmanships in local and national contests. The green ones with red lines and red teeth, the green ones with red lines, the green ones with white lines, and green-golden-winged ones are the ones followed. In addition, green ones with ink-color teeth and black-head silver-wing ones are superb, with strong elegant bodies and excellent fighting records. Although limited in number, they are not that hard to find.

As an entertainment for the folk, catching and keeping crickets for fighting have a long history in Ningjin and great impact on locals' lives. The time for catching crickets in the year is during the Beginning of Autumn and the White Dew. After 11 p.m. each night, people go to wheat straws and corn and bean fields to catch them. Then, these crickets are divided into different categories according to their fighting abilities and kept carefully in the house. The high-quality ones are especially popular. People observe them, listen to their voice, and can hardly stop enjoying the process. Then cricket fighting begins and everyone invites their friends and relatives. Crickets are divided into different groups according to their size, put into round pits or basins, and induced to fight and kill each other. Gradually, cricket fighting has become a folk custom and is still popular nowadays.

Ningjin people have been paying much attention to their cricket fighting culture. As early as the early 1990s, a cricket research center was founded and cricket cultural festivals have been held. From 1991 to the present, nine festivals have been held, each festival witnessing more activities and larger size. The festivals are significant in that they greatly enrich locals' lives. Cricket fighting has become an integral part of Ningjin people's lives as well as a highlight of the place.

Nowadays, Ningjin Cricket Fighting Custom has become more and more well-known. We need to protect and carry forward this great intangible cultural heritage.

Abacus Culture (Shandong Abacus Association)

In 2016, "Abacus Culture" of Shandong Abacus Association was listed in the fourth batch of provincial intangible cultural heritage by Shandong Provincial People's Government.

Abacus is a tool for numerical calculation. It is acclaimed as the fifth great discovery of China. In 2008, it was listed in the second batch of national intangible cultural heritage by the State Council. On December 4th in 2013, it was listed in the intangible cultural heritage of humanity by the UNESCO.

Abacus has a long history. In the year of 190, Liu Hong, a Shandong local, invented this tool. It was first recorded in *Mathematical Heritage* by Xu Yue (a local of Laizhou, Shandong) of the East Han Dynasty, in which he mentioned "Abacus" in his book as was said by his master Liu Hong. Liu Hong also taught the calendar calculation and *Qianxiang Calendar* to his pupils Yang Wei and Han Yi. Through transmission and education, abacus was spread first to surrounding cities and then to the whole nation. During the Tang and Song Dynasties, abacus had been perfected and gradually replaced other calculation techniques, methods, and tools. During the Yuan and Ming Dynasties, it became the dominating calculation tool. Since the 16th century, it spread to the surrounding countries and greatly promoted their economic and cultural development. Abacus made a great contribution to Japan's mathematical development. In the Qing Dynasty, abacus was widely used in all fields, having a large impact on every aspect of people's lives, which can be shown by the popularity of proverbs stemming from pithy formulas for the tool.

In the Guangxu 29th year of the Qing Dynasty(1903), the issued *Authorized School Regulation* stipulated that students of the fourth and fifth years of the lower primary school as well as those of the second, third and forth years of the higher primary school were required to learn abacus for the purpose that they could learn the daily calculation, know how to make a living, and become more careful and prudent. Since then, abacus had been a course till the end of the 20th century.

During the Republic of China (1912—1949), with the development of the Chinese national industry and commerce, the domestic market expanded, trading ports increased, financial exchange and deposit business developed, leading to increasingly heavier calculation work. Under this circumstance, abacus was developing accordingly. There was a saying at that time, "Since the 20th century, the business has witnessed unparalleled development... All merchants use abacus for trade. Its popularity and simplified usage have become a Chinese feature. Westerners speak highly of it and also want to have it." To cater to the social needs, main finance universities, middle schools, and primary schools offered abacus courses, not only publishing quality abacus textbooks, but also proposing abacus-written mixed calculation for teaching. Some reforms were not realized, but abacus education never stopped. The tool became more and more popular. During the war of liberation (1946—1949), the support crew of the People's Liberation Army used cloth to fold abacuses during marching and unfold them when using. After the foundation of the People's Republic of China, abacus continued to play an important role in economy. Abacus courses were still offered in primary schools, with textbooks and teachers' books. Later, oral-written-mixed abacus calculation greatly facilitated the spread of abacus. In November of 1963, the Chinese Mathematics Society held a "Meeting for Abacus and Auxiliary Tools", proposed reforms for abacus teaching, and created the mimeograph periodical *Abacus Teaching and Research Communication*, greatly promoting the development of abacus. In 1979, the Chinese Abacus Association was founded. Since then, abacus teaching, application and research have developed quickly and thrived again.

As the hometown of the abacus inventor Liu Hong, Shandong has played an important role in the development of abacus. In 1981, from 12th to 15th in September, the first National Abacus Contest was held in Shandong. As a result, abacus contests spread quickly in both official and folk circles. It seemed everyone was beginning to study abacus in the province. At the same time, a lot of researchers had made great achievements in abacus fields. In June of 1982, the second academic discussion meeting for Chinese abacus history and the first abacus history research meeting in Shandong were held in Mengyin county. During that meeting, Jing Yushu, the leader of the abacus history research team in Shandong, made it clear that Liu Hong was the abacus inventor. Then he published many papers such as *Hong Liu's Mathematical Level and Values and Contributions of His Abacus*, which solidified Shandong's status as the hometown of abacus. In 1994, *A Collection of Mathematics in Chinese History* edited by Jing Yushu was published, which made Chinese ancient calculation methods known to the public and laid a solid foundation for the status of Shandong algorithm research in the nation. In 2003, Shandong government began a project about mental calculation with abacus, sponsored by the Education Ministry and Finance Ministry. The project took five years and through the contrast of a large amount of experimental data, the subject Mental Mechanism Research for Using Mental Calculation with Abacus to Train Children's Intellect was completed. The research showed that mental calculation with the abacus could train functional areas in the brain, and therefore the project strongly demonstrated that such a mental calculation can facilitate intellectual development. In April of 2010, the Chinese Society for the Study of Folk Literature and Art sent an expert team to Mengyin. The experts spoke highly of the protection and development of its calculation saint culture, and the place was officially named as "Home for the Chinese Calculation Saint Culture". In December of 2013, just before abacus was listed as the intangible cultural heritage of humanity by the UNESCO, Jing Yushu presented *Mathematical Heritage* of a cut-block printing version, the only one of its kind to the Chinese government, offering a valuable material to prove the inventor and invention year of abacus and helping successful application of the cultural heritage.

Abacus has developed with society and the calculation speed requirement. In history, abacus gradually replaced rod-arithmetic because the latter was limited in speed and space. The invention of abacus is significant and has made great contributions to mankind. As an excellent intelligence product of the Chinese, abacus has great research values and practical application, deserving our transmission and protection.

Shandong Pancake Custom

In 2016, "Shandong Pancake Custom" of the Shandong Folk Society was listed in the fourth batch of the provincial intangible cultural heritage by Shandong Provincial People's Government.

Chinese pancakes are made of mixed grains. Grains are ground into paste, put on hot griddles, and flattened with a special rake. Pancake is the most typical food in the mountainous areas of Taiyi, Shandong, as well as a traditional food in the north of the country. It has a history over 2,000 years in Shandong. The iron griddle unearthed from Juxian proved that Taiyi first used griddles as early as the Western Han Dynasty. Shandong Pancake Custom refers to a series of daily production and living customs, folk religion, festivals, folk legends and stories, proverbs and Chinese two-part allegorical sayings related to pancake making and eating.

1. Production and living customs

1.1 Production customs

The Taiyi mountainous area is the main production site of Shandong pancakes. Pancakes are made from drought-tolerant crops such as corn, wheat, millet, beans, sorghum, and sweet potatoes. Main tools for making only include griddles, oil brushes, scoops, rakes, and shovels, but the procedures and techniques are complex. There are almost ten steps such as washing grains, crushing them, grinding pastes, mixing cooked and uncooked grains, spreading firing, and storing. Fermentation is required if you want to make sour pancakes.

To make pancakes, one can use flattening, rolling and scraping methods. It does not take a long time to make a pancake but it is quite technical. For example, when using stone mills to flatten the paste, one should add ingredients frequently but with a little amount each time. Also, the flattening should be slow so that the paste can be flattened evenly. When fermentation is required, fermenting should be in accordance with temperature and made timely. There are also requirements on the duration and degree of the fire. A big fire results in burnt pancakes while small fire affects the speed and makes it difficult to take out the pancake. Therefore, soft firewood such as straws and weeds are preferred. In addition, one needs to have flexible wrist when flattening pastes on griddles. Otherwise, the pancake will not be even.

1.2 Diet customs

Shandong pancakes are made from basic grains and therefore it's green and healthy food. It is easy to carry, eat, and store, hence deeply loved by locals. Different places in Shandong have different eating habits on pancakes, the most typical of which is putting green Chinese onions into them. Other ingredients like vegetable, seafood, pork head meat, beef residues, fried yellow croakers and crucian carps, dried shrimps, shredded kelp, small bean curds, pickles, and even sugar, lard and boiled eggs. In addition, pancakes with lard, chopped green onions and salt can be put into boiled water to eat; cold ones can be roasted by fire with sesame and salt on them. You can also steam pancakes in pots. Another interesting way is to fry bean curd, vermicelli, and Chinese chives with oil, put them into pancakes evenly, fold the pancakes into rectangles, and bake both sides with added oil in the pot until they have golden colors. All these methods can bring you a very enjoyable eating.

1.3 Household customs

In rural areas, pancakes are daily food and making pancakes is a part of everyday life. The process of making pancakes, from preparation to storage, requires efforts of all family members. Hard work such as getting water, cleaning grains, and grinding mills is done by men, but in most cases, grinding mills is done by all family members. Women are mainly responsible for pancake making and storing. During the whole process, household members have specific tasks. Their cooperation can help deepen their emotional ties and make the family more harmonious.

In the past, a golden standard for the qualification of a wife was whether she could make good pancakes. Therefore, girls from an early age learned how to make pancakes so that she would be a good wife in the eyes of the husband's family.

2. Social customs

2.1 Festivals

People in Linyi and other places in Shandong often prepare a lot of pancakes when the Spring Festival is coming, so that they can have more time to enjoy the festival. Pancakes are important new year gifts. Wives prepare pancakes for both their parents' homes and husbands' homes. There is a local saying, "so many daughters to marry, so busy during the festival", which means that pancake making often starts from the beginning of the twelfth month of the lunar year but can be hardly finished when the festival arrives. Pancakes are often put below all kinds of fried food prepared for the festival to make it more cleaning and oil-saving. Oil-saturated pancakes have a special aroma and make one's mouth water. This is the Spring Festival custom.

In the southwest of Shandong, there is a saying, "the second day of February brings strong wind, and it's time to gather firewood for making pancakes." On this day, it is said that pancake making is to commemorate the Dragon King who was punished for giving rain to the world without being ordered to do so. Eating pancakes on that day is also called eating the "dragon's scales", and it has become a custom.

2.2 Folk religious customs

One custom is using pancake to "mend the sky". According to *Realm of Ci Poetry* of the Song Dynasty written by Yang Shen of the Ming Dynasty, "The 23rd day of the first lunar month is named Tianzai Day by the Song Dynasty, on which day the goddess Nüwa mended the broken sky with her powerful magic. On the day, the folks put pancakes on the roof to imitate the goddess. This custom stems from the Sky Leaking Day, which is on the 23rd day of the first lunar month, just around "Rain Water" Day. Using pancakes to "mend the sky" is a symbol of praying for good weather for the crops.

In Jining and other places of Shandong, there is a custom of using pancakes to cure headache. In the past, around the Beginning of Spring, paper cattle were made with pancakes inside, and the cattle was called the spring cattle. Beside cattle, a pit was dug with a bamboo tube set up in it. In the tube there were chicken feathers. As the temperature rose around the Beginning of Spring, the feathers were pushed out by the warm air inside, and people used wooden sticks to beat the paper cattle, hence the Beginning of Spring is also called Dachun (hit the spring). Then, everyone went for the pancakes insides the cattle because they were said to have the function of curing headaches.

2.3 Language customs

Vernaculars related to Shandong pancakes include baking pancakes, raking pancakes, scraping pancakes, flattening pancakes, steaming pancakes, saucing pancakes, edge warping, oil brushes, chizi (a tool like a small rake), rakes, and griddles.

Proverbs and ballads related to Shandong pancakes are mostly about life. For example, "sorghum pancakes with peppers make one strong", "wheat pancakes with sesame oil make one slim", "wheat pancakes with eggs make one study harder" , "one pancake after another, food is better anyway" , etc.

There are also two-part allegorical sayings related to pancakes. For example, "roll pancakes with thumbs—bite yourself while eating" , "making pancakes on palms—a skilled hand" , "emperors eat pancakes—evenly made ("even" and "emperor" have the same sound in Chinese). All these show the folk intelligence and passion for life.

2.4 Folk stories

There are many folk stories related to pancakes. The most popular three ones are as follows.

The first story is that pancakes were invented by Zhuge Liang. In the beginning he served as a military counsellor at Liu Bei's army, which was often pursued by Cao Cao's army because it was not strong initially. One time Liu's army was surrounded between the rivers of Yi and Shu. The army had lost its cooking utensils and soldiers were hungry and exhausted. Zhuge Liang asked the chef to make a paste, put the tool gong on the fire, and use wooden sticks to even the paste. The pancakes were thus made. After eating pancakes, the soldiers regained strength and fought their way out. The locals learned this way of making pancakes, but replaced the gong with iron-made ones because the original coppery-made ones were expensive and easy to break. This method of making can still be found in Yimeng and many other places in Shandong.

The second one is a love story. It was said that under the mountain of Yimeng, Sister Huang and Liang Ma fell in love, but Huang's sly and greedy stepmother did not agree upon their marriage. She accepted money from a rich family under the condition to marry Huang, who refused to do so. She decided to set an evil plan for Liang by inviting him to her house for study and said that he could marry Huang after passing the test and having an official rank. She prepared a study room and the writing brush, ink stick, ink slab and paper and asked Liang what else he needed. Liang said as long as books and brushes were available he needed nothing else. The stepmother was too glad and told the servant to keep an eye on the man and not to give meals to him. Liang studied until the dusk, but no one brought food to him. He suddenly realized that he was in a trap. The stepmother was making him hungry and forcing him to escape so that she could make a false charge of him stealing. That would give him a bad reputation and very likely their love would come to an end. Having learned what a condition her lover was in, Huang was angry and worried. Suddenly she had an idea. She made a pile of white cakes as square as white paper, shaped the green Chinese onions into brush forms, and asked a maid to send them to Liang. The servant saw nothing strange and let the maid go into the yard. With such "paper" and "brushes" to eat, Liang became better spirited day after day. The stepmother was surprised and asked him what happened. Liang said gods were helping him and told him he would be the number one scholar in the future. This completely changed her attitude and she began to treat him well. Later, it happened that he indeed became the number one scholar in the imperial examination, and he brought Sister Huang to the capital. The story spread far away since then, and eating pancakes with the Chinese green onions became popular.

The third story is about Pu Songling, author of *Strange Stories from a Chinese Studio*. Once there was a mother and a daughter who made their living in Zichuan of Shandong (also Pu's hometown) by selling pancakes. The business was small and not able to afford rolled food, they had to cut onions and mixed them with other ingredients made by themselves in the pancake. Few customers came. One day Pu passed the shop, saw their condition and decided to help them. He wrote a couplet and put it on the door. The first line was "round griddle even paste big size", the second line was "many onions little sauce long roll", and the horizontal scroll in the middle read "eat it short". The public thought this was very well written and began to buy pancakes from the shop, whose business became prosperous.

Nowadays, traditional hand-made pancakes have witnessed half or total mechanization production. However, in some rural areas of Shandong, the hand-made methods have been kept. The pancake culture of Shandong has enriched itself continuously in its long history and has formed its unique local culture with widespread influence. Meanwhile, Pancake Custom in Shandong is significant for researching the food culture, farming, food processing, traditional festivals, folk religions, folk literature and vernaculars in Taiyi areas of Shandong.

Temple Fair for the Fishing Ancestor in Dongyi

In 2016, "Temple Fair for the Fishing Ancestor in Dongyi" in Chengyang district of Qingdao City was listed in the fourth batch of provincial intangible cultural heritage by Shandong Provincial People's Government.

Chengyang District lies in the south of the Shandong Peninsula. There is a Han folk custom village affiliated to Han village in the district. In the village, there is a temple for the fishing ancestor Langjun (the legendary figure Fu Xi was thus called in Dongyi), and the temple is called Langjun Temple. According to *Chinese Fishing History*, Langjun came to Shaohai (nowadays Jiaozhou Bay) in the Era of Yan and Huang, teaching locals how to make webs and boats and how to fish. He was beloved by locals and was called the fishing ancestor out of respect. To commemorate him, locals built a temple, but the building time could not be known because it was too long ago.

During the Jiaqing Reign (1796—1820) of the Qing Dynasty, locals expanded the temple and added a statue. Under the suggestion of Han Bingren, the temple fair for the fishing ancestor was reorganized. During the Tongzhi Reign (1862—1874) of the Qing Dynasty, merchants from Jiaozhou, Jimo, Haiyang and other places attended the fair, which was set in a wide place. It started from the eve of the Tomb-Sweeping Day and lasted for three days. The fair was held at a time when people were outing for spring, and merchants and pilgrims came from very far-away places such as Jimo, Jiaozhou and Pingdu. Commodities for trade included fishing tools, wood for making boats, iron anchor, dry seafood, livestock, agricultural tools, furniture, grain, vegetables, daily necessities, and various local food. At the end of the Qing Dynasty, one could also find fishing baskets and bamboo-made tools from Jiangsu and Zhejiang provinces, forks, rakes, brooms and other agricultural tools from Laiyang, bellows from Pingdu, mountain products from Laoshan, as well as various local seafood and specialties. The most popular business was bars along the streets, because pilgrims and merchants who had no relatives in the village came one or two days earlier for the fair had to live in the bars. There would be a one-day holiday for school students and short-term and long-term workers. On the day before the Tomb-Sweeping Day, incenses were nonstop, firecrackers were always heard, storytellers and performers were very active on the streets where one could also enjoy the Mao opera from Jiaozhou, Liu opera from Jimo, as well as the bench play.

After 1897, the Yin Island (nowadays the Red Island) where the temple was located and was occupied by Germany as a concession. The relatively stable environment made it possible to hold the temple fair regularly. Many foreigners from Qingdao also attended the fair and it developed continuously. After 1931, the stable society, new roads built, specialties from other places in the country made the fair develop smoothly. However, after 1937, Qingdao was again occupied by the Japanese army. Frequent wars and poor security slowed down the development of the fair. Few people came, and there were even bandits. Finally, the fair stopped.

In 2000, Han Pingde began to restore the temple. Since then, worshiping the fishing ancestor has been regularly held every year during the Tomb-Sweeping Day, with pilgrims and merchants from all over the country. For people in the surrounding villages and towns, the temple fair has become a good occasion for travelling, visiting, spring outing, and relaxing. The traffic is convenient, the economy is thriving, the culture is rich, and the scenery is breath–taking, all of which, combined with the rich cultural elements of the Han folk village and the marine culture, constitute an ideal regional advantage.

Nowadays, the temple fair for the fishing ancestor in Dongyi of the Han folk village is the only costal place in China where the fishing ancestor is worshiped. Every year during the Tomb–Sweeping Day, local fishermen always hold solemn worshiping ceremonies before they set out to the sea, to show their respect for the fishing ancestor and wish to have a safe voyage as well as bountiful gains from the sea. Locals greatly value the temple fair, planning one month earlier by booking worshiping items. The fair host and the main worshiper are usually the village party secretaries or people highly respected in the village. The host is responsible for making and scheduling procedures for the fair as well as announcing for the ceremony, while the main worshiper is responsible for reciting congratulatory message, leading the public to salute, toast, and incense. When the Tomb–Sweeping Day comes, the temple fair starts with a parading team with local features of the Han folk village. The team consists of hundreds of local artists, who wear coarse clothes with dark colors and shoes sewn with pig skins with fur on them. Such traditional outfit is to show how fishermen worked on the boat in winter. They will show visitors wedding ceremonies of the fishermen, walk on stilts, leading donkeys, two–ghost wrestling, and acrobatics, so that visitors will know what it was like when ancient fishermen prepared to set out to the sea. Then, the fisherman trumpet blows and the solemn worshiping begins. During the ceremony, the main worshipper instructs the team to blow the trumpet and sacrifice livestock, invites gods to the position, and leads the team to worship, recite, and kowtow. Fishermen who are proud of the sea and prosper owning to the sea show their gratitude and respect for the fishing ancestor through the ceremony, wishing for propitious winds and rains, a good harvest for agricultural families, bountiful gains for fisherman families, as well as health and happiness for friends and relatives. After the worshiping, there are still many pilgrims left, most of whom are locals. There are merchants from both the local and other places such as Jimo, Laiyang, and Pingdu. Local seafood is the main trade item, other products including dry seafood, handicrafts, toys, and clothes. There are many operas widely liked such as the Liu and Mao operas as well as acrobatics each year. In the folk village, people can ride horses, take bridal sedan chairs, cast fishing nets, fish, swing, and row boats with ancient-style sails. Also, visitors can follow fishermen to catch fish, go to the fishery salt exhibition hall and folk museum to learn the evolution of the Chinese fishery salt history, hear stories of the ancient items, and witness life traces of previous generations.

The temple fair for the fishing ancestor in Dongyi was first started to commemorate the fishing ancestor. Later, it incorporates worshiping elements for smooth voyages. The fair has a strong local feature of the Chinese coastal areas, and is an integral part of the Chinese folk culture.

Zen Tea Ceremony in Boshan Zhengjue Monastery

In 2016, "Zen Tea Ceremony in Boshan Zhengjue Monastery" in Boshan district of Zibo City was listed in the fourth batch of provincial intangible cultural heritage by Shandong Provincial People's Government.

China is the hometown of tea, and the discovery and drinking of tea has a long history. It is recorded in Shennong's *Classic of Materia Medica* that the divine farmer Shennong tasted 100 herbs and encountered 72 kinds of poisonous ones one day, but were all cured by tea. This shows that tea drinking has been a custom in China for a long time, and in later generations, it has developed into tea ceremony and tea culture. Tea culture originated in China, and tea ceremony came from the practitioners. Tea ceremony has a profound relationship with Zen meditation, and Boshan Zhengjue Monastery, as a Zen meditation shrine, has a deep relationship with tea ceremony.

In the Western Han Dynasty, Wu Lizhen planted seven tea trees on Mengding Mountain in Sichuan Province, pioneering the first example of artificially cultivating tea in the world, thus is revered as the "Tea Ancestor". Wu Lizhen found in the process of planting, brewing, and drinking tea that the hard work of tea cultivation is like the ascetic practice of monks, and when the tea leaves are brewing in boiling water, they symbolize the ups and downs of life. The tea tastes light and refreshing, leaving a fragrance in the mouth, just like Buddhist ascetic practice, with all the great compassion for the world in one's heart. Wu Lizhen believed that tea and Zen Buddhism are inextricably linked, so he coined the term "Buddhist Tea Family", and was revered as "the Dharma Master of Sweet Dew" by later generations.

Master Daoxin, the fourth patriarch of Zen Buddhism, advocated paying equal attention to agricultural labor and the meditation and enlightenment of Zen Buddhism. Monks should engage in self-cultivation and self-sufficiency while concentrating on Zen meditation, cultivating their own crops and engaging in Zen meditation and enlightenment during their work. Because Zen monasteries are mostly built in secluded mountains, monks' agricultural production is mostly planting trees and creating forests while ploughing farmlands and planting tea trees. Therefore, monks follow the habit of drinking tea after picking and processing tea leaves. There's almost no monastery without planting tea or no monk without drinking tea. Monks practice, meditate and engage in self-cultivation in the tea garden. Master Daoxin called monk labor as "Outside the Slopes" (to engage in labor, such as cleaning, washing, carrying, planting, etc.). This term has been passed down to folk people, and is still used by farmers in Anshang Village and nearby areas in Boshan.

The Book of Jin records, "The monk Shan Daokai sat in meditation, without sleeping day and night, taking several pills of medicine as big as Chinese parasol seeds to guard and fortify several meridians and organs of the body every day, which had the smell of pine honey, ginger, cinnamon and tuckahoe while drinking one or two liters of tea altogether." During meditation, thinking while sitting quietly for a long time can easily make people tired and absent-minded, so monks drink tea to refresh themselves and assist their practice. During the Northern and Southern Dynasties, Zen Master Bao Zhigong, National Master assisting Emperor Wu of Liang, the representative figure of the Tathagata Zen, presided over the formulation of the *Water and Land Fairs Ritual*, which included the words "incense lights, tea and fruit" and "tea cooking, fragrant and tender". This shows that tea has not only been used as a refreshing drink for monks, but also become an essential offering for devoutly offering Buddhas.

It can be seen that there is a strong atmosphere of tea and Zen culture in China, and Boshan Zhengjue Monastery, where Zen meditation and tea culture are well developed, is a representative area of Zen Tea Culture.

Boshan is a charming mountain city with beautiful scenery, long history, rich culture, developed economy, profound cultural heritage and vibrant atmosphere, which is well-known as the "Water & Mountains Gallery of the Central Lu (now Shandong Province)" and the "Back Garden of Zibo". In addition to its unique geographical environment, Boshan has a strong cultural atmosphere and is a famous cultural city as well. Boshan is located at the crossroads of Qilu, the intersection of Qilu culture, and is known as the "Garrison of Central Lu (now Shandong Province)", rich in many cultural landscapes.

The Boshan Zhengjue Monastery was originally built in the Eastern Jin Dynasty and repaired in the Song and Jin Dynasties, with a history of more than 1,600 years. It was once the ancestral temple of the Buddhist Zen sect, and the representative figure of the Tathagata Zen, Zen Master Bao Zhigong became a monk and practiced here. The third ancestor Sengcan and the fourth ancestor Daoxin had both practiced here. Later, it was severely destroyed and disappeared in the wild mountains. In 2002, Master Renda came to this place and was very sad to see the desolate scene here. So he led the people to rebuild the Boshan Zhengjue Monastery, which had also undergone several repairs prior to this one. According to the inscriptions on the reconstruction stele of the Zhigong Pagoda and the Zhigong Temple, in the reign of Emperor Liang Wu in the Southern and Northern Dynasties, a Zhigong Pagoda was rebuilt with a golden statue inside; the Buddhist temple was repaired in the tenth year of Zhizheng of the Yuan Dynasty(1350); in 1552, the disciples of the Heshan mountain monks and laymen were inspired by the patriarch of Zhigong to rebuild the Buddhist scriptures again and a stone hall of Zhigong Temple was built in front of the Zhigong Pagoda.

Zen Master Bao Zhigong, National Master of Emperor Wu of Liang in the Northern and Southern Dynasties, is widely recognized as the embodiment of Guanyin Bodhisattva. There are still ruins such as "Zhigong Terrace" and "Zhigong Pogoda" in Boshan District. According to Buddhist rituals and local folklore, Zhigong Pogada is the place where the relics of Zen Master Bao Zhigong are placed, and Zhigong Terrace is the place where Zen Master Bao Zhigong practiced. Boshan Zhengjue Monastery is one of the few monasteries in the country dedicated to Zen Master Bao Zhigong.

The purpose of tea brewing (Chongcha) is Zen practice, and the essence of Zen is self–awareness. Master Renda , the 46th generation successor of the Linji Zong of Zen Buddhism and the abbot of Boshan Zhengjue Monastery, inherits the spiritual cultivation method of Zen meditation and enlightenment, and based on the jungle tea ceremony, refers to *The Zen Forest Standby Code* and *Baizhang Code* for exploration and organization of the "Zen Meditation & Tea Ceremony" . In order to facilitate the practice of Zen for the world, Master Renda compiled 12 Zen tea poems and *Zen Tea Ceremony 100-Sentence Three-character Classic*, explaining the twelve processes of Zen Tea Ceremony, the mental method and practice essentials of each process, as well as the inheritance and connotation of Zen Tea Culture. The Zen Tea Ceremony originated from Boshan Zhengjue Monastery, spread and flourished. The monks who practice Zen meditation in the monastery all understand and love tea ceremony.

Today, Zen Tea Ceremony has become a comprehensive cultural manifestation integrating Zen meditation, tea ceremony, poetry, music, and health preservation. As the origin of Zen Tea Ceremony, Boshan Zhengjue Monastery still retains the tradition of practicing Zen Tea Ceremony. Moreover, local people in Boshan also like to calm their minds and gain insight into their true nature through Zen Tea Ceremony when they are troubled and unable to calm down. During the practice of Zen Tea Ceremony, people should carry out the following twelve procedures.

1. Light the lamp and burn incense, meditate on Zen and chant the praises of tea.

2. Boil the water and wait for the tea to steep, like the roaring sound of the ocean.

3. Clean the cups and rinse the tea vessels with hot water to wash away dust and dirt.

4. Appreciate the tea, infuse it with a joyful heart, as if plucking up a flower and smiling.

5. Observe the color, inhale the aroma, savor the secret and appreciate the roundness.

6. Rinse the tea with boiling water, and let go of the inner shackles.

7. Calmly brew tea, encompassing the vastness of universe.

8. Share tea as fate brings us together, and spread compassion.

9. The fragrance of tea condenses, like nectar, and provides sustenance for all beings.

10. Take a small sip and drink slowly, taste and meditate.

11. Thank you for the tea invitation, and may our good fortune last forever.

12. Zen and tea are interlinked, and the nature of the law is the same.

With the help of tea sets, tea leaves, incense, lamps, water and other main tools and materials, the concept of Zen meditation is integrated into every action of the twelve procedures while completing the rituals of tea ceremony, thus achieving the purpose of calming body and mind, nurturing the temperament, understanding the spiritual connotation of Zen, and enhancing the realm of life. The wonderful and profound Zen theory is carried by tea, forming a unique Zen Tea Culture that attracts literati and scholars, followed and studied by the public.

In the Zhengjue Monastery of Boshan, from the elders and masters to every ordinary monk, they all attach great importance to Zen Tea Culture and actively spread the culture of Zen tea through various means, making Zen Tea Culture continue to grow. Zen Tea Culture enriches peoples' spiritual life and gives people living in the fast-paced modern society a chance to meditate and calm down.Boshan Zhengjue Monastery holds tea ceremony workshops all year round, hoping to let more and more people understand, love and cultivate a tranquil and compassionate heart through Zen tea, which also promotes Buddhism and benefits society in another way.

Penglai Pavilion Temple Fair

In 2016, "Penglai Pavilion Temple Fair" of Penglai City was listed in the fourth batch of provincial intangible cultural heritage by Shandong Provincial People's Government.

Penglai City is affiliated to Yantai City, Shandong Province. It has a history of more than 2,100 years. It is a famous historical and cultural city full of myths and legends. Penglai Pavilion, which is known as one of the four famous buildings in ancient China, is well-known at home and abroad. The Penglai Pavilion Temple Fair was gradually formed with the completion of Penglai Pavilion.

The Penglai Pavilion Complex began to be built in the Song Dynasty Jiayou sixth year (1061). It is mainly composed of the Queen of Heaven Palace and the surrounding Dragon King Palace, Tzusun Palace, Mi Tuo Temple, Sanqing Hall, Lu Zu Hall, Su Gong Ancestral Hall, and Penglai Pavilion. It is composed of halls, attics and pavilions. The local immortal culture arose in the Warring States Period. By the Ming and Qing Dynasties, there were dozens of local immortals recorded in the county chronicles. All of these have put a layer of mystery on Penglai Pavilion, so Penglai has been known as a "Fairyland" since ancient times, and the Penglai Pavilion temple fair originally thrived with the worship of the Sea Goddess. The Sea Godess, also known as the Queen of Heaven, is the "Mazu" in the South. She was good at helping the world during her lifetime, and she often rescued fishermen in distress at sea. After her death, people set up ancestral temples for her to show their gratitude and pray for her protection. The belief in Mazu started from this, and Putian, Fujian and Taiwan were the places in which it was the most prosperous. Since the Ming and Qing Dynasties, with the development of the North–South maritime shipping, the belief in Mazu has gradually spread to the north, and Mazu has also become one of the sea goddess generally worshiped by coastal fishermen. There are a large number of Mazu Temples built in the coastal areas of our country. The most representative Mazu Temple in the north, the Queen of Heaven Palace, is located in the Penglai Pavilion complex on the top of Danya Mountain in the north of Penglai city.

Penglai people, especially the fishermen along the coast, have infinite admiration for the Sea Goddess. People still extol her deeds of fighting the wind and waves and courageously saving ships in distress, and her virtues of healing those in weakness and helping those in distress. It goes in the legend that the Sea Goddess can patrol the country around the border to expel demons and eliminate epidemics and pests. The 16th day of the first lunar month is the birthday of the Sea Goddess. Penglai has the custom of inviting the Sea Goddess for a parade on this day every year, which is commonly known in the local area as "Walking Away All Diseases" . In fact, this is just borrowing from the local habit of "Playing on the 15th and Making a Noise on the 16th" to extend the Lantern Festival one more day and create a holiday climax. The "birthday" is just an excuse for joining in. Since the Song Dynasty, the people in Penglai have celebrated this day as a festival, and it has the old saying that all the people in Penglai "go to the temple fair on the 16th day of the first lunar month" .

The early form of the Penglai Pavilion Temple Fair was only a solemn blessing activity. Later, with the development of social economy, various rural areas organized theatrical troupes and Yangko teams to perform slang folk dramas and big Yangko in the theater opposite the Queen of Heaven Palace, and a large number of local and Penglai People from the surrounding areas will come to the Penglai Pavilion to rush to the temple fair to celebrate the birthday of the Queen Mother and pray for the safety of the fishermen. The festive atmosphere is very strong. This custom has lasted more than 900 years and has gradually evolved into the "the Penglai Pavilion Temple Fair" . Now the Penglai Pavilion Temple Fair has become an indispensable folk activity for Penglai people to meet their daily and spiritual needs.

Every year in the early morning of the sixteenth day of the first lunar month, the Penglai Pavilion is already full of tourists, bustling with excitement, and full of a strong festive atmosphere everywhere. A grand worship and blessing ceremony will be held on the Penglai Pavilion Panorama Plaza, and the blessing ceremony will be carried out completely in accordance with local traditional customs. Due to the prestige of the Penglai Pavilion temple fair spreading to the surrounding counties and cities, various theatrical troupes, Yangko teams, and cultural performance groups from the Jiaodong region who participated in the temple fair ceremonies came to the square early to prepare in advance. In the square, gongs and drums are noisy, and firecrackers are humming, attracting visitors to stop and watch. The Penglai Grand Pole ranked at the top of the team, as the "Pioneer" kicked off the whole ceremony. The heroic grand horn music expresses people's blessings and hopes for the new year. Immediately afterwards, folk arts such as dragons, lions, dry boats, donkeys, waist drums, and free funny Yangko made their grand debut. The agile lions scramble and play sometimes; the soaring dragon flashes and moves up and down; dry boats, donkeys, exaggerated costumes, and vivid performances of various shapes can be described as diverse and unique; the Qi Family Army of Penglai Water City "Mandarin Duck Array, Chinese Shadow Boxing of the Qi Family Clan (Qijiaquan)" performed on-site and won warm applause from the audience. There are also great dramas, monkey snakes, acrobatics, swallowing swords, spitting fire and magic, drawing foreign films, etc. There are all kinds of things. In the performance team, there are elderly Yangko enthusiasts over the past few years, as well as innocent and lively children, and various folk art performances are mixed in, which is very lively. Temple fairs have become a place to invigorate the cultural life of the masses, and also enable people to appreciate the charm of local folk culture.

At the same time, the Queen of Heaven Palace and the Dragon King Palace also worshiped and prayed in accordance with traditional etiquette. Bells and drums were sounded in the temple, and smokes swirled around. The majority of fishermen went to the Queen of Heaven Palace to worship the Sea Goddess, praying for a safe journey to the sea, and return with a full load; farmers entered the Dragon Palace to worship the Dragon Lord, and prayed for good weather and good grains for this year; Buddhists can go to Mi Tuo Temple to worship Sakyamuni, and Taoist people can go to the Penglai Pavilion and Sanqing Hall, praying for blessings and happiness for the whole family. Because the temple fair has attracted tens of thousands of people of different beliefs to come to worship the gods during the temple fair, the Penglai Pavilion is filled with incense, flow of people, smoke in the halls, and bright candle lights. In front of the Penglai Pavilion Theatre, there is a surging crowd. The Lu opera performances, folk music performances, singing and dancing performances here attract people to stop and appreciate.

On the day of the temple fair, people from townships and merchants from other cities gathered in one place, and there was a hustle and bustle. Shop stalls were set up everywhere, and there were all kinds of strange things in department stores. The shouts came and went, the buyers and sellers had their own attitudes, and the business was booming. Because of the needs of temple fairs, people formed into a market, forming a street in your ancient city, and later gradually formed today's small commodity market. The famous local flavors and special snacks in Penglai gather here, such as Penglai small noodles, sesame sugar, noodle fish, braised donkey meat,

Spanish mackerel dumplings and other traditional famous foods performed on the spot. They are made and sold and are very popular among the tourists. Featured arts and crafts, such as yayao painted gourds, painted ball stones, root carvings, etc., such children's toys like windmills, shell products and etc. are everywhere.

Nowadays, in addition to traditional programs, the Penglai Pavilion Temple Fair has also added a variety of modern exhibitions such as photography exhibitions and Spring Festival couplets exhibitions. Many programs are also combined with local folklore, adding fascinating colors and charm to the temple fair. As a kind of folk culture, the Penglai Pavilion Temple Fair has been deeply rooted in people's hearts. While maintaining blessing activities, it has gradually integrated into bazaar trading activities and entertainment activities. It has now become a folklore of technology exchanges, commodity trade, and leisure and entertainment. The cultural event is hailed as "a blend of elegance and vulgarity, and a blend of business and entertainment".

The formation of the Penglai Pavilion Temple Fair has profound social and historical reasons, and has a close relationship with the faith activities of the local people. It developed along with the folk belief activities. The Penglai Temple Fair integrates various cultures and can satisfy groups of different beliefs. It is a kind of folk activities with strong local characteristics. It not only enriches the cultural life of the local people, but also plays an important role in protecting folk culture.

Yuhuangding Temple Fair

In 2016, "Yuhuangding Temple Fair" of Yantai City was listed in the fourth batch of provincial intangible cultural heritage by Shandong Provincial People's Government.

Temple Fair, also known as 'Temple Market', is a folk religion and seasonal custom of the Han people, and one of the forms of market trade in China as well. The formation and development of the temple fair are related to religious activities. It is usually held on festivals or specified dates of temples, mostly in and around the temple. Yuhuangding Park, located in the central area of Zhifu District, Yantai City, still holds a regular temple fair with a history of more than 600 years—Yuhuangding Temple Fair. After years of development and changes, it has now become a cultural and economic activity widely participated in by the masses, and has continued for a hundred years with great prosperity.

At first, it was not called Yuhuangding. In the Yuan Dynasty, because of the Yuhuang Temple built on the top of the mountain, it was named "Yuhuangding". In 1890, Liu Ciyuan, a scholar from Yantai, visited here and exclaimed: "How strange! Isn't it a blasphemy to name the mountain after the Yuhuang Peak? Moreover, this mountain range extends from the peak, with its shape winding and twisting, as if gasping for breath while rushing towards a destination. Glanced from afar, it looks like a thirsty horse galloping towards a spring and converging here. And in its east, there are numerous towering peaks stretching for miles. In its west, there are layered forests and mountains, steep and abrupt. Surrounded by mountains and forests, the scene is clear and impressive. Only the middle of the West Mountain is lush and green, rising above the mundane world. This place was originally a large town in our village, full of vitality and the fine spirits of the universe. Now, can we rename it as Yuhuang instead of Yuhuang Peak?" From then on, "Yuhuang Peak" has been changed to "Yuhuangding", and has been used ever since.

According to current inscriptions from the Ming and Qing Dynasties, the Yuhuang Temple was first built in the late Yuan Dynasty. It is said that a Taoist priest happened to pass by this mountain in the late Yuan Dynasty and discovered that the cave on the mountaintop emitted golden light straight into the blue sky. To explore its secrets, he sneaked into the cave and saw a golden toad with its mouth open and closed, emitting golden lights. The Taoist monk exclaimed, "This is truly a sacred mountain!" Therefore, he collected donations and funds to build a three-room temple on the mountain to worship Yuhuang, who is of the highest ranking and has the most powerful authority in Taoism, and thus the Yuhuang Temple came into being. The Ming Dynasty rebuilt and expanded it, forming a quadrangle style temple building. In the following centuries, it was repaired and expanded many times in different eras. In the 23rd year of the Wanli Reign of the Ming Dynasty (1595), the official and gentry Liu Weiye gathered funds to rebuild the Yuhuang Temple, and built a new Yuhuang Hall on the site of the original three-room temple, adding the bell tower and the drum tower, and east and west wing rooms. The Yuhuang Temple was built and expanded in Xianfeng, Tongzhi and Guangxu years of the Qing Dynasty. In the 19th year of Guangxu Reign of the Qing Dynasty (1893), the scale of the expansion was relatively large, thus forming an architectural complex composed of a theater, a mountain gate, a bell tower and a drum tower, the Yuhuang Hall, a back hall, the east and west wing rooms, a back garden, the Lvzu Temple, Xiangruo Pavilion, and a stone memorial archway and etc.

The early Yuhuangding Temple Fair originated from a solemn prayer event. According to the *Glorious Record of the Newly Built Yuhuang Temple in the Ming Dynasty*, "In times of disaster or drought, people climb to the top (now known as Yuhuangding) to pray, and their prayers are always answered, and thus leading to favorable weather, peaceful people, and abundant crops." Since then, the Yuhuang Temple at Yuhuangding has become an important place for Jiaodong people engaging in religious activities. The ninth day of the first lunar month is the birthday of the Yuhuang. Every year since the Yuan Dynasty, the people of Yantai spontaneously come to the Yuhuang Temple to pray, worship, and engage in other activities, which gradually formed the Yuhuangding Temple Fair.

"The Year on Duty (Zhinian)" activity of the Temple Fair has been passed down to this day. During the Ming and Qing Dynasties, there were 13 villages in Zhifu, including Dongmen Village, Ximen Village, Nanmen Village, Beimen Village, etc. They established an autonomous association (also known as Qishan Community) under the jurisdiction of Fushan County. Each of the 13 villages elected a leader to take turns in "governing" and each village served one year, which was called "The Year on Duty (Zhinian)". The handover work was carried out during the Yuhuangding Temple Fair in the back living room of the Yuhuang Temple (now the Queen Mother [Wangmu] Hall). During the meeting, besides discussing important issues among the 13 villages, the transfer of power was also conducted, with the previous leader handing over the "powers" (accounts) to the newly elected leader.

The Yuhuang Temple was the center of early religious culture in Yantai and can be called a living fossil of Yantai's regional religious culture. It contains the unique folk cultural value of Yantai. The Yuhuang enshrined in the temple is the king of all gods in Taoism and holds the greatest religious authority. On the ninth day of the first lunar month every year, the abbot at the Yuhuang Temple will hold a Taoist ritual to pray for favorable weather and rainfall in the new year. People from all around will come to worship the Yuhuang, pray for blessings with peace and safety, and make vows to thank God. Nowadays, a large folk activity of "Praying for Good Fortune and Returning Home with Blessings" is held during the temple fair every year.

The entertainment activities at Yuhuangding Temple Fair are also extremely rich. There is a theater building built in front of the Yuhuang Temple Square, which is a reconstruction of the original site according to its original appearance. The original theater building was built in the eleventh year of the Xianfeng Reign (1861), with funding from the social, business, and public sectors. It is used for annual temple fairs and serves as the entertainment center of the temple fair. On the day of the temple fair, the performances on the stage are mostly local performances and charity performances, without the need to purchase tickets, and are popular among the people. The current temple fair still retains custom of singing full-scale drama in the theater, and each temple fair has time-honored opera performances. As the famous overseas Chinese Mr. Qu Zhengmin wrote in his article "Memories of Childhood in 1994", "Yuhuang Temple is supported by 13 villages, so Beijing Opera must be performed on the stage of each Yuhuang's birthday, at least until the Lantern Festival on the 15th day of the 1st lunar month. At this time, the temple gate is wide open for virtuous men and women to offer incense. On the ninth day of the first lunar month every year, the representatives of the villages, including gongs and drums teams and Yangko teams, come to worship with the sound of firecrackers setting off all the way under the flags, umbrellas and fans. At this time, the mountain is bustling with vendors, storytelling, martial arts, magic and other variety shows. The festival of the Yuhuang's birthday is the most significant event in the local area."

Commodity trading is also an important function of Yuhuangding Temple Fair. Every time the temple fair is held, local and surrounding vendors gather here to buy and sell goods. After worshiping and making wishes, people attending the temple fair can not only watch performances, but also purchase various items necessary for daily life and work. According to elderly people's recollections, during the temple fair, the narrow alleys around Yuhuangding were filled with small vendors selling items such as sugar, glass balls, and needlework, with a wide variety of stalls; there were also local snacks such as pancake soup, Chaotian pot, and Fushan noodles with soup of three delicacies. One unique custom is that several stalls sell wax wood poles at the temple fair every year, and almost everyone who attends the temple fair buys a wax wood pole. It was originally used as a walking stick for mountain climbing, but since then, it's been widely believed that using a walking stick to ascend mountains can ensure a safe and peaceful life.

In recent years, the Temple Fair has been themed on "promoting traditional folk culture and building a brand of cultural progress", inviting performances such as Haiyang Dayangge, Wuqiao Acrobatics, Acrobatic Lift, Jiaodong Drum Dance, Bagua Drum Dance, Flower Piercing Dance, Mantis Boxing, Shadow Boxing, Daganhao, and Shadow Puppetry, etc. Traditional programs such as Lü opera, Peking opera, acrobatics, gongs and drums, variety shows, martial arts, and Yange Dance are also rich and colorful; Some new forms of performance have also been integrated into it, such as magic and hip hop, attracting more young people to participate. In addition, during the temple fair, the column expert group of CCTV-2's "Treasure Appreciation" also joined in a series of highly interactive and participatory theme activities with the public, including large-scale folk treasure hunting activities, traditional cultural public welfare lectures, calligraphy and painting exhibitions, photography competitions, blind dates, riddles, couplets, etc., providing a set of exquisite and rich cultural feast for residents and tourists.

Nowadays, the Yuhuangding Temple Fair has become a major folk event in the local area. Tourists, vendors, and performance groups who come to participate in the Temple Fair are spread throughout the Shandong Peninsula and even all over China, and the number of visitors received reaches a new high every year. What's even more valuable is that the current temple fair has excavated and cataloged a large number of folk cultures that have been nearly forgotten. The Yuhuangding Temple Fair has made great contributions to the inheritance of Jiaodong culture and is an important carrier for promoting traditional folk culture.

Shouguang Vegetable Production Customs

In 2016, "Shouguang Vegetable Production Customs" of Shouguang City was listed as in the fourth batch of provincial intangible cultural heritage by Shandong Provincial People's Government.

Shouguang City is located in the north-central part of Shandong Province, under the jurisdiction of Weifang City. In the 1990s, Shouguang City was named by the State Council as "The Hometown of Vegetables in China", and the influence of its vegetable cultivation has spread all over the whole country. Since 2000, Shouguang City has successfully held 14 sessions of "China (Shouguang) International Vegetable Sci-Tech Fair".

Shouguang has a long history of vegetable production, with records dating back to Dynasties of Xia, Shang, and the Spring and Autumn Period. By the Northern Wei Period, Jia Sixie, a native of Shouguang, wrote *Qimin Yaoshu* (*Important Arts for the People's Welfare*), which contains 27 chapters on crop cultivation techniques and 16 chapters dedicated to the cultivation and processing of vegetables. In the 37th year in the reign of Emperor Kangxi in the Qing Dynasty (1698), *The Shouguang County Annals* during the Republic of China, the 1990 edition of *The Shouguang County Annals* and other ancient books also recorded the inheritance and development of vegetable production in Shouguang.

The vegetable production customs in Shouguang include soil preparation, breeding, planting, management, harvesting, storage, and consumption, etc. This custom is followed by Shouguang people in accordance with The Laws Of Nature and The Twenty-Four Solar Terms. For example, in spring, there are "On the second day of February, storing the soil, planting cucumbers, and offering sacrifices to the Kitchen God", which means the farming activities related to vegetable production from the second day of February onwards—storing the soil, offering sacrifices to the Kitchen God, and praying for a good harvest in the coming year; in summer, there are "planting green onions in mid-May", "planting radish in the First Heat and mustard in the Second Heat, and planting cabbage in the Third heat"; in autumn, there are "planting celery at the Autumn Equinox and planting garlic at the White Dew"; in winter, there are "planting green onions at the Start of Winter and digging cabbage out of the ground at the First Snowfall", and so on.

There are many varieties of vegetables in Shouguang, among which the representative ones are Jiuxiang Yellow Chives, Guihe Celery, Shouguang Chicken-drumstick Green Onion, and Fuqiao Green Radish. The production customs of each are unique as follows.

1. Jiuxiang Yellow Chives. Jiuxiang Yellow Chives are planted in two seasons: spring (late March to mid-April) and autumn (late August to mid-September). The production process is divided into five stages: selecting high-quality seeds and plots, leveling the plots and making ridges, cultivating yellow chives, monitoring the vegetable plots, and harvesting. Before sowing, the soil layer should be deeply tilled about 30 cm and exposed to the sun for about 7 days. Then, the plots are leveled for ridges, and the soaked seeds are sown with a layer of thin fine sand covered on top followed by the fertilization of well-rotted organic fertilizer. After that, timely topdressing, watering and weeding are required. Fertilizing that combines water

and fertilizer are applied, controlled and stopped respectively in the early, middle and late autumn. When the chives grow to 5 cm, new soil is added for the first time; after about 10 days, the upper green chives are cut off and new soil is added for the second time. When the chive seedlings grow to 10~16 cm, a straw mat is placed over them to maintain the humidity inside. When the yellow chives grow to about 50 cm, they are harvested with a special sickle for sale. *The Shouguang County Annals* in the 37th year in the reign of Emperor Kangxi in the Qing Dynasty (1698) records, "In the early spring, chives are the earliest vegetables to grow, just like Jiuxiang Yellow Chives in Shouguang, which are not just about to grow in spring. Even in the cold snowy and icy winters, they can still be served on the table, with their delicious sweetness and crispness far surpassing other ingredients like meat."

There are also folk sayings like "To make chives flourish, one needs to add ash as fertilizer," "Chives are sold on the street in March," "The prime of chives or cucumbers is their heads." There is also a record in the Chapter of *Sunflower Vegetable Sowing in Qimin Yaoshu* written by Jia Sixie that "Chives should not be harvested at noon."

2. Guihe Celery. First, prepare the soil to create a seedling bed about 1 meter wide, composed of 6 parts of farmland soil and 4 parts of well-rotted organic fertilizer. After the soaked seeds are sown, a straw mat or sunshade net is covered on top to reduce water evaporation. When the seedlings grow to 1~2 true leaves, they are thinned and planted in permanent rows. When the plants have been cultivated for 50~60 days and reach a height of 10~20 cm, they are transplanted. The ridge-bordered planting plots are fertilized with 5,000~10,000 kg well-rotted organic fertilizer per mu, and then ploughed, tilled and leveled to make a planting bed about 120 cm wide. The next day after watering, holes are dug with a pointed spade for planting, and then the plots are watered immediately once again. After that, well-balanced temperature management, timely fertilization and watering are required.

Fried bean powder and organic fertilizers are mainly used in topdressing. Harvesting is determined by market demand and plant growth. The celery is stored in a cellar, which is excavated to a depth of 70 cm and a wall is built at a distance of 30 cm from the edge. Bamboo strips are used to support the top of the cellar covered with straw mats. Coverage or ventilation is adjusted according to the exact temperature conditions. After about 60 days of winter storage, Guihe Celery is bright yellow, crispy, and fragrant, and can be used in salads or stir-fries.

Due to its meticulous management, there is a saying among the people that lazy people should not plant celery, and those who plant celery should be diligent.

3. Shouguang Chicken-drumstick Green Onion. Shouguang Green Onions look like inverted chicken drumsticks, and are planted either in spring or in autumn. Manure is applied in planting seedlings, then the surface of plots are ploughed and leveled to make ridges, and shallow ditches are opened along the ridges with the coverage of fine soil after sowing. During the seedling stage, timely soil loosening, weeding, fertilizing, and watering are required. Seedlings are to be thinned out after the autumn seedlings green up or the spring seedlings grow true leaves, and the intermediate seedlings are planted from mid-June to early July. In planting, ditches are to be opened narrowly (about 25 cm) but broadly in the north-south direction with fertilized manure applied at the bottom, and then the plots are to be tilled to mix the manure into the soil. Planting is usually done by means of "Water Insertion Method", which means that water is poured thoroughly into the planting ditch, and then the green onion seedlings are planted while wet after watering, so that the false stem is vertically erect and aesthetically pleasing. After the green onion seedlings are planted, it's time for topdressing (the first topdressing at the beginning of vigorous growth, and then topdressing once every 20~25 days), adding soil (twice, in middle and late August), watering (water 2~3 times each time after soil adding and topdressing), and harvesting after the seedlings are protected with slow growth in

summer into thriving prosperously in autumn full of false stems. Generally speaking, spring-planted green onions can be harvested in autumn, while overwintering green onions can be harvested in middle and late November.

The best storage effect is achieved by freezing after harvest, which is called frozen storage (Dongcang). Keep the sorted green onion bundles at a low temperature of −5~0℃ to slow down the respiratory consumption and water loss. Bulk storage mainly uses the natural low temperature in winter, that is, green onion bundles (root down) are discharged in the shady site of a building to facilitate ventilation management. Before freezing, the bundled green onions are left exposed; after freezing, the false stems are covered with soil and a straw mat is placed on top to protect against rain and temperature changes, stabilizing the green onions in a mild frozen state for easy transportation and sale.

The production customs of proverbs include "Plant green onions in the middle of July." "Green onions in July will grow green, while green onions in August will harvest none." "Green onions are to be planted deep, while garlic is to be planted shallow." "Frozen onion, dry garlic." "Drowned cabbage, dry green onions", and so on.

4. Fuqiao Green Radish. First, select high quality planting farmland, use decomposed manure as base fertilizer, plough deeply, rake and level the ground well for flat beds. In mid-August, it's time for ditch digging, seed selecting and sowing, soil covering and plot leveling. If the weather is dry, water in small amounts several times to keep the surface of the plots moist. Thinning the seedlings for the first time after they all spring out and then thinning for the second time when they grow to 3~4 true leaves. After planting, it's time to fertilize and then water 2~3 times to exert its effects and promote the growth of leaves. Afterwards, It's time for shallow hoeing, topdressing, watering, inter-tillage and soil loosening, weeding and soil moisture conserving. During the early stage of fleshy root expansion (that is, the vigorous

growth stage of leaves), it is necessary to promote vigorous leaf growth and preventing excessive leaf growth as well. At the end of the early stage and the beginning of the peak stage of fleshy root expansion (2~3 days before the Autum Equinox), a large topdressing should be carried out. After fertilization, it's time for timely tillage and soil loosening to mix the fertilizer into soil, followed by watering. After that, the plant entered the peak period of fleshy root expansion, it's necessary to supply water appropriately to keep the soil from too dry or too wet and to prevent root cracking as well. The tail of the fleshy root is fully enlarged and round, indicating that the fleshy root has been long and is a sign of the harvest period. In general, after several frosts in middle and late October, their quality becomes better, so the Start of Winter is the harvest period of radishes stored in winter. After harvest, cut the top of the radish root and put it into a shallow trench cellar 30 cm deep and 100 cm wide, covered with a layer of moist soil for cooling in advance before storage. It's advisable to transfer them into the cellar 7~8 days later for storage when the weather has turned cool in the afternoon and sprinkle a thin layer of moist fine soil while placing a layer of radishes. Generally speaking, 4~5 layers can be placed to make the height of the radishes in the cellar reach 60~80 cm. 8~10 cm moist fine soil is covered on the top of the uppermost layer of radishes. As the weather gets cold, more soil will be added several times.

There are many proverbs in production customs. For example, "Plant radishes during the first period of hot weather, mustard during the second, and Chinese cabbage during the third." "(Harvesting) radish at the Start of Winter, and Chinese cabbage at the First Snowfall." "The more times to hoe, the more conducive to the growth of radish." "Radish in winter and ginger in summer keeps the doctor away." "Yantai apple, Laiyang pear, not as good as Weifang radish skin."

Shouguang Vegetable Production Customs are closely related to people's daily life. For instance, a local wedding banquet in Shouguang must include "One chicken, two fish, three cold dishes, followed by Four-Pleasure braised pork meatballs" . To entertain a new son–in–law at the Spring Festival, it must be "Fried eggs with leeks, a nephew then at that year see the dish immediately" . For a wedding event, two washbasins are placed in the wedding room, one of which is filled with wheat and inserted with green onions, implying "the wedding basin is inserted with green onions, and a son will be born to serve the court" .

Shouguang Vegetable Production Customs, an important part of Chinese folk customs, is summed up by the local people in long–honored vegetable production practices with distinct regional characteristics, rich in common people's production wisdom and colorful vegetable culture.

Qingzhou Buddhist Preaching Scripture

In 2016, "Qingzhou Buddhist Preaching Scriptures" was listed in the fourth batch of provincial intangible cultural heritage by Shandong Provincial People's Government.

Qingzhou City, with a long history and prosperous culture, is one of the nine states in ancient China, the source of the Silk Road, and the birthplace of Dongyi culture. A long history and splendid culture breed many intangible cultural heritages, among which Qingzhou Buddhist preaching scriptures is a typical representative.

After Buddhism was introduced into Qingzhou during the Western and Easten Han Dynasties, it soon took root, germinated and blossomed in this land. According to *the Records of Yidu County* in the period of Guangxu Reign of the Qing Dynasty, Ningfu Temple, the earliest temple in Qingzhou, was built in 302, the first year of Tai'an in the Western Jin Dynasty. Its former site, Ta'erpo, is near Nijia Village, Zhengmu Town, Qingzhou City. During the period of Sixteen States, the monarchs of Later Zhao, Fomer Yan, Fomer Qin and Southern Yan who ruled Qingzhou believed in Buddhism, which made Buddhism develop rapidly in Qingzhou. In 469, after Qing Qi (referring to Shandong) was brought into the Wei Dynasty, religious culture and art developed greatly here. On the sites of Qiji Temple, LongXing Temple, Guangfu Temple and Xingguo Temple, a large number of exquisite Buddhist statues have been unearthed and handed down. Now Longxing Temple in Qingzhou is the only existing large-scale temple site built before Tang Dynasty in China.

According to relevant historical records, it can be inferred that Qingzhou Buddhist preaching scriptures originated from the temple chanting activities in the Tang Dynasty. It's recorded that in the eighth year of the Yixi reign(412) of the Eastern Jin Dynasty, the famous monk Fa Xian traveled to the west to seek Dharma and collate a large number of scriptures. He returned to the motherland by sea from the Lion Kingdom (today's Sri Lanka) and landed on the Laoshan Mountain in Guangjun, Qingzhou. He once collated Buddhist scriptures and preached in Longxing Temple, Qingzhou, and lived there for about a year. In 840, the Japanese monk Yuanren recorded a popular preaching in temples in the Tang Dynasty in his work *Seeking Dharma travel to the Tang Dynasty*. Monk Yuanren once lived in Longxing Temple in Qingzhou. As a master of folk speaking, he left precious and rich materials for the folk speaking and singing activities in Qingzhou.

Most of the folk religions in Shandong originated from the Pure Land Sect of Buddhism. In the Southern Song Dynasty, they were called White Lotus Sect, and later called White Lotus Society. Historically, Shandong and its neighboring provinces had been the most extensively influenced. White Lotus Sect has its own unique scriptures, and each folk secret religious activity also has its own unique scriptures. They are aimed at preaching doctrines, and these scriptures have the names of reciting scriptures, preaching scriptures, preaching Buddha, persuasive book, and etc. In the Song Dynasty, most of the preaching and chanting arts such as "preaching scriptures" in temples and fairs were transferred to the entertaining place named as Washe. The combination of monks' "chanting scriptures" and "expounding karma" with folk story-telling and singing broke away from the content of religious disaster relief and blessing, and became a popular form of folk art relying on Buddhism to tell stories.

Since the Yuan and Ming Dynasties, Buddhist reciting scripture, a form of folk art, has been quite active in central and southwest Shandong. Buddhist reciting scripture in Qingzhou was popular in the Ming Dynasty. During the Yongle period of the Ming Dynasty, Tang Sai'er, the leader of the peasant uprising army in Qingzhou, called himself "mother of Buddha" and organized the uprising in the form of Buddhist Chanting in the form of White Lotus sect. After the middle period of the Ming Dynasty, folk religion developed rapidly, and treasured scriptures became more and more popular. In the period of Tianqi of the Ming Dynasty, Xu Hongru, a native of Juye, launched the peasant uprising, and he also made use of the scriptures of Wenxiang sect of White Lotus society to launch the uprising. It is obvious that Qingzhou is one of the areas with frequent activities of folk religion sects, and the preaching scripture of various sects are widely spread throughout the province. The development of folk secret religion led to the prosperity of Qingzhou treasured scriptures. After the reign of Kangxi in the Qing Dynasty, the Qing government suppressed the local folk religious groups on a large scale and destroyed the scriptures they used. According to the records of the Qing government, Treasured scriptures found most were in Shandong, including Qingzhou treasured scriptures. But until the end of the Qing Dynasty, treasured scriptures were still very popular in Qingzhou.

During the period of the Republic of China, all kinds of scripture preaching activities popular in Qingzhou were called "Shanshu" (talking and singing activities of persuading beneficence). Since the 1980s, believers often gathered and sang in Qingzhou area, mainly distributed in Qingzhou city, Huanglou town, Shaozhuang town, Miaozi town, Wangfen town, etc. The temple fair of Yunmen Mountain in Qingzhou is held on March 3rd and September 9th of the lunar calendar. During the temple fair, believers gather in the mountains, burn paper and incense to worship the

Buddha, and then disperse in front of the temple, behind the temple or among the hillside forests. They sit around on the ground and sing scriptures, which is called "Praying to Buddha" . The number of believers is often thousands. Singers who make the pilgrimage to the temple on the famous mountain are mostly middle-aged and old women, and there are also young singers and dancers with the gaily decorated basket on their shoulder. Among the hillsides, the sounds of praying chant rise and fall one after another, and stop at dusk.

There are various forms of preaching scripture performance in Qingzhou, such as sitting in the hall and reciting the scriptures, group singing, walking and singing with the gaily decorated basket on their shoulders(actually Dan Scriptures) in the temple fairs, etc. most of the tunes used are from folk songs.

Some of Qingzhou preaching scriptures are only sang but not spoken. For example, the libretto of "Buddhist Mantra" :

From nine doors to the Eastern Heaven, / there is the First Emperor, Qin Shi Huang/access to the Three Pure Ones./ The God of Goumang was busy with military affairs and transport / up around rosy clouds /of 90 million layers / with a left waiter in green waist / and a right guard prodigy./ The recruitment of official dispatch / was submitted in a list to the superior./ Today's disciples / were welcome to give accounts./ May Gods and Goddesses / listed in the green book / came back to the spiritual drive / and reshaped like babies. / Peacefulness cures the liver / incurring brightness. / Sit naturally /and the spiritual state will be fine. / Heaven and Earth are infinite / enough to enjoy banquets and luxurious houses. / In the Anzhen Spirit Prison / with the help of the feather carriage / twelve flying dragons / Clearly drill the inscriptions on the jade slips / approved fairy name /wrapped red books in body / whose names were imprinted in the ginseng hall / to my room / two mixed together / spiritual flows glow/ gold face and fresh appeared / and the body became alive forever.

There is only a libretto but no preaching speech.

Some preaching scriptures are the combination of words and sentences. For example, "Buddha Mantra for Shroud" :

There's a mystery of fate on the way to the west and 72 copper news. The weaver–girls came to work hard on the loom from the ninth sphere of the heavens and weaved silks into a garment for birthday. The weaver–sister was actually smart in weaving and tailoring, and the garment was quite fit to her body without too thin or too heavy and too big or too small. The embroider–sister was actually smart in ironing, and was skillful in embroidering a variety of flowers and grasses with steel needle yarn at hands. The bright moon loomed above Xi River was embroidered on the front panel and a seahorse–shaped sunrise was on the back panel. The two banks of the milky way was embroidered on the sleeves and a picture of the Weaver–maid and the Cowherd on the shoulders. Ducks playing in the water was embroidered on the big flap and peony and Phoenix on the bottom flap. Guardian warriors and a Picture of Bagua was embroidered on the edge of the garment and Heaven Marshal holding a tower on hand on the corner of the garment. Two dragons diving into the sea was embroidered on the collar of the garment and flowers falling into the Heaven on the belt tied to the garment. The Weaver–girl presented the fairy clothes to the Queen Mother after the embroidery and rode the clouds to the west to see the Yuhuang. She was required to do good deeds and detach from the life transmigration cycle into a Buddha, and was rewarded with blessings for longevity and good fortune.

This is called "Buddhist treasured scriptures" , which is a mixture of ancient and modern languages, with combination of seven–character and ten–character sentences.

Some are combination of singing and talking. For example, the lyrics of "Big Dipper Mantra" :

Yuhuang Supreme Deity of Taism/the emperor in charge of Ziwei fate plate/in circumferential horizon/thoughtful even to tiny dust/no matter what kind of misfortune cannot be diminished,/no matter what kind of fortune cannot be blessed./The righteous spirit of the emperor/comes and joins me./What the Big Dipper refers to is/ that days and nights turn constantly./Common people on the earth/prefer to bless for good wishes./May the witness of your respected appearance/and pray for longevity./ The virtual essences of the Three Terrace Constellations /and the Six Chun Star of Fortune, Wealth and Longevity / give birth to me and raise me / and protect my body and shape.

Speaking each character after singing: Kui, Shuo, Quan, Xing, Bi, Pu, and Piao.

The places for scripture preaching is very flexible, such as temples, families, forests in the mountains and so on. Before preaching the scriptures, preachers still need certain rites. They will wash their hands first, pick incense, and kowtow to the Buddha statue hanging on the wall. Then, the main preacher would knock on the wooden fish, chime, dharma drum or dharma bell, and meanwhile, there are many people chanting beside. They can also recite the scriptures without musical instruments. The main preacher should memorize the content of the Buddhist scripture roll, have a certain eloquence, and pronounce accurately. The scripture roll can be spread on the table or held in the hand to remind the preachers.

Qingzhou preaching scriptures truly records the customs and social changes of Qingzhou, Shandong Province. It is a valuable "information bank" for us to study the history of Shandong social customs. The singing of all kinds of treasured scriptures gradually absorbed a lot of folk art, which has the value of folk custom and folk art. Qingzhou preaching scriptures exhorts people to do good, accumulate virtue and show filial piety to their elders, which plays a positive role in purifying social atmosphere and maintaining social stability.

Worship for Sun Bin

In 2016, "Worship for Sun Bin" of Changyi City was listed in the fourth batch of provincial intangible cultural heritage by Shandong Provincial People's Government.

Changyi City, located in the northwest of Shandong Peninsula, is subordinate to Weifang, Shandong Province. Sun Bin (about 380–320 BC), formerly known as Bin, was born in the State of Qi. He was a representative of the military school in the middle of the Warring States Period and an outstanding militarist. He was the descendant of the famous militarist Sun Wu. Sun Bin was very interested in marching and fighting when he was young, and liked to study the art of war. He inherited and developed the military thoughts of Sun Wu, Wu Qi and others, and formed his own military theory.

Sun Bin studied the art of war with Pang Juan when he was young. Pang Juan later went to the State of Wei, but he was always secretly envious of Sun Bin's talent. He was afraid that Sun Bin would surpass him, so he secretly sent someone to invite Sun Bin to the state of Wei and planned to frame Sun Bin. After Sun Bin's arrival, Pang Juan trump up some charges to frame Sun Bin, causing corporal punishment called penalties of Bin and Qing(cutting off the part of leg under the knee, branding the face). Pang Juan cut off Sun Bin's feet and stabbed words on his face, trying to destroy Sun Bin in this way. However, Sun Bin's outstanding talent was discovered by an envoy of the state of Qi, who secretly drove Sun Bin back to the state of Qi. After his arrival, he helped Tian Ji, the senior general of Qi, win the horse race. Tian Ji thought that this man was a rare talent, so he recommended Sun Bin to the king of Qi, and Sun Bin was highly valued by the king of Qi. In the later battle of Guiling, Sun Bin performed well. In the battle of Ma Ling, he used the strategy of "Encircling Wei and Rescuing Zhao", which made Wei lose its hegemony. Sun Bin became famous after the battle of Maling. King Wei of Qi bestowed Duchang (now Changyi of Weifang) on him as his fiefdom, and the same record can be found in *Honorable Land*, Volume 5 of *Changyi County Annals* in 1742.

Because of the popularity of novels about Sun Bin, such as *Stories about Yueyi Attacking the State of Qi, Nations' War:Chronicles* and *Biography of Sun Pang—the seven nations since the Song and Yuan Dynasties*, people's worship for Sun Bin gradually rose in Duchang.

Duchang was established as a county in the Qin Dynasty with a history of more than 2000 years. With a long history, Dong Yong'an Village of Duchang Street in Changyi City is a key historical and cultural village in Duchang residential district. Sun Bin once lived in Xitu Port of Dong Yong'an Village. Sun Bin Temple was built in the Wanli Reign of the Ming Dynasty to commemorate the military strategist Sun Bin.

According to the inscriptions in front of the Sun Bin Temple, during the Xianfeng Reign of the Qing Dynasty, a group of ferocious bandits came here, burning, killing, robbing and plundering. The people here suffered a lot, and the villagers hated them. After their discussion, all villagers decided to take the initiative to drive the bandits away and protect their homes. So all villagers gathered in Sun Bin Temple with enclosing walls at that time, and took it as a stronghold to rise up against the bandits. Seeing that the Sun Bin Temple could not be attacked for a long time, these bandits converted to attack with fire. They wanted to force the villagers in the temple to surrender by smoking. Just when the villagers were about to give up their fight, a strong wind suddenly blew up, blowing the fire and smoke in the opposite direction, driving the bandits away, and the villagers and the Sun Bin Temple survived. The villagers believed that Sun Bin had protected them. Since then, the villagers had become more devout in their worship for Sun Bin.

People, full of the worship for Sun Bin, carried out a series of folk activities centered on Sun Bin. The 14th day of the first lunar month is the birthday of Sun Bin. Since the Sun Bin temple was built in the Wanli period of the Ming Dynasty, the 14th day of the first lunar month of each year has been designated as the Sun Bin Temple Fair to commemorate this outstanding military hero. It is said that every time Sun Bin won, he always sat in a chariot pulled by a fierce, tall and powerful bull with one horn. Therefore, every year on this day of the Sun Bin Temple Fair, a folk memorial ceremony of "burning the bull" was held, which has a history of more than 400 years. Every year, there are many people in the Sun Bin temple fair and folk art teams from different places, which add a strong cultural atmosphere to the local tourism.

"Burning the bull" is one of the most distinctive activities in the series of activities of worship for Sun Bin. Generally speaking, there are five steps to be completed from the beginning to the end of this folk custom activity.

First of all, it is "Making the bull". On the sixth day of the first lunar month of each year, people in Dong Yong'an village begin to prepare with great piety. They begin to tie the framework of the old bull with plant straws with proper hardness such as local beads, cotton and locust sticks, sunflower stalks and sorghum stalks. On the twelfth day of the first lunar month, after the frame was tied up, the women cut yellow colored paper to be the bull's hair, and various colored paper to be the saddle, broadsword, bell and other decorations which were glued to the bull. The whole binding process required more than 140 procedures. The bull with power and magnificence is 5 meters high, 10 meters long and the horn is 1.8 meters long.

Secondly, there is the activity of "Parading with the Bull". At 8 a.m. on the 14th of the first month, villagers set off firecrackers in front of the Sun Bin temple, and the bull was surrounded by the crowd, the parade starts.The whole team of "Parading with the Bull" is magnificent. In the front, the firecracker team leads the way, the gongs and drums team, the Yangko team and the stilts team follow. After them, the team of lifting the bull is composed of more than 20 young adults, and the other villagers are at the back. The route of the parade is: walk along the North–South Street adjacent to the east of the village committee to the crossroads, then turn to the west side, and finally stop in the empty space in the west of the Sun Bin temple. Along the way, gongs and drums were noisy, firecrackers were blaring together, and it was very lively.

At the end of the parade, the third stage of activities—sacrifice begins. This activity usually starts at about 10 a.m. people set up offerings in the open space, burning paper and incense for Sun Bin, and kowtowing to pray. At the same time, activities such as twisting Yangko, dragon dance, playing waist drum and singing L ü Opera, which were spontaneously organized by villagers, also begin to be staged. At the scene of the performance, the solemn Sun Bin temple, the powerful bull and the lively artistic performance in the open space in front of the temple contrast finely with each other.

After the end of the these activities, they begin to "Touch the Bull". People flocked to the scene, competing to "touch the bull, and pray to the bull for the take–away of the disease". Villagers have been saying for generations, "Touch the head of the bull and you'll not worry about food and clothing; touch the buttocks of the bull and you will never get sick; touch the horn of the bull, you won't have acne on your body; touch the saddle, there will be no scar on your body." The villagers believe that on the fourteenth day of the first lunar month, "Bull Touching" can get rid of all kinds of diseases and bring good luck to the family for a whole year.

The last activity is "Burning the Bull". "Burning the Bull", also known as "Seeing off the Bull", is usually held between 11 a.m. and 12 a.m.. Before "Seeing off the Bull", some pious villagers have knelt in front of the sacred objects, devoutly singing divine songs, and their excitement and expectation are beyond expression. As soon as the time comes, the villagers carry the bull over the ready-made incense paper pile, reciting the name of "Master Sun", and warning the bull not to "Scare the Master", until the organizer yelled "See off the Bull", and the bull is immediately ignited, and the sky is filled with the flames and smoke. The delicately made bull finally is burned into smoke and goes to the heaven. The villagers believed that only the burning bull can ascend to heaven so as to bring people's piety and wishes to Sun Bin.

The Sun Bin Worship also includes legends, craftsmanship, artistic performance and so on. A series of folk activities arising from the worship of Sun Bin have brought the relationship between the neighboring villages closer, enriched the spiritual life of the local people, and formed a unique local culture. This folk activity should be inherited, innovated and developed continuously.

Yishan Fair

In 2016, "Yishan Fair" of Zoucheng City was listed in the fourth batch of provincial intangible cultural heritage by Shandong Provincial People's Government.

Zoucheng City is located in the south of Shandong Province. As early as the Neolithic age, there were ancestors living here; During the Spring and Autumn Period and the Warring States Period, it became the capital of the State of Zou. Together with the State of Lu, it was also known as the "holy land of Zou and Lu". It was also a place of cultural prosperity at that time. Zoucheng is the hometown of Mencius, known as "the birthplace of culture, the hometown of Confucius and Mencius". In such a famous historical and cultural city, there are many folk cultural events of which Yishan Fair at the foot of the mount Yishan is a very famous one.

Yishan is located about 12 kilometers southeast of Zoucheng City, with an altitude of 550 meters. It is known as "land of beauty, wonder of the south of Mount Tai". Since ancient times, Yishan has formed four wonders, including 24 landscapes, 36 fairylands, 228 temples and hundreds of palaces and nunneries after many times of development. Such beautiful scenery naturally attracts tourists and pilgrims from far and near.

Yishan Fair is set at the foot of Yishan. It is held on February 2nd of the lunar calendar every year and lasts for 3–5 days, up to 7 days. The management organization of the Fair is called "guild", and the broker's deal or stall–setting is called "declaring the deal". The commodities to the fair are categorized into different stands, including cattle and horses market, furniture and farm tools market, black shed (for steamed stuffed bun sale), white shed (for cloth sale), etc. The front of Yishan is took as the center of the fair which is from Majiagou in the east to Liujiagou in the west, with a square of five or six *li*. The fair is the most influential and large–scale historic one among the local people. At that time, there are people coming to the fair from the neighboring counties and provinces, some praying for gods and worshiping Buddhas, some making vows and returning vows, some buying and selling things, and some acting storytelling and singing operas, and some juggling. Generally speaking, people going to the fair will first go up to the temple and offer incense, then go down the mountain to listen to the opera, and finally buy some necessities. Commodity trading reached its peak on the second or third day, and numerous people attended the fair.

The origin of the Yishan Fair is related to the earliest sacrificial activities. The specific origin is not clearly recorded, but there are two kinds of legends. First, Liu Hui of the later Han dynasty recorded in his book *History of Zoushan* that February 2 was the day when the Dragon raised its head. People gathered in Yishan to pray for good weather and harvest in the whole year. Second, on February 2nd, 615 B.C., Zhu Wengong, who understood the decree of the Heaven, established his country in the south of Yishan. Therefore, February 2nd was the day of celebration. There were activities on this day every year, and later gradually evolved into the Yishan Fair.

In the later development, the functions of the Yishan Fair was no longer limited to offering sacrifices and praying, but added many new content. On February 2nd every year, many pilgrims gather on Yishan, particularly, there is the "incense society" organized by the village. The so–called "incense society" is a literary and artistic group organized by the elders or leaders of the village. Generally, young people who are good at singing and dancing are selected from their own villages, rehearsing entertaining programs such as "dragon lantern dance", "stilt walking" and "gaily decorated boat rowing" based on rural customs. The incense society collects some of the money and grain according to the householder (or population of the family) for collective expenditure, and the well–off families will pay more. The time of the above activities is usually from the first day of the first lunar month to the second day of February. On the day of the fair, the members of the incense society hold high the colored flag with the words of "× × incense society", "× × pilgrimage group", with the sound of gongs and drums, they walk toward Yishan. On the way to Yishan, they set off firecrackers when passing through villages or places where people are concentrated. After they enter the mountains, they have to go to the Dragon Temple to offer the incense and worship, then, give performance. The louder the cheers of the audience around, the harder they perform.

Individual pilgrims are praying for having children or grandchildren, being free of diseases and disasters, and consulting fortune. They will put incense into the censer and light it, then they will kneel down and pray devoutly. Many of the villagers around Yishan come here to pray for having children, and some of their grandparents, parents and grandchildren come together to "pray for having children". On the day of the fair, they all dress up, take paper money and incense, and light a stick of incense at home before leaving, hoping for the protection of their ancestors, praying silently along the way and praying for the blessing of their children. Moreover, the devout people kowtow at every step when they go up the mountain. After entering the temple, under the witness of a priest, they light incense, kowtow, report their names and living places, and give a "vow" to fulfill his promise on a certain day of the next year. Then, plead with the priest for the stone (getting kid in pronunciation)or the clay doll.

The person who vows takes the stone, ties it with a red rope (or red cloth) prepared in advance, puts it in his/her arms and returns home. On the way home, he/she still chants the words "kid, come home with me" again and again. When he/she gets home, he/she puts the stone on the bed. If there is really any kids in his/her family, the person who vow will take the offering to the mountain to fulfill his/her promise. Some will sew a "longevity lock" with colored threads after the birth of the kid. The "longevity lock" in the shape of a Yuan Bao (shoe–shaped gold ingot) is sewn with seven color silk thread and hung on the baby's chest. According to local customs, children who are "tied up" on the stone from the mountain can't climb Yishan for their whole life to avoid being kept by immortals.

Today, the Yishan Fair has developed into a cultural material exchange fair integrating offering incense and praying, mules and horses trade. There are all kinds of snacks, as well as a variety of special cultural commodities at the fair. According to a stone inscription at Baiyun palace in the fourth year of Wanli period in the Ming Dynasty (1576), there are 38 firms, halls and shops in the areas of Yishan. According to historical records, in the late Ming and early Qing Dynasty, the Shanxi guild hall once monopolized the market of Yishan, dealing in hundreds of varieties of goods.

The special snacks at the Yishan Fair are full of distinct cultural characteristics. Among them, Bahua treasured porridge (porridge made by eight treasured ingredients) and liquor–saturated jujube are the most famous. Bahua treasured porridge appeared in the Tang and Song Dynasties and flourished in the Yuan, Ming and Qing Dynasties. The so–called "Babaohua Treasured Porridge" refers to the porridge made by eight local products, such as cowpea, mung beans, red and white adzuki beans, glutinous rice, red jujube mud, peanut grits, yellow lentils and watermelon kernels. They are put in the pot one after another by different timing, with sweet dew and spring water, simmered gently. These eight ingredients are boiled to be blossom–shape. After it's done, the taste is excellent, suitable for all ages, so it is often called "surname–

forgetting porridge", which means that the porridge is so delicious that you will forget your name for a while. "Liquor" of liquor-saturated jujube comes from Sweet Dew from Heaven, a special Baijiu of Yishan, which is brewed by using the water from Sweet Dew pool of Yishan. Legend has it that Zhuzhuang, the 18th monarch of the state of Zhu, was full of praise and named it as "Sweet Dew from the Heaven". Liquor-saturated jujubes are made by the following steps. Take the fresh long jujubes, put them into "Sweet Dew from Heaven" with chopsticks and soak them for several days. After taking them out, put them into porcelain pot or pottery pot and seal it in a cool place indoors for eating on the new year's Eve or selling at the Yishan Fair. The jujubes are crisp and delicious, giving off the smell of fragrance of Baijiu, and the their color is kept fresh, which have the effect of increasing appetite. In addition, the famous delicacies are Golden Phoenix Facing Morning Sun (pheasant), Baiyuan Immortal (white hare), Recumbent General (crab), etc.

Yishan Fair has left a deep mark in the production and life of local residents, and it shines with the light and color of Yishan in Zoucheng on the land of China.

Mount Tai Tofu Feast

In 2016, "Mount Tai Tofu Feast" of Tai'an city was listed in the fourth batch of provincial intangible cultural heritage by Shandong Provincial People's Government.

Mount Tai Tofu Feast has a long history, which accompanies the ancient emperors' activities of offering sacrifices in Mount Tai. The emperors came to Mount Tai to express his gratitude for the Heaven's mandate. In order to show his sincerity, he had to "bathe and change clothes, and have vegetarian diet to express his devout heart" before he came to the temple. As a result, Mount Tai Tofu, a common food for ordinary people, became the emperor's exclusive diet.

Mount Tai Tofu is made of high-quality soybeans which are ground by hand-made stone mill and spring water from Mount Tai. Its color is as white as jade, tender but not loose, so it is called "Magical Tofu", and it is also one of "Three Beauties of Mount Tai" together with Huangya cabbage and spring water of Mount Tai. The Mount Tai Tofu Feast made with it is an indispensable part of the emperor's activities of offering sacrifices to the Heaven, and it has been handed down to the present day.

Since Emperor Wu of the Han Dynasty, tofu has been an important part of offering sacrifice to the Heaven. In the Song Dynasty, it reached a prosperous period, and in the Ming and Qing Dynasties it reached its peak. Tofu feast has become an integral part of Mount Tai culture. Mount Tai Tofu Feast is rich in variety of dishes, focusing on the combination of nutrition and taste, variety and culture. The twelve main courses and more than a hundred common dishes reflect the eating habits of the emperors. For example, the dish "Auspicious Luck" is evolved from the vegetarian culture on the basis of inheriting the production technology of "Bag-shape Chicken", a royal dish in the Kangxi period of the Qing Dynasty. "Good fortune" comes from the traditional Shandong cuisine "Dry-fried Tofu Balls". After Emperor Qianlong tasted this dish, he praised it and named it "Dragon's Eyes and Golden Balls". It can be seen that Mount Tai Tofu Feast is a perfect combination of royal cuisine culture and local traditional diet. Mount Tai Tofu Feast has absorbed cooking technology of dishes made by tofu in the process of inheritance, into which Mount Tai culture, culture of sacrificing to the Heaven and the Earth, and folk culture are integrated, and gradually become a unique feast with local characteristics. *Tai'an County Annals*, which was revised in the reign of Emperor Qianlong, once recorded, "In the early hours of the morning, there are the sounds of the clapper in the streets, tofu fragrance in the evening, tofu workshop in Taicheng's family." It can be seen that at that time, it was a normal life for every household to make tofu.

Mount Tai Tofu Feast is one of the representatives of Shandong cuisine. Mount Tai Tofu Feast, using tofu as the main ingredient, has experienced three developing stages.

The first stage is the period of germination and integration. The emperors had to eat vegetarian food in order to show their sincerity to the Heaven. Therefore, the local mountain delicacies and wild vegetables once became the main component of sacrificing food for emperors. Tofu was introduced to Mount Tai in March of the fifth year of Yuanfeng (106 BC). Emperor Wu of the Han Dynasty also went to Mount Tai during his southern tour and offered sacrifices to Emperor Liubang in the ceremonial hall. In addition to cattle, sheep, pigs, jade and silk, there were also "Li Qi" (another name of tofu) as the sacrificial offerings. Due to its tender taste and rich nutrition, tofu was gradually introduced into imperial food for sacrificial ceremony .

The second stage is the developing period. Tofu can be processed and cooked in different ways to produce dishes with different tastes and shapes. Since the Tang and Song Dynasties, tofu has become the main courses of imperial cuisine. In the Song Dynasty, bean curd processing workshops flourished in Taicheng. But at this time, it is just tofu dishes, not a real system banquet.

The third is an important development stage, represented by the Ming and Qing Dynasties. The large-scale processing of tofu has also promoted the reform of tofu processing techniques. Tofu dishes have gradually developed from the original "frying, pan-frying, and deep-frying" techniques to a "cultural cuisine" with tofu as the main ingredient and using cooking techniques to integrate them into local culture. Special dishes such as "tofu vegetarian chicken" and "tofu vegetarian fish" have emerged, which laid a solid foundation for tofu dishes to turn to tofu banquet. By the Qing Dynasty, tofu feast became mature. During the period of the Republic of China and the early days of the founding of the People's Republic of China, the methods of making tofu dishes spread among the people, and tofu banquet became an important representative of Taishan food culture in the cultural space at that time.

Mount Tai Tofu Banquet is influenced by Mount Tai sacrificing culture. It is made of vegetarian food to reflect the emperor's idea of eating vegetarian food and sincerely respecting the Heaven; In terms of technology, steaming, deep-frying, pan-frying, frying, quick-frying, braising, and stewing are all available; Serving dishes with four small plates, four side dishes and nine main dishes can achieve the goal of "eating fish but no fish, eating chicken but no chicken, only enjoying its taste without cooking the real ones" . The serving procedure is to serve the small dishes first, then the side dishes, lastly the main courses and various snacks. In the course of serving dishes, the interpreter will introduce the historical origin and cultural connotation of the dishes, so as to reflect the style of imperial cuisine of local culture.

Mount Tai Tofu Feast is improved on the basis of retaining the traditional techniques. The main dishes are: Taiji happiness and longevity soup with the shape of Taiji, which embodies Yin and Yang by black seaweed and white tofu, and implies harmony. Auspicious Luck with Ease and Comfort, young-chicken-shaped, is filled with tofu, sea cucumber, shrimp and beans. Showing Emperor Kangxi's principle of vegetarianism during his six tours to the south, three visits to Mount Tai and two visits to the top of the mountain; Jade Emperor's blessing, honeycomb-like bean curd and beef under it is used to reflect the lofty of Mount Tai, and Yuhuang grass is added to nourish yin and supplement yang, strengthen spleen and replenish qi. Kyllin Fish with Soybean Mosaic, made from perch, bean curd, carrot, mushroom and Polygonatum, can be eaten in two ways, and it's originally made for the calm-down of the people's resentment and sacrificial ceremony in Mount Tai by Emperor Zhenzong of Song Dynasty. Based on "Braised Intestines in Brown Sauce", "Braised Tofu Intestines in Brown Sauce shows the religious and cultural characteristics of Mount Tai culture; More than 400 dishes, such as "Dragon eye and golden balls", Taishan Treasured Soup made by three Mount Tai treasures (cabbage, tofu, water) and "Blessed Land", which is known as "Magical tofu".

Mount Tai Tofu Feast has distinct characteristics, and it is the cream of imperial tofu dishes for emperors' Mount Tai ascents and sacrificial ceremony in the past dynasties. The dishes show the fusion of thousands of years of Buddhist culture and folk culture, reflecting inheritance of Fu (blessing and happiness) and the development culture in traditional catering culture. Nowadays, the tofu banquet for the ancient emperors is put on the public dining table, which not only enriches the food culture of Mount Tai, but also reflects the absorption and inheritance of traditional culture by the common people. People use "tofu" to signify "Doufu (all blessings)", which express people's pursuit of a better life and hope for a happy life.

Mount Tai Jade Custom

In 2016, "Mount Tai Jade Custom" in Daiyue district of Tai'an City was listed in the fourth batch of provincial intangible cultural heritage by Shandong Provincial People's Government.

Mount Tai Jade is known as the national jade by domestic experts for it combines the dignity of national mountain and the Reiki of national stone in one which come from the essence of the sun and the moon of billions of years, and the history and culture of Mount Tai of thousands of years. Today, Mount Tai Jade attracts the majority of jade collectors for its unique deep dark green and fine texture.

Mount Tai Jade has a long history, dating back to the Neolithic Age. At that time, the ancestors of the Wenhe Valley had already made jade spades, arm rings, ornaments and other works of art with Mount Tai Jade. It is recorded in *the Book of Shangshu: Yu Gong* that "Mount Tai grotesque-stone" was a tribute to Da Yu in the Xia Dynasty. In *the Book of Mountains and Seas*: *Dongshan Classic*, there is also a record that "There are many jades on Mount Tai, golds below it, and water jades in the water around it" . There is a clear record of Mount Tai Jade in Cao Zhi's poem, "Drive and scold with a duster, east to Fenggao City. So mystical is Mount Tai, the most famous one of the five sacred mountains... There are Yongli spring and beautiful jade on it..." During the Five Dynasties Period, the Taoist book *Lucky Land Records* recorded: "There are many lucid ganodermas, cordyceps sinensises and jades on Mount Tai." Until the contemporary *The Records of the Five Sacred Mountains*, there is a record of "Mount Tai is forty-four square circumference, with many lucid ganodermas and beautiful jades".

Before the Qin and Han Dynasties, Mount Tai Jade was so popular with the people that it was even sold as "stone to protect mountains" and "stone to keep away evil spirits". When emperors such as Qin Shihuang and Emperor Wudi of the Han Dynasty went to Mount Tai to worship, they all worshiped the standing stones on the summit. Jade was an important prop in the ceremony. After the Tang and Song Dynasties, Mount Tai Jade began to be popular among the people. As a talisman, Mount Tai Jade has become the spiritual sustenance of people at this time. People believe that Mount Tai stone can drive out disaster and insurance safety. The Mount Tai Shigandang customs influenced East Asia, Kyoto Museum of Ethnology in Japan has a collection of Mount Tai Shigandang stone unearthed in Okinawa.

As the saying goes "famous mountains produce famous jades", Mount Tai Jade is precious for the 2 words "Mount Tai" with the extraordinary implication and blessing of "Safety and Good luck". Mount Tai Jade is considered as jade to protect house, lucky jade, jade to keep away evil spirits, Gandang jade, and jade to keep safe for it is endowed with the meaning of keeping safe and helping families flourish. As the saying goes, "without jades, the garden isn't elegant, the hall isn't magnificent, the house isn't safe, and the people aren't beautiful". Mount Tai Jade is widely popular among the people, and it has become a kind of custom to collect Mount Tai Jade.

Fancy stones in the world are countless, only Mount Tai Shigandang is the most fancy. At the foot of Mount Tai, the wall of every household is inlaid with a "protective god" —Mount Tai Shigandang, The faith of "a Mount Tai Shigandang can ensure family security" has been deeply rooted in the hearts of the people. In order to pray for peace, Mount Tai tourists do not forget to take a Mount Tai Shigandang back home.

Jade has been used as medicine since ancient times. It has a very good effect on treating diseases and keeping fit. Wearing Mount Tai Jade frequently not only can beautify the jade, but also is beneficial to health. No matter from the perspective of natural gas field or scientific medical treatment, we can not ignore its role in human health care. According to scientific verification, Mount Tai Jade contains many trace elements needed by the human body. Wearing and using Mount Tai Jade frequently can help these beneficial elements through skin into human's body, so as to balance the imbalance of Yin and Yang in human body, conducive to promoting human health. These trace elements can not only maintain the normal physiological needs of human body, the amount of them in human body will also affect the intellectual development of human. In addition, Mount Tai Jade has a certain magnetic field effect, which helps to speed up blood circulation and enhance metabolism, and improve people's immunity. Containers made of Mount Tai Jade can moisten heart, lungs and throat, refresh brain and prolong life, etc.

Mount Tai Jade is preferable mineral raw materials of ornamental stone, carving crafts or jewelry for it is suitable for grinding and polishing, and easy to drill, saw, cut and grind, carve, etc. as the mineral particles of it are fine and evenly distributed with compact structure. Mount Tai Jade not only has a high artistic value, but also has a more profound spiritual and cultural connotation for the color of Mount Tai Jade is dignified and elegant, in line with the masculinity of Mount Tai Shigandang.

Mount Tai Jade carving industry enduring prosperity for it's profound cultural heritage. Mount Tai Jade carving skill well inherited the Chinese traditional jade carving techniques and characteristics, absorbed the advantages of hundreds of schools. At the same time, Mount Tai Jade become a jade version of the "Mount Tai Encyclopedia" for it innovate boldly and stand in the height of carrying forward

Mount Tai culture, integrating Mount Tai culture, customs and scenery into it. In recent years, with the protection and development of Mount Tai Jade, Mount Tai Jade carving works have been widely recognized by all sectors of society. Mount Tai Jade has become one of the representatives of the high standard of modern jade carving technology and has gained a broad market. It not only has a place in Tai'an, but also was successfully sold to the major cities of China. At the same time, it also spread the profound culture of Mount Tai in all directions.

Since the Neolithic Age, Mount Tai Jade has been widely loved by Chinese people. Mount Tai Jade is considered as the symbol of gentleman and the representative of distinguished man for it has fine texture, black and crystal appearance, elegant temperament and gentle introspection. Mount Tai jade has a Confucian connotaion at the same time for Mount Tai is closely connected with Confucianism. The statues of Confucius made of Mount Tai Jades have frequently appeared in the gifts exchanged between Chinese leaders and friends from all over the world. Mount Tai Jades were specially chosen as the cornerstones in many buildings on Tian'anmen Square in Beijing. The foundation jade of the new Chinese Embassy in the United States comes from Mount Tai. On the main hill of Beijing Olympic Forest Park, a 5.7-meter-high, 63-ton Mount Tai landscape jade stands on the peak. This stone has become one of the iconic landscapes of the Olympic Forest Park, and was named "Tianjing", which means "as steady as Mount Tai, as peaceful as Mount Tai".

Along with people's general attention, the value of Mount Tai Jade is gradually revealed. On April 10, 2010, the Shanghai World Expo licensed products "Mount Tai Jade, Expo Emblem" and "Mount Tai Jade, China Pavilion" were launched simultaneously in Beijing and Shanghai. "Mount Tai Jade, Expo Emblem" and "Mount Tai Jade, China Pavilion" set off a Mount Tai Jade collection upsurge for their highly ornamental and collection value. They embody strong Chinese elements and represent the spiritual temperament and verve of Chinese culture.

Mount Tai Jade's noble sentiment would rather be destroyed than be broken, would rather be break than be bend and unyielding inspired the Chinese people to struggle for the great cause of the nation. With infinite respect for Mount Tai and praise for Mount Tai Jade, people place their good hopes and wishes with Mount Tai Jade.

Mount Tai Sacrifice Custom

In 2016, "Mount Tai Sacrifice Custom" of Tai'an City was listed in the fourth batch of provincial intangible cultural heritage by Shandong Provincial People's Government.

Mount Tai has enjoyed a high reputation since ancient times, being called "Magical Mountain" and "Sacred Mountain" by people. "Mount Tai Sacrifice Custom" starts from people's fear, prayer, admiration, worship and integration of nature, and integrates politics and belief in the form of Chai Wang, Buddhist worship and pilgrimage to the mountains. It has a profound influence on the formation and development of the Chinese nation's spirit and is one of the most important intangible cultural heritages of Tai'an City.

In *the Book of Shang Shu*, an early Chinese classic, there is an account of the sacrifice on Mount Tai. Such as the Book of *Shang Shu*: *Shun Dian* said, "In February, hunt in the east, to Daizong, Chai, according to rank sacrifice mountains and rivers." Among them, the so-called "Chai", refers to burn wood to worship heaven; The so-called "Wang" means sacrifice mountains and rivers. Shun's Daizong "Chai Wang" and relevant records in ancient books show that Mount Tai not only played an important role in the development of the culture of the Eastern

Yi, but also had an important influence on the formation of the tribes of the Eastern Yi. Mount Tai is not only an object of worship for our ancestors, it has also become a cultural symbol.

Mount Tai Sacrifice in ancient times derive from ancestor's fear, worship and prayer to the nature. They find the living space and way of life suitable for their survival between heaven and earth, and use the natural conditions to seek development. The formation of Dawenkou culture created material conditions for the worship and sacrifice of Mount Tai. In the eyes of ancient people, they could not only avoid flood disasters with the help of mountains, but also obtain the necessary living and production resources from mountains. People revere and worship mountains and need to strengthen their cognition of nature with certain forms to express their awe and worship to nature. Primitive sacrifice also came into being. From the pre–Qin period to the Tang and Song Dynasties, Mount Tai sacrifice was a political ceremony to announce that the emperor had been ordered by heaven and had achieved prominent achievements.

The specific rituals of Mount Tai are full of symbolism, Ban Gu once explained, "Therefore, those who offer sacrifices to Heaven will also increase in height; Under the Zen Liang father base, wide thick also; He who carves a stone and a mark will do his own good. The Heaven is high for respect, and the Earth is thick for virtue, so increase the height of Mount Tai to report to the sky, attached to the father's address to report to the Earth, tomorrow the Earth's orders, success and success, beneficial to the Heaven and Earth, if the high is high, thick is thick." There is also a deeper meaning about offering sacrifices to the Heaven: to harmonize the relationship between human and God, and finally achieve the harmony between spiritual will and external behavior. In the Xia, Shang and Zhou Dynasties, Mount Tai was gradually regarded as a symbol of power, and the right to sacrifice to Mount Tai was also exclusive to emperors. This sacrifice which stand for political power evolved into offering sacrifices to heaven in the Warring States period. Since then, Mount Tai has also become a symbol of imperial power, that is to say, Mount Tai denotes the legitimacy and rationality of the divine right of Kings. Qin Shihuang patrolled the east in 28 years (219 BC), first he offered sacrifice on Yi mountain and carved stone in praise of the Qin Dynasty's achievements. At the same time, he called Confucian scholar of Qi, Lu to verify etiquette of offering sacrifices to heaven. All Confucian students have their own views. Qin Shihuang revised the ritual system by himself, repaired the mountain path and then climbed Mount Tai from the sunny side to held the ceremony of endowment at the top of Mount Tai, and erected a stone to offer eulogy. After that, a total of 12 emperors came to Mount Tai to worship and offer sacrifices.

From the Ming and Qing Dynasties to the modern times, Mount Tai worship changed from worship of the Heaven and the Earth to worship of Mount Tai Gods—Emperor Dongyue and Goddess Bixia. The ritual of Mount Tai worship gradually moved from the royal court to the people, and gradually became secular, universal and diversified. During the Ming and Qing Dynasties, great changes took place in the worship ceremony with strong political color. Emperor Taizu of the Ming Dynasty advocated there will be no longer "Worship Ceremony" , but only sacrificial activities. Since then, the emperor's sacrifice on Mount Tai became secular, and the secular sacrifice gradually turned to be religious.

The custom of Mount Tai sacrifice and the appeal of Mount Tai belief spread from the north to the south, from the Han region to the minority areas, and from home to abroad. Since the Tang Dynasty, Mount Tai sacrifice has spread to foreign countries across the ocean. Up to now, there are God Mount Tai, Goddess Bixia and Taishan Shigandang in Japan, the republic of Korea, Malaysia, Philippines, India and overseas Chinese living places, which shows its far-reaching influence.

In the inheritance and development process of Mount Tai Sacrifice Custom, the physical form and material form mutually combined together, folklore, performing, temple fairs and opera coexisted and mutual supported with ancient cultural relics, ancient buildings, sacrificial vessels such as Qin Stone, Han Cypress, Tang Cliff, Double Beam Tablet, Bixia Temple, Dai Temple, Mount Tai Triratna on Mount tai, accumulated into a broad and profound Mount Tai culture.The large–scale real landscape performance "Chinese Buddhist Ceremony" was popular among people since it was performed in public in 2010. The Mount Tai Temple Fair has also formed custom and the influence of it has been continuously broadened. expanding its influence; The imitation Song–Dynasty–style performance of offering sacrifices to heaven was performed all the year round in the Dai Temple, welcomed and loved by tourists at home and abroad.

Chengshan Sun Sacrifice

In 2016, "Chengshan Sun Sacrifice" of Rongcheng City was listed in the fourth batch of provincial intangible cultural heritage by Shandong Provincial People's Government.

Chengshan Sun Sacrifice refers to the sacrificial activity held by people in the Chengshantou District of Rongcheng City to express their respect to the Sun. It is the inheritance and continuation of the sacrificial culture formed for the local people's respect for the ancient "Eight Lords" (the Heaven, the Earth, the Army, Yin, Yang, the Moon, the Sun and the Four Seasons).

Chengshantou, also known as "Chaowu" in ancient times, which means "dancing toward the morning sun", is the first place in China to see the sunrise over the sea. Chengshantou is a rare tourist resort for its magnificent green peaks and towering cliffs and its unique geographical environment connected to the land on the one side and surrounded by the sea on three other sides. This unique geographical environment gave birth to its unique myth worship.

Chengshan is an important birthplace of Chinese Sun worship culture. Sacrificial activities to the Sun express Chengshan people's devout belief in the Sun God and their good wishes for life. This ritual has a long history and has lasted for more than

2,000 years, which can be traced back to the Warring States Period. At that time, a hundred schools of thought contended with each other to discuss the origin of the universe and the world. Under such cultural background, thinkers in the State of Qi (Chengshan belongs to the State of Qi in ancient times) arranged and combined the local natural beliefs by virtue of nature worship that had already existed in the region, and classified the eight belief modes of gods: "the Heaven", "the Earth", "the Army", "Yin", "Yang", "the Moon", "the Sun" and "the Four Seasons". Each of these eight gods has its own place and form of worship. The seventh god was the "Sun God", also known as "Sun Lord", whose place of worship was the present Chengshantou. It is recorded in *The Records of the Grand Historian* that "the mountains enter the sea, and they live in the northeastern corner of Qi to greet the sunrising". This sentence means Chengshantou stands steeply on the seashore at the northeast end of ancient Qi State, and is famous for being the first place to greet the sunrise from the sea.

In the Qin and Han Dynasties, the Sun God worship was still very popular here. In 1979 and 1982, two batches of jade wares were unearthed in front of the Shihuang Temple in Chengshantou. According to research and textual research, the first batch of jade was buried here by Emperor Wudi to offer sacrifices to the Sun God. The second batch was buried by Qinshihuang on the earlier day to offer sacrifices to the Sun God. Burying jade Gui and jade Bi was the highest ritual in the national memorial day in the Qin and Han Dynasties.

According to historical records, Qinshihuang made four eastward patrols, two of which destinations are Chengshan. There are two purposes of his first visit to Chengshan. First, the State of Qi was one of the seven powerful states of the Warring States, it was finally destroyed by Qin. Qinshihuang followed the example of Yao and Shun to visit the people for he was worried about the State of Qi at the beginning of uniting the country. "To show his strong power and be approved by the people", and declared that "he had made more achievements than the Three Sovereigns (Suiren, Fuxi and Shennong) and higher virtue than Five Emperors (Zhuanxu, Huangdi, Diku, Yao and Shun)". In order to show off the strength of the Qin Dynasty and the dignity of the emperor, Qinshihuang was escorted by 600 Huangmen Langzhong, 6,000 HuBen troops, and 60,000 elite Qin troops to deter the remaining forces of the Qi State. Second, to offer sacrifices to the Lord of the Sun, Chengshantou was the eastern polar region of the Qin and was called the "East Gate of the Qin" at that time. Belief in the Mandate of Heaven, Qinshihuang worshiped the Heaven and the Earth at Mount Tai, and then toured to Chengshantou to worship the Lord of the Sun. This inspection left historical relics such as the "Qin Bridge Relics" "Qin Dynasty Stone" "Shooting Shack Platform" and Qin Prime Minister Li Si's calligraphy "the end of the heaven, east gate of Qin" as a stone landmark. The so-called "Stone Mark" is "stone table", is "the national boundary monument" to distinguish the boundary of the border, known as the "law stone tablet" among the people. In 210 BC, accompanied by the Prime Minister Li Si and his young son Hu Hai, Qinshihuang went on a tour "from Langya to Rongcheng Mountain" once again. The purpose of this expedition was to go to Fairy Mountain on the Sea in search of the elixir of immortality to improve health and prolong life. According to *the Historical Records of Qinshihuang*, Xu Fu and others from the State of Qi wrote to Qinshihuang that there were three sacred mountains in the sea, called Penglai, Fangzhang and Yingzhou, where the immortals lived, and there was the elixir of immortality on the mountains. Xu Fu deceived the emperor, saying, "I have gathered a magic potion, but there are a large number of mermen on guard and the men they bring are bitten by mermen. The only way to get the magic potion is to shoot them." Qinshihuang mistakenly believed him and began his second eastward tour. When Qinshihuang visited Chengshan in the east, he built a palace on the west side of Chengshantou, which was called "Shihuang Palace". Later it collapsed due to years of disrepair, and later a temple was built on the site of Shihuang Palace. This temple is the only "Shihuang Temple" existing in China.

During the Western Han Dynasty, Emperor Wudi of the Han Dynasty also climbed Mount Cheng. Once, Emperor Wudi of the Han Dynasty led the civil and military officials from Chang'an, passing through Mount Tai and patrolled east until they reached Chengshantou. They were shocked by the magnificent scenery of "Sunrise at Chengshantou" . So they worshiped Sun God ceremoniously and built the "Sun God Temple" to thank the Sun God for his grace. Today, Chengshantou still remains the Sun Worship platform of Emperor Wudi and the Sun Worship Statue of Emperor Wudi led his ministers at the coast.

In the Song, Yuan, Ming and Qing Dynasties, the Sun Worship declined to some extent. But from the Temple of the Heaven, Temple of the Sun, Temple of the Earth and Temple of the Moon built in the city of Chang'an, it can be seen that the worship of the Sun as a cultural custom was retained in many places. In particular, the Sun Sacrifice in Chengshan has been inherited and carried forward among the people and continues to the present day. However, it evolved from the original national sacrifice to the folk sacrifice, but there were still altars, strict schedules, ritual plans and sacrifices.

Later, the folk custom of the Sun Worship at Chengshan had its inheritors. At first, it was inherited by families, and then from masters to apprentices. According to the existing historical records, the original representative successor was Tian Wanqing in the early Qing Dynasty. After several generations of inheritance, the current representative inheritor is Tian Wenhu, the seventh-generation inheritor who is over 70 years old. Tian Wenhu was born in a fisherman's family in Chengshan whose ancestors have been fishing for generations. Like his peers in the village, he followed his ancestors to worship the Sun in Chengshan since he was young. In 2014, he was approved as the representative inheritor of the municipal intangible cultural heritage because of his deep feelings about the historical and folk culture of the Sun Worship in Chengshan.

With the development of modern society and economy, the act of praying like the worship of the sun and the sea are gradually integrated. Both the state sacrifice of ancient emperors and the folk sacrifice today have clear ritual steps. First of all, an altar should be set up, and on the offering table should be placed Tailao (three animals—ox, sheep and pig), Shaolao (only sheep and pig, no ox), fresh fruits, etc. Secondly, the detailed ceremony program should be determined, presided over by the respected elders to salute, sun-worship, read out the eulogy of sun-worship. Thirdly, dance performances is performed to show that the country is prosperous and the people are in peace. Finally, the festival is celebrated, families kill pigs and sheep to celebrate the festival, and pray for the well-being.

As a folk culture with a long history, the worship of the Sun in the mountain reflects the ideal pursuit of advocating beauty and striving upward of the Chinese people. It is an important medium to maintain regional unity and promote social harmony. The protection, inheritance and promotion of this folk custom will have an important impact on the inheritance and development of traditional culture that cannot be ignored.

Hungry Ghost Festival Custom

In 2016, "Hungry Ghost Festival Custom" in Laicheng District of Laiwu City (Laiwu District of Jinan City today) was listed in the fourth batch of provincial-level intangible cultural heritage by Shandong Provincial People's Government.

Every year, on the 15th day of the seventh lunar month, people in Laiwu District will celebrate the local traditional custom festival—Hungry Ghost Festival. The Hungry Ghost Festival is commonly known as "July 15th", "Filial Son Festival", "Reunion Festival", "Ghost Festival", "Half a Year", "Ancestor Worship", "Melon Festival" and so on. The representative village of the Hungry Ghost Festival is Zhanggongqing Village. In the third year of Hongwu in the Ming Dynasty (1370), the Zhang family moved to this village from Zaoqiang County, Hebei Province. As there was an iron mine to the east of Genggongqing Village, all the neighboring villages were named as "Kuangkeng (mine pit)". Zhang's family also changed the name of the village to Zhang Kuangkeng, which later became Zhang Gongqing. There is the "Zhang Ancestral Hall" existing in the village built in the period of Hongwu in the Ming Dynasty.

The Hungry Ghost Festival custom in Laiwu District originated in the reign of

Emperor Qianlong in the Qing Dynasty and has a history of more than 270 years. According to *Laiwu County Annals*, in the 13th year of Emperor Gaozong's Reign in the Qing Dynasty (1748), plague broke out among the people, killing countless villagers. Zhang Bingyi served as a Chenghuang (the God who guards the city) in Hongdong, Shanxi Province. In order to save the villagers in Hongdong, he was instructed by An Qisheng, an immortal of Laiwu, and drove away the God of Plague by offering sacrifices to his ancestors. Later, this ancestor sacrifice gradually evolved into a regional local custom. During the Reign of Emperor Jiaqing of the Qing Dynasty, custom activities were developed. The Zhang family in Zhanggongqing Village set up a hall in the ancestral hall, where they offered sacrifices of fruits, wine and dishes to their ancestors, forming a sacrificial scale. In the Reign of Tongzhi, Li Quan decided to hold family sacrifice activities at home due to the change of the "Hungry Ghost Festival" sacrifice activities among clans. He organized his family, set up the altar in the main room, hung up the axles of the family hall painted by others, and personally burned incense outside the village to ask his ancestors to go home to receive incense. Since then, the family sacrifice activities of the Hungry Ghost Festival has been developed and Li Quan has become the successor of the first generation of the present Hungry Ghost Festival sacrifice custom.

Li Hai'an, the successor of the second generation, inherited and carried forward the family sacrifice of traditional activities and shouldering the responsibility of offering sacrifices to ancestors and educating descendants. At this time, the family sacrifice activities had become more and more perfect, the ritual of offering sacrifices to the ancestors became more and more exquisite, and the wine, dishes and cooked wheaten food were constantly updated. Li Zixiu, the inheritor of the third generation, was in a turbulent era. Although the Hungry Ghost Festival was sometimes simple and sometimes complicated, it never stopped. Li Hongjun, the inheritor of the fourth generation, shouldered the responsibility of inheriting the customs and educating his descendants. During the war period, he offered sacrifices to his ancestors in the simple form of melon sacrifice, and told the touching stories of his ancestors to his descendants, in order to make them know how to be grateful to their ancestors. Up to now, Li Naidong, the fifth generation inheritor, has studied the historical origin of the custom, the culture of filial piety and morality, the inheritance and development, and the significance of festival and custom, and sorted out more than 100,000 words of customs information.

Nowadays, the Hungry Ghost Festival custom in Laicheng District still inherits the ritual steps of "Qingjiatang (inviting the ancestors' soul go home at Spring Festival)", "offering sacrifices" and "Songjiatang (sending the ancestors' soul to leave after Spring Festival)".

When it comes to "Qingjiatang", local people will clean the courtyard, set up an altar, hang a Jiatangzhou (A scroll of genealogy) on the wall, and put a basin under the altar for holding tea, wine and burning paper for sacrificial offerings at the morning of the 15th day of the 7th lunar month. The male host is the chief priest, who is responsible for writing ancestral tablets and arranging sacrificial tools and articles. Ancestor tablets are divided into two categories: colorful tablets and plain coloured tablets. Fold a piece of yellow cover paper into a square, and fold the upper end into a triangle. Write the names of the last three generations of ancestors and their wives' surnames on it respectively in the order of the left male and the right female, thus forming "ancestral tablets". The memorial tablets should be placed in a clear order, with "Gaozu (great-grandfather's father)" in the middle, "Zengzu (father's grandfather)" and "Xiankao (the dead father)" from the middle to the two sides, or from left to right, from the youngest to the oldest. The hostess led female family to fold Yuanbao (an ancient currency made of precious gold or silver) with gold and silver paper for the sacrifice. It is particularly important to note that pregnant women and women who have just given birth are not allowed to attend the ceremonies.

At 10 o'clock in the morning, after memorial tablets, tea, bowls, cups and chopsticks be set, chief priests burn incense with their children and carry wine jugs to the road outside the village to welcome the ancestors' soul. They generally choose a place in front of the village beside the road to welcome ancestors' soul, pile soil into a censer, pour a cup of wine, face the road, hold incense and bow to pray, "Ancestors, the elderly, please follow me home to sit at the table!" They put a wick of incense in the incense burner, pour the wine on the ground, kneel on the ground and kowtow for three times. Then they take the other incense (commonly known as "Xinxiang" (Chinese Buddhism and other religions hold that incense is the cause of faith. When burning incense, gods and Buddhas will know their wishes, so it is called incense of faith) home. When they come to the door of the home, the first thing is to insert a wick in the left side of the door frame, with a stick in the door, commonly known as "block the door stick" . There are two sayings of "block the door stick" . One is to prevent ghosts from entering after the ancestors' soul enter the door. Second, when one's ancestors' soul have entered the house, no one other than his own clan may enter. If people from outside the clan have important matters to enter the door, they must kowtow to the hall table. Incense is also inserted in each door of the courtyard, and sticks are used to block the door. After inserting incense on the family immortal and the kitchen king's altar, the last three incenses are inserted into the incense burner of the home hall table. The whole family should kowtow before the table at home, with the male in the front and the female in the rear, to welcome the ancestors' soul home to the banquet. After Qingjiatang is completed, followed by the sacrificial activities.

"Sacrifice" refers to offering sacrifices to the ancestors of the family who go home by the chief priest according to the traditional way of offering sacrifices. Firstly, lay out the refreshments. Put refreshments (basically are cake, fruit, biscuit, crisp, honey etc.) in dish. The chief priest fill the tea bowl in front of the memorial tablets at the altar table with tea and offer tea according to the generation of the ancestors.

Custom stresses that tea should be pour seventy percent full, wine to eighty percent full. Fresh fruits should be prepared, the main fruit is watermelon, cut watermelon into lotus petal shape into two like a lotus which is a symbol of good luck, family reunion, prosperous days; Put on apples, bananas, grapes instead of peaches and pears. Peach has the function of ward off evil spirits, ancestors may not dare to sit if peaches are offered; "Pear" and "Li (to leave)" are homophones, ancestors and descendants may be unfamiliar with each other if pears are offered.

Then put Gongcai (dishes for the ancestors). The number of Gongcai is singular, three, five, seven or nine, the essential main course are chicken, carp, meatballs, tofu, celery and so on. Put a little spinach on the meat dish, commonly known as "Caicaitou". The difference of the Jiatang on July 15th and the Jiatang on Spring Festival is that three animals—raw chicken, raw fish and raw meat are not served on the Jiatang on July 15th. The dishes should be placed from the middle to the two sides for Gaozu sit in the middle (except those from left to right). Avoid using dog meat. There is a folk saying that dog meat can't be served on feast. Leek, green onion, onion and other vegetables with peculiar smell also can't be served. Sacrificial cabbage should be wrapped in red paper, or put some carrots, meaning prosperous. After Gongcai are laid out and the wine cups are poured, the chief priest happily explains to his children the ancestors on the memorial tablets one by one, especially those who have made outstanding achievements, made contributions to their hometown, had a good reputation among the villagers or worked hard to study, to encourage their descendants. The whole family get together and talk freely. At lunch, steamed buns should be placed on the altar, and a toast and tea should be offered. When toasting and serving tea, the chief priest should piously say, "Please get enough to eat and drink!" After that, the family has lunch in front of the Jiatang table (the table in the central room of a house).

Around 5 p.m., it's time to "Songjiatang (sending the ancestors' soul to leave)" . The chief priest personally or ordered his son to print paper (print flower money with wooden money mold, commonly known as "Zhiwozi (a kind of paper cutting)" , flower paper (the utility model relates to a printing pattern process paper on the surface of a backing paper, to cut the paper to burn which have been print into flower paper and folded them good standby). The hostess cooked the dumplings with meat stuffing (the Spring Festival with vegetarian stuffing) and filled them in a tea bowl. She put a bowl in front of a memorial tablet and two dumplings in each bowl. At "Songjiatang" , people pour wine, tea, dumplings before the memorial tablet (pour into the basin under the table to toast the ancestors with wine and tea), the memorial tablet should be put in order from "Gaozu" to "Xiankao" in a pan or plate with paper to burn, wine, tea, dumpling soup, firecrackers. The chief priest stand before people with incense from the censer in hand and guide the whole family, old and young, to go to the road outside the village to send the family off. "Block the door stick" should be taken away when one go out. In legend, if the wooden stick used to block the door is not taken away, the ancestors cannot get out.

"Songjiatang" would also be held beside the road outside the village.First, pile up an incense burner with sand and stick the burning incense in the incense burner. First are the tablets of Gaozu, the tablets should be arranged in a line according to the generation. Put a tablet on each hundred of paper to burn, and hold them down with a wick of incense, and draw a half circle on the paper to burn and tablet, commonly known as "circled money" . Light the paper to burn, then pour it with wine, tea, dumplings soup from the half circle, the chief priest face the road ahead, piously say, "Hope the old people leave safely!" The whole family kowtow, and then set off firecrackers, the sacrificial ceremony of "Songjiatang" end.

On the fifteenth day of the seventh lunar month, Laiwu people come back to their hometowns from all over the world to hold the traditional ceremony of "Qingjiatang" , and the whole family gets together. Hungry Ghost Festival customs have a history of more than two hundred years,they have not been cut off although there are always war and chaos. The inheritance and development of the Hungry Ghost Festival custom is of great educational significance for respecting ancestors and caring for the elderly, and also contributes to the formation of a good moral trend of harmonious coexistence.

Bead Counting Culture (Mengyin)

In 2016, "Bead Counting Culture" of Mengyin County was listed in the fourth batch of provincial intangible cultural heritage by Shandong Provincial People's Government.

Mengyin County, which belongs to Linyi City, Shandong Province, is the hometown of Liu Hong, the first creator of bead counting. It is proved that Liu Hong was the sixth grandson of King Liu Xing, the nephew of Emperor Guangwu Liu Xiu of the Eastern Han Dynasty, who loved a leisurely and quiet life and hated hooking and playing with power by nature. In order to escape from the world, he came to live in seclusion in a manor called Longyan Guanzhuang of Taishan County, the territory of King Lu, which is today the Village of Zhaozi Guanzhuang of Mengyin Street, Mengyin County, and the site of Liu Hong's former residence is 200 meters west of Zhaozi Guanzhuang of Mengyin Street, Mengyin County.

Bead counting is a kind of calculating method using the abacus as a tool, *Mathematical Heritage* records, "Abacus controls four seasons and three talents of longitude and latitude. The plate is divided into three parts, the upper and lower parts are divided into stop swimming beads, and the middle part is divided into the arithmetic position. Each position has five beads. The upper bead is different from the lower four beads. The beads of the other colors should be five, and the lower four beads should be one." The invention of bead counting has made a great leap in people's computing power, and abacus has become the fifth invention in addition to the four great inventions of China.

"Bead Counting" was first seen in the Eastern Han Dynasty—Xu Yue's book *Mathematical Heritage*, Xu Yue said in the book, "Liu Kuaiji, erudite and knowledgeable, adept in mathematics...worked as the official Lishou and began to count. And bead calculation was one of his inventions." Liu Kuaiji mentioned in this article is Liu Hong. After many scholars' arguments, Liu Hong is the founder of abacus. In 190, Liu Hong invented the abacus and created bead calculation, and then passed it to Xu Yue and Zheng Xuan; from the year 196 on, Liu Hong accepted disciples and taught the skills of calendar calculation, and taught the skills of bead calculation and the astronomical work *Qian Xiang Calendar* to Yang Wei, Han Yi and others, and then passed on from generation to generation by his disciples. In this way, it was passed down to future generations. In addition to calculation methods, Liu Hong's invention of the abacus, a calculation tool, contributed greatly to the advancement of calculation methods. The abacus invented by Liu Hong inherited the advantages of the five-to-ten calculations, the set-dispersion calculation method and the position system, and overcame the shortcomings of the vertical and horizontal counting and the inconvenience of placing chips in the abacus, which was a very advanced calculation tool before the emergence of electronic computers.

Mengyin, As the hometown of Liu Hong, the creator of bead counting, there has been a very strong culture of bead counting from ancient times to the present, and the local people are quite familiar with bead counting and are proud of it.

In 1994, an 8-episode TV series *The Sage of Abacus*, the first literary work depicting Liu Hong's journey of inventing the abacus, was premiered in Beijing by Shandong Film and TV Drama Production Center. Soon, the TV series was broadcasted on CCTV and aired three times in a row, causing a great response, and the bead counting of Mengyin came into the view of common people through the dissemination of mass media like TV series. In April 2010, the Chinese Folk Artists Association sent a group of experts to investigate Mengyin County, and they gave high praise to the preservation and development of "Culture of the Abacus Sage" in Mengyin county and soon named MengYin county as the only "Township of the Sage of Beading Culture in China". In May, 2010, the World Expo was held in Shanghai, and each participating region exhibited the most representative culture of region. Among them, the Shandong Hall had a total of four display cases, and the third one showed the bead counting and abacus invented by Liu Hong. On December 4th, 2013, the eighth meeting of the UNESCO Intergovernmental Committee for the Safeguarding of the Intangible Cultural Heritage was held in Baku, Azerbaijan, at which a resolution was adopted to officially inscribe Chinese bead counting on Representative List of the Intangible Cultural Heritage of Humanity, with a special introduction: "Bead counting is a major invention of ancient China, which has accompanied the Chinese people through their experiences and experiences. It is a major invention of ancient China and has accompanied the Chinese people for more than 1,800 years. With its simple calculation tool and unique connotation of numerology, it is known as 'the world's oldest computer'."

The scientific method and the programmed and mechanical way of thinking embedded in the culture of bead counting have also promoted the creation and invention of car and boat manufacturing, bridge building, navigation, etc., and have had a profound impact on commerce and the military. Many elements of bead counting are also often found as symbols in language, literature, architecture, painting and sculpture, and have had a significant impact on all aspects of people's lives. In 2007, the British newspaper *The Independent* and the Indian newspaper "*The Times of India*" ranked Chinese bead counting in the first place in their ranking of inventions that changed the world.

Nowadays, more and more people are willing to understand and learn bead counting culture, and many parents encourage their children to learn bead counting from childhood, so as to improve their children's reaction ability, memory and reaction speed. Bead counting is getting closer and closer to people's daily life, and bead counting culture is also known by more and more people.

Jiaodong Variegated Steamed Bun Custom (Qixia)

In 2016, "Jiaodong variegated Steamed Bun Custom" of Qixia City was lised in the fourth batch of extended provincial intangible cultural heritage by Shandong Provincial People's Government.

Qixia City is part of Yantai City, Shandong Province, located in the northeastern part of Shandong Province. Qixia variegated steamed bun, a kind of biscuit, is a traditional folk art created by local rural women according to the characteristics of regional culture and combined with festivals and customs.

Qixia variegated steamed bun had its prototype as early as in the Han Dynasty, but at that time the variegated steamed bun only made the dough into a certain image. It was recorded in Wu Zimu's *Mengliang Records* in the Song Dynasty that flower-shaped steamed variegated buns were used in the Spring Festival, the Mid-Autumn Festival, the Dragon Boat Festival and wedding celebrations. In the Ming Dynasty, the skill of steamed variegated buns continued to be improved. At this time, Qixia variegated steamed buns were mostly used for the Spring Festival, the Lantern Festival, the Qingming Festival, the Mid-Autumn Festival and Festival on the 23rd or 24th of the 12th month of the lunar year, when sacrifices are made to the kitchen god. Later on, it was extended to weddings and funerals, and later on, to show the grandness of the ceremonies, representing good blessings more and more in front of the shrines and on the tables of ordinary people. In modern times, under the influence of the Mou clan, the content and form of Qixia variegated steamed buns have become more and more sophisticated and perfect in terms of expression and skills, based on the traditional dough sculptures and the integration of the fun of ancient and modern people's lives. After thousands of years of inheritance and management, Qixia variegated steamed buns have been deeply rooted in people's daily life and have formed their own unique characteristics.

Qixia people use flour as the main source to make variegated steamed buns by using tools that they are comfortable with and accustomed to, such as knives, scissors, pens, brushes, bamboo strips and some homemade tools. There are two types of variegated buns: cooked variegated buns, which are mainly made by the processes of "making dough—developing dough—kneading dough—pinching—sculpting—steaming—coloring"; and raw variegated buns. "The other is raw variegated buns, which are mainly made by "making dough—kneading dough—kneading (coloring)—gluing—air—drying".

During different festivals, Qixia people make different kinds of variegated buns with a variety of themes and expressions. They are made in different shapes and colors, and they carry people's wishes for a happy life and their simple aesthetics and traditional totem beliefs.

During the Spring Festival, a traditional festival in China, people make variegated buns called "sacred worms". The "sacred worm" is a kind of variegated bun that people offered as sacrifices during the Spring Festival. It is shaped like a dragon with spines and a copper coin in its mouth to attract wealth and treasure. Most people put the "sacred worm" into the jar of flour, meaning that they will have endless food for the coming year. In addition, the dragon's power is used to suppress all kinds of pests, so that the owner's family will not suffer from food losses.

On the 15th day of the first lunar month, families in Qixia start to make various kinds of bean–flour bowl lamps. The Doumian (bean–flour) lamps are made by mixing water, peanut oil and bean–flour in a certain ratio and then kneading them together, and they are shaped into a cylindrical shape of 8 to 10 cm high, with a "small bowl" of suitable size on top. The people of Qixia are very particular about the bean–flour lamps, and twelve bean–flour bowl lamps are kneaded according to twelve months, with only one fold on the small bowl in January and two folds in February, and so on. On the night of the fifteenth day of the first month, the cotton wick and the peanut oil are put in the twelve bean–floured bowl lamps and lit, which month of the bean–floured bowl lamp burns for a longer time, it means in the year of that month life is smooth and prosperous; people also observe what crops the flow of lamp oil may form like, foretelling what crops can be bountiful in the coming year. In addition to the December lantern, people also make "Watchman" lamps. After lighting the lamp, the host holds the lamp and shines it around the courtyard, which means to protect the family.The bean–flour lamp burnt out can't be thrown away. It can be sliced and cooked the next day with a unique taste. While celebrating the festival themselves, people do not forget their deceased relatives, and usually make round or pillar–shaped bean–flour lamps and light them up to light the way for the dead.

When it comes to the Qingming Festival, every family makes a special kind of variegated bun called "chicken bun" for their children, and those who are well–off also boil a few eggs for their children. In fact, the shape of "chicken bun" is more like a swallow, and it was called "swallow bun" in the early days, but it was called "chicken bun" in the long process of inheritance. The meaning is that children will be healthy if they eat "chicken bun".

It is also a traditional folk custom of Qixia to eat Qiaoguo (a kind of variegated bun) on the seventh day of the seventh lunar month. The most common type of variegated bun is fish–shaped, but there are also other types such as lotus–shaped bags, old-aged-man shapes for lucky, long-lived and rich, various small animals, pomegranates, lotus flowers and lotus puffs. Most of these different shapes are carved out of molds. When making the fruit, the dough is pressed into the mold and then put into a pot and cooked, and the different shapes of the fruit are ready. Then they are strung together with thread and a corn stalk is found as a handle. The children gather together with a string of variegated buns in their hands to show off to each other and see who has more patterns and numbers. July 7th on Chinese calendar is the festival begging for good luck, and children's eating the variegated bun on this day signifies that they will be skillful.

In addition to these variegated buns during festivals, there are also wedding variegated buns, birthday variegated buns and variegated buns for setting housing beams and for newly-born babies on the day of a full month or a hundred days.

The wedding variegated buns are the most complicated, with the size generally exceeding the diameter of the mouth of a copper basin (washbasin), and are placed on a copper basin and taken by the bride to the groom's home, hence the name "Copper Basin Variegated Bun". It is a representative local culture that has long been formed in traditional wedding customs and practices. Its shape is large, with a diameter of 50 cm to 60 cm and a height of 40 cm to 50 cm. The base is a lotus petal, on which are finely molded twelve zodiac shapes, including dragon and phoenix (prosperity brought by the dragon and the phoenix), gourd(as a homophonic for good fortune in Chinese), goldfish (gold and jade fill the hall—avariegated bundant wealth or many children in the family) and mandarin ducks (flying with wings—happy couple). There are as many as 20 embellished components. The variegated buns are finely embellished and vividly shaped, forming a strong artistic effect that sends the blessings of loved ones, enhances the festive atmosphere and enriches the content of folk wedding customs. These exquisite copper-basin variegated buns are brought to the groom's house by the bride's family on the wedding day. When the bridal party arrives at the bridegroom's village, two people from the bridegroom's house will welcome the bride and groom and take them back to the bridegroom's house and place them in a conspicuous place for the guests to enjoy. The bride will also feel honored by the unanimous praise of the guests for the well-done variegated buns. Therefore, the bride's family will make a great effort to make a beautiful copper-basin variegated bun, and those who are not as skilled will often seek help. The groom's family usually doesn't want to eat the good-looking copper-basin variegated buns right away, and will set them up for a while before eating them.

The full-moon day for newly-born baby is also quite elaborate. The main forms of full-moon day buns are "tiger's head", "Buddha's hand", "hundred-year-old child" and "cow's hoof", etc., expressing people's sincere blessings to their children and their love for them. The "hundred-year-old" bun is a kind of variegated bun sent by Grandma's family after her daughter has given birth to a child for 100 days. The main forms are "long spike", "sugar bun", "sugar cap", "hanging flower", "tiger's head", etc. It means that the elders hope for healthy growth of their grandsons.

The Beam-raising bun. Building a new house with a big beam is one of the more important activities in rural areas. On this day, at noon, the owner of the new house will hold a ceremony of "Beam-raising" and the hostess will make some small and exquisite variegated buns, mainly in the form of "Dragon and Phoenix", "lion holding the door", "treasure gourd" and so on. Which means that the dragon will raise its head, the phoenix will fall on the treasure ground and the family will be prosperous. During the ceremony, the carpenters and masons hold the variegated buns in a "Bucket", chanting a jingle to express their blessings, and then raise them on the roof to the audience who come to watch. The audience will compete for the variegated buns below, and the one who gets them will be blessed by the owner of the house.

The longevity buns are made in a shape of peach for the elders at their 60s in the family to wish them a long and healthy life and to express their filial respect for them.

There is also a kind of daily variegated buns. This is the most common type of variegated bun, and can be made on any holiday. They are made in a semi–circular shape, and some of them have a bulge on the top. They are first made into ordinary variegated buns and put aside, and then decorated with ornaments shaped like plum, orchid, bamboo, chrysanthemum, flowers and birds, according to personal preference, and pasted on top. According to the old artists, the decorated dough should not be fermented, but should be used raw (cold). This way, the variegated buns will not be deformed after steaming. After the variegated buns are steamed and cooled, they are then colored with brushes according to their needs, mainly in pink, yellow and green.

Qixia variegated bun inherits the tradition of the ancestors' love for flowers, birds, fish and insects, but also incorporates a little bit of ancient and modern people's life into it, making it more vivid and interesting. For thousands of years, Qixia variegated buns have been gradually integrated into people's daily life and shine in the folk art world with their strong local flavor.

Jiaodong Variegated Steamed Bun Custom (Laizhou)

In 2016, "Jiaodong Variegated Steamed Bun Custom" of Laizhou City was listed in the fourth batch of the extended provincial intangible cultural heritage by Shandong Provincial People's Government.

It is not known when the practice really began, but it has been known for at least 1,300 years, judging from the dough figurines and piglets excavated from the Tang Tombs in Turpan, Xinjiang. The *Reminiscences of the Eastern Capital Bianliang* has a record on the kneading of dough figurine, "Smiling dough figurine made of oil, sugar and honey." At that time, the dough figurines were edible, called "Fruit Foods" . There is also a folk legend about the dough figurine. According to legend, during the Three Kingdoms period, Zhuge Liang conquered the southern barbarians, and when crossing the Lu River, the wind suddenly blew up, and the wise Zhuge Liang ordered his attendants to make dough figurines and animals out of flour, so as to worship the gods of the river. Strangely enough, the river did calm down, and the team crossed the river and pacified the southern barbarians successfully. From then on, all the variegated bun makers worshiped Zhuge Liang as the grand master.

Laizhou variegated steamed buns originated as a flour offering for festivals in the countryside. There are two types of variegated steamed buns: variegated steamed buns in the coastal fishing village and variegated steamed buns in the plain mountain areas. In the coastal fishing villages, there are many variegated steamed buns with images of fish, shrimp and clams, i.e. a dough man or woman in costume with a fish or clam behind or under their feet; in the plains and mountainous areas, there are many variegated steamed buns with images of sacred worms (the dragon) , longevity peaches and dramatic characters.

The Laizhou variegated steamed bun is made of wheat flour. In addition to small figures, there are also various animals and flowers and many patterns. During the Ming and Qing Dynasties, they were mostly used for the Spring Festival, the Lantern Festival, the Qingming Festival, the Mid-Autumn Festival and other festivals; later, they were extended to weddings and funerals; later on, they were increasingly used in front of the shrines and on the offering tables of all households to express the grandness of the ceremony. According to the *Laizhou County Chronicles*, Laizhou variegated steamed buns have a history of more than 600 years and were once one of the four major local tributes. In the early Ming Dynasty, there was a variegated steamed bun workshop in Ye County (now Laizhou), which specialized in the production of variegated steamed buns. Later, through the exploration and innovation of successive generations of bakery craftsman, the variety of bakery products in Laizhou was constantly increased and the skills were significantly improved.

As a result, Laizhou variegated steamed buns have become a folk artwork for people to liven up the atmosphere and show their own craftsmanship during festivals. During the Spring Festival, most local villages and towns hold variegated steamed buns exhibitions. Thousands of people participate in the competition, and there are variegated steamed bun professionals. In 1986, more than 140 pieces of Laizhou variegated steamed buns were exhibited at the Yantai Arts Festival; in 1987, Yang Ketai of Zhang Village, Zhuqiao Town, made sacred worm (dragon) variegated steamed bun and participated in the "One of the Best Chinese Folk Art" exhibition sponsored by the Chinese Ministry of Culture in Shanghai. In 1988, more than 10 pieces of Laizhou variegated steamed buns were collected by the Shandong Provincial Art Museum, including "Double Lions" by Shen Zhanmin in the Zhuyou village and "Fushou Magpie" by Liu Xiyun in the Xibeiyu village.

Laizhou variegated steamed buns are unique folk artworks in China, as are other variegated steamed buns from all over the country, but Laizhou variegated steamed buns are different from other varieties because of their unique characteristics.

One is that Laizhou variegated steamed buns have been perfected over time and have gradually developed a round, thick, vivid, smooth and flamboyant artistic style.

Secondly, the forms of Laizhou variegated steamed buns mostly take after animals, flowers, birds, fish, insects and traditional mythological characters and episodes, the most representative ones being "variegated bundant-year fish" and "Mandarin ducks for an affectionate couple".

Thirdly, Laizhou variegated steamed bun is produced in family workshops, and different styles of production are formed due to the differences in each family's interests and hobbies, which makes the variety of Laizhou variegated steamed buns colorful.

Fourthly, because of the abundant variegated local raw materials, variegated steamed buns are simple and fast to make. "Every family has skillful workers, and every household produces fine products."

Fifthly, the main mode of inheritance is that the father passes on to the son and the master takes on the apprentice.

Sixthly, it is easy to operate with abundant variegated raw materials, low price and wide marketing.

The production of variegated steamed buns. Usually, an appropriate amount of white sugar is added to the refined flour, and then a dough is made. The dough is then kneaded, rolled, selected, twisted, and shaped into a basic form, and then raised, dotted, and cut with simple tools to make it distinctive and vivid, and after steaming, painted with color. For larger variegated steamed buns, each part should be steamed separately, colored and then combined. Some particularly delicate characters, flowers and words placed on the main body should be finished with raw dough, while the rest should be made of leaven dough. Specific production steps are as follows.

The first step is "making". Mixing high-quality wheat flour from Laizhou, water and yeast together in proportion to make the dough uniform, firm, smooth, neither too soft nor too hard , not sticky hands, not sticky board.

The second is "kneading". That is to knead dough, the purpose is to make a variety of raw materials mixed evenly, so that the protein in the flour to fully absorb water to form an elastic gluten network, increase the dough tendon, so that the dough is smooth, soft and moist.

The third is "rolling". The dough is rolled out to the shape of the variegated steamed buns according to the pattern you want to make.

The fourth is "pinching". That is, pinching the dough, refining it by hand on the basis of the existing ones, "the chest of a scholar man, the belly of a military man, the back of an old man, the waist of a beautiful woman."

The fifth is "cutting". Using knives, grates, needles and other tools, we cut, dot and other fine processing of the variegated steamed buns, so that the image made of the variegated steamed buns is lifelike, full and vivid.

The sixth is depicting". The image can be colored with oil paint, Chinese painting, watercolor, gouache and other paints. In order to make the variegated steamed buns look bright, sometimes fluorescent colors are also used, creating the characteristic of bright and colorful variegated steamed buns in Laizhou.

Like paper-cutting, Laizhou's variegated steamed buns are made with soft lines, which are slim and light. Birds' feathers, whether traced or cut, have the feeling of being moved by the wind. In addition, the taste of Laizhou variegated steamed bun with refreshing smell is sweet and soft, and the color, fragrance, taste and shape are all intact, which makes them very popular.

The form of Laizhou variegated steamed buns comes from all aspects of human life and is the essence of art created by Laizhou people during their long-term labor practice; it expresses their desire for beauty; it is the flower of art created by generations of artists; and it is the treasure of traditional Chinese customs. Therefore, we should inherit and develop it, keep integrating innovative elements into it, and keep it alive forever.

Jiaodong Variegated Steamed Bun Custom (Muping)

In 2016, "Jiaodong Variegated Steamed Bun Custom" of Muping District, Yantai City, was listed in the fourth batch of provincial intangible cultural heritage by Shandong Provincial People's Government.

The custom of making dough figurines has been handed down throughout the Yellow River Basin, but it is called differently in different places. The Muping area is unique in that it is commonly known as "big variegated steamed buns", "date variegated steamed buns", "big peaches" and so on. Muping variegated steamed bun has a history of more than 300 years, and is an art style created by women in Jiaodong according to the regional characteristics, festivals and customs of Muping, with distinctive artistic features and interest in life. Muping variegated steamed buns are mainly found in Muping Wanggezhuang Town, Jianggezhuang Town, Longquan Town and other towns and surrounding areas.

At the end of each year, women in Jiaodong make many jujube steamed buns for ancestor worship, offering and consumption in the Spring Festival. The bun is round in shape, with seven holes picked up on it and red dates set into the holes. According to the local elderly, the seven holes represent the eyes, ears, mouth and nose of a person.

Variegated steamed buns are the characteristics of the Jiaodong Region. Every year, from the 23rd to the 28th of the twelfth lunar month, every family has to steam steamed buns and make variegated steamed buns. It is a tradition left by the old generation to make variegated buns for the Spring Festival, which means family reunion, prosperous days, and a good year.

Smart and hard-working rural women in Muping make their favorite styles of dough, such as "reunion buns", "five blessings buns", "jujube buns" and "sacred worm buns" and so on. The "sacred worm buns" are stored in the steamed bun jar during the Spring Festival to ensure a good harvest, while the "jujube buns" are used to worship the ancestors, expressing the people's wish for a rich life. When steamed, the buns look thicker and are decorated with flowers and birds on the surface, they look bright, full and lifelike. They are not only delicious, good-looking, but also blessed, which are very popular with people. This artful household food gradually became a vivid piece of art, both edible and ornamental.

People take dough as the main processing object and use knives, scissors, pens and other tools to create the food. The flowers, leaves and animals in the meat and potatoes should be in even numbers, and the days should be double, so as to make good things double, which has distinctive artistic characteristics. The popular sayings around Muping, such as "The chicken follows the toad, and the child lives to 99" and "Grandma on father's side sends a pair of chickens, grandma on mother's side sends a pair of ducks back, and the child lives to 98" (in Chinese, Ya (duck) and Ba (eight) are homophonic), reflect the beautiful aspiration of Muping people for a happy life.

There are two types of variegated steamed buns according to their functions. One type of buns is used for collection, usually made of refined flour, salt, preservatives and honey. The process is as follows: dough mixing—kneading—dyeing—shaping—bonding—air—drying. The other type is edible biscuits and cakes, which are mainly made of flour and go through several steps: dough mixing—dough fermentation—

kneading—shaping—carving—steaming—coloring. There are three types of dough: leavened dough, dry dough (flour) and cold water dough. The color treatment is divided between monochromatic red dots and colored dots. The technique varies from region to region.

"Children's Haircut" Bun

When a child comes into the world, the first haircut is rather grand, usually in the first half of the two month. Grandmother on father's side sends a pair of chickens and the grandmother on mother's side sends a pair of ducks to wish the child a long life.

"Hundred-year-old" Bun

The "Hundred-year-old" bun is to celebrate a hundred days of children's arrival in the world. The number of buns is 99, and they are made in the form of chickens, ducks, apples, phoenixes, gourds, bats, hedgehogs and so on.

"Wedding" Bun

The requirements for wedding buns are high, and the practice is even more elaborate. The most common types are "rich peony", "dragon and phoenix", "magpie on the plum", "red durian flower", "precious jade gourd" and so on, respectively, means happy, many children, many blessings, life is red and hot, attracting wealth into the treasure. There is also a basin bun for the bride to hold in her hands, usually with a lotus flower bottom and a peach or fish on top. The buns in the bride's box are four large longevity peaches and a pair of fish on the corner of one box.

"Birthday" Bun

Instead of flowers, four longevity peaches are usually made on top of the buns for the elderly, signifying longevity and solidity.

"Housewarming" Bun

Usually 8 large longevity peaches are made, steamed cakes (the size of the cakes is as big as the pct) are made, and the cakes are also made to support the pot, usually two, six or eight, etc. The number is even.

"Beam-raising" Bun

"Beam-raising" bun is a variegated steamed bun made when building a new house. It is generally 8 longevity peaches, as well as pig-headed buns, implying a rich life and a prosperous family.

"The Spring Festival" Bun

Every year, from the 23rd to the 28th of the twelfth lunar month, every family starts to steam variegated buns, make jujube steamed buns and "sacred worm" buns. The "sacred worm" is placed in the jar containing steamed variegated buns to ensure that the harvest will not be cut off, and the jujube buns are used to worship the deceased and express the people's desire for a better life.

The types of Spring Festival's buns include "reunion buns", "sacred worm buns", "five blessings buns" and "surplus for the year buns". They mean family reunion, prosperity and surplus.

"Ritual" Bun

Only the large white longevity peaches are used for "sacrificial" buns. If the other elderly person in the family is still alive, 5 large longevity peaches are made, and if both of them have passed away, 10 large longevity peaches are made.

"June 6 Rabbit Birthday" Bun

On the sixth day of the sixth month of the lunar calendar, it is commonly known as the birthday of the rabbit, and the type of variegated steamed buns made is the rabbit. There are two types of buns, one is a squat rabbit and the other is a lying rabbit, and each pair is made.

The materials used in Muping variegated steamed buns are very common, mainly made of flour we eat daily, but they are pristine, malleable and expressive with deep historical, artistic and practical values.

Postscript

Shandong Provincial Intangible Cultural Heritage Popular Edition Folklore Volume (*Book Two*) is a book of a collection of folklore originated from and popularized over prefectures in Shandong Province. The current book is but a drop in the ocean of the Shandong provincial intangible cultural heritage folklore, but it is already rich in content and profound in folklore culture. Therefore, This book is a good way to communicate with the rest of the world, for readers both at home and abroad, to obtain a glimpse of Shandong provincial intangible cultural heritage folklore.

The entries in the book are classified into 25 topics, among which in the first draft of translation Pan Shuaiying accomplished the preface and the former five folklore translation from *Laiyang Bean-flour Bowl Lamp Custom* to *The Custom of "Stringing the Yellow River"*, Yu Bo assisted in drafting a preliminary translation of the next four from *Cricket Fighting Custom in Ningjin County* to *Temple Fair for the Fishing Ancestor in Dongyi*, Pan Shuaiying translated the next four from *Zen Tea Ceremony at Boshan Zhengjue Monastery* to *Shouguang Vegetable Production Customs*, Chang Juanhua assited in drafting a preliminary translation of the next four from *Qingzhou Buddhist Preaching Scripture* to *Mount Tai Tofu Feast*, Xiang Lijun aided in the initial translation of the next four from *Mount Tai Jade Custom* to *Hungry Ghost Festival Custom*, and Guo Qiaolan aided in the initial translation of the next four from *Bead Counting Culture* (*Mengyin*) to *Jiaodong Variegated Steamed Bun Custom* (*Muping*). After the first draft, Pan Shuaiying was in charge of the revision and the final draft of the translated version of the whole book.

As this translated manuscript is about to be printed, I would like to express my gratitude to Professor Zhang Zhizhong for his recommendation to Editor Sun Yuchen, to my husband Dr. Jin Xin for his understanding and support, and to four colleagues in my studio team Yu Bo, Chang Juanhua, Xiang Lijun and Guo Qiaolan for their indigenous work. Without them, this translated manuscript could not have completed and published on time. I sincerely hope that the publication of this English translated book can help promote the external communication and dissemination of Shandong Provincial intangible cultural heritage folklore.

As this is my first experience in translating a book of this kind, there might be errors and misinterpretations in it. I sincerely hope our readers will kindly point them out when any is found so that I can correct them when the book has a chance to be reprinted.

Pan Shuaiying

Xinquan Campus, Kashi University

Dec. 22nd, 2023

山东省级非物质文化遗产普及用书

民俗卷（下）

序　言

习近平总书记指出："文化是一个国家、一个民族的灵魂。文化兴国运兴，文化强民族强。中华优秀传统文化是我们最深厚的文化软实力，也是中国特色社会主义植根的文化沃土。要积极推动中华优秀传统文化创造性转化、创新性发展。"在悠悠五千年的历史长河中，中华文明绵延不绝，历久弥新，孕育了丰富的精神文化财富。非物质文化遗产是中华优秀传统文化的重要组成部分，代表中华民族鲜活的文化基因，是民族历史的传承和民族精神的凝缩，是自古以来劳动人民智慧的生动展现。传承和弘扬中华优秀传统文化，挖掘和保护中华民族非物质文化遗产，研究和利用齐鲁大地的优秀文化遗产，是时代的要求，是历史的必然，是人民的期盼。

山东是孔孟之乡，礼仪之邦，拥有悠久的历史和灿烂的文明，是中华文明的重要组成部分。在这片广袤的齐鲁大地上，生长着韵味十足、特色鲜明的非物质文化遗产。神秘动人的民间文学、地域鲜明的民俗传统、风格迥异的传统音乐、独具神韵的传统舞蹈、意味无穷的传统美术、丰韵绵长的戏剧曲艺、通灵入化的体艺杂技、创意灵动的手工技艺，都饱含着齐鲁儿女的创造力，深藏着齐鲁大地的智慧，是齐鲁文化的重要代表。灿烂的非物质文化遗产充分展现了齐鲁儿女独具品位的审美个性和别具一格的思维方式，是山东文化发展的见证。

山东是非遗大省，非物质文化遗产资源极其丰富，非遗保护工作一直走在全国前列。目前，我省共有联合国教科文组织认定的"人类非遗代表作名录"项目8个，国家级名录173项，省级名录751项，现有国家级传承人51名，省级传承人296名，3家企业被文化和旅游部命名为"国家级非遗生产性保护示范基地"，共有68个省级非遗生产性保护示范基地，有1个国家级、9个省级文化生态保护实验区。为弘扬中华优秀传统文化，充分展现我省非物质文化遗产的博大精深和独特魅力，山东省文化和旅游厅组织编纂了“山东省级非物质文化遗产普及读本”系列丛书，首套共5册，其中民间文学类共3册，包含80个省级民间文学项目；民俗类2册，包含50个省级民俗项目，以后会陆续编纂其他系列的丛书。本套丛书的内容主要是以各市申报省级非物质文化遗产代表性项目的素材资料为依据。

本套丛书通过故事叙述与文化阐释相结合，以图补文与多方视角来讲述，涵盖历史渊源、基本内容、表现形态、传承发展、社会价值等方面。相信此套丛书的出版，必将使广大读者更加全面、系统地了解山东省非物质文化遗产的传承历史、表现形态、文化内涵及保护现状，必将进一步增强广大群众的文化自信和文化自豪感。下一步，我们将深入贯彻落实党的二十大精神，深入贯彻落实习近平总书记系列重要讲话精神和视察山东重要讲话、重要指示批示精神，以习近平新时代中国特色社会主义思想为引领，统筹推进“五位一体”总体布局，协调推进“四个全面”战略布局，不断弘扬中华优秀传统文化，不断推动文化建设向纵深发展，为满足人民群众对美好生活的向往，为丰富广大人民群众的文化生活，保障广大人民群众的文化权益，为深入推进经济文化强省建设，实现中华民族伟大复兴的中国梦而贡献更大的力量。

山东省文化和旅游厅厅长　王　磊

莱阳豆面灯碗习俗

2013年，莱阳市的“莱阳豆面灯碗习俗”被山东省人民政府列入第三批省级非物质文化遗产名录。

莱阳豆面灯碗习俗通常被称作灯碗，是当地特有的一种民俗活动，流传于辖区内的十几处镇街。其中，万第镇、谭格庄镇、沐浴店镇、照旺庄镇、团旺镇因此民俗活动的规模具有广泛影响力，被公认为莱阳豆面灯碗习俗的代表。

元宵节燃灯的习俗起源于汉代；到了唐代，国家繁荣，民风开明，赏灯的活动就更加兴盛了。宋代更加重视元宵节，南宋孟元老《东京梦华录》记载：“民间用面塑造花鸟、鱼虫祭祀，做贡品等。”从明代开始，人们从元宵节这一天开始，连续赏灯十天。明马理《澄城县志》记载：“正月十五日蒸荞麦面为灯盏，注油燃灯，次早食之。”这里所说的灯盏便是面灯了。

莱阳豆面灯碗的形式多种多样，常见的豆面灯碗有十二属相灯、十二月灯、看场佬灯、福禄寿喜灯、灶王爷灯、家禽走兽灯等20余种，每盏灯都有特殊的寓意。譬如，捏一盏狗灯放在大门口，寓意能够看家护院，保平安；把圣虫（蛇）灯放在窗台上，寓意能够百毒不侵；将马灯放进马厩，寓意来年马壮无恙；点燃猪头灯则寓意猪肥满圈。除此之外，福禄寿喜等吉祥的寓意则可以用相应的动物和植物来代替，如蝙蝠灯取谐音寓福，喜鹊灯取谐音寓喜，鸡灯则寓意吉祥，求生育多用莲子灯，取多子之意。

莱阳豆面灯碗中最出名的可以说是十二月灯了。点燃十二月灯，可以凭借火花的大小占卜来年十二个月的兴衰，灯盏熄灭后，盏内余油的多少预示着来年十二个月的旱、涝情况。清康熙年间《莱阳县志》载：“又做面盏十二照月序蒸之，以卜水旱。”也就是说，在康熙年间莱阳就有面制灯碗了。

关于灯碗，在莱阳还有一则流传甚广的故事。故事是这样说的：相传，古时姜子牙封神，把所有的神封过之后，却发现没有封自己，最后姜子牙只好封自己为元宵夜灯神。这天晚上，姜子牙看到世间哪里亮着灯，就到哪里去解决问题。无论是祈愿还是告状，他都会逐一办理。若时间来不及，他便会等来年的元宵节接着办理。

莱阳豆面灯碗习俗是从元宵节闹花灯、放烟火的习俗演变而来。如今花灯、烟火跳出山沟，进入官方组织的专题活动现场，而豆面灯碗作为农民心灵的寄托，依然以它特有的淳朴自然，悄悄地在每家每户生存着。

莱阳豆面灯碗习俗分为“捏灯”和“送灯”两个部分。

首先是“捏灯”。莱阳豆面灯碗是以黄豆磨成的面为主要原料，做灯前先用食油掺和豆面揉成面团，加油后的豆面很有筋力，所以豆面灯碗能够做得十分精细，点燃后能透出黄金色的光晕，也叫“金灯”。

在莱阳豆面灯碗中，普通简单的灯碗不改变面的本色，用于供奉祖先；家谱和喜庆用灯多采用色面制成。色面是将蔬菜汁直接调和在豆面里反复揉和，直至蔬菜的颜色成为面的本色。莱阳豆面灯碗所用的色以大红、大绿、黄色为主，其他色彩则作为点缀，整体上是一派大富大贵的调子，好像古埃及人在制作好了的雕像上加彩绘一样。

制作豆面灯碗，先要把捏制的各种灯的胚胎进行粗加工，成为雏形；然后利用梳子、剪刀、绿豆、火柴棒、竹片、硬币等工具，进行局部的精细加工，像猪的头、龙的鳞、刺猬的眼睛等，整个捏制过程随意性很强，基本上是边创作边制作，作品形态各异，惟妙惟肖；最后用火柴棒缠上棉花作为灯芯，插在灯碗上，到此一盏可爱的豆面灯碗就做好了。

莱阳豆面灯碗不仅寓意祝福，而且可以反映民生。如家境贫穷的人家往往会多做虎灯、天狗灯等，虎寓意强大，天狗口叼元宝，有得“天财”的意思；经常闹虫灾的农户，则多做金蟾灯、青蛙灯，将它们放在田间粪堆上，寓意希望来年无虫害。有些灯碗寓意丰富，如有余（将灯碗置于粮囤中表示有余）、洁净（将灯碗置于水缸中表示洁净）等意。不同的环境，所用灯碗的含义也不同。

除了“捏灯”外，“送灯”也是莱阳豆面灯碗习俗的重要组成部分。“送灯”是极为恭敬的，整个“送灯”过程默默无声，除了必要的念词和招呼之外，人们很少说话。“送灯”时，各家各户的男主人会盘坐在炕头闷声抽烟袋，他们会看着儿子从老婆手里送出去一盏盏灯碗，他们偶尔会去猪圈或牛棚里转转。各家的女主人们会在送灯时倒油点灯。实际上从正式送灯开始，整个气氛已经染上了神圣的色彩，人会不由自主地恭敬起来。

送灯的顺序一般是从灶王爷开始，这对农民来说极为重要；接下来是将圣虫灯放入粮囤面缸，送看场佬灯去场园，再依次将马灯、狗灯、猪灯、鸡灯送出，送灯的顺序基本上是按照神、吃、住、畜禽，属相灯从来不可少。

送灯习俗还包含着特有的诗意性。例如，送灯时会唱一些这样的歌谣：“照照锅台前，蝎子不蜇老娘；照照炕头，蝎子不咬老头；照照窗台，蝎子不蜇小孩。”送看场佬灯时要绕场院正转三周，倒转三周，边走边唱：“看场佬，满场跑，打的粮食吃不了；看场佬，满场转，打的粮食吃不繁（完）。”

总之，灯碗习俗的活动内容与人们的现实生活和感情紧密相连。当夜色逐渐浓厚时，父亲会带领孩子往自家的祖坟上送灯，送灯时很少哭泣，据说是因为正月十五的时候，家中已逝去的长辈喜欢安静。父子两代轮流对地下的先人说着“悄悄话”，无论是感恩、祈愿，还是喜、怒、怨、恨，都要“告知”地下的先人，以达到天遂人愿的淳朴之心。

莱阳豆面灯碗的习俗，是农耕文化的典型代表，在内容和形式上都极为丰富。它不仅是农民祈愿的一种活动形式，而且是民俗文化的重要组成部分。莱阳豆面灯碗是莱阳人民根据自己的地域特色、节日和生活习俗而创造的一种艺术形式，它植根于劳动者深厚的生活土壤，具有鲜明的艺术特色和生活情趣。这种流传于民间的灯碗习俗，实际上是集传统的祭祀、祈愿于一体的活动，它源于人类对自然力量的恐惧和崇拜，对命运的忧患和生活的美好向往。通过“做灯”“送灯”等一系列活动，民间传统的心态和审美情趣就会自然而真实地流露出来。

莱阳豆面灯碗具有深厚的历史价值和实用价值，是研究胶东历史、民俗、美学不可忽视的实物资料。从莱阳豆面灯碗习俗中汲取有价值的内容，有助于我们深刻理解莱阳文化，也会为我们继承和发扬莱阳传统习俗提供许多珍贵的经验和素材。保护好这一民俗文化遗产，对于反映地域文化特点、延续中国传统文化有着重要意义。

东镇沂山祭沂

2013年，临朐县的“东镇沂山祭沂”被山东省人民政府列入第三批省级非物质文化遗产名录。2014年，张孝友（男）被山东省人民政府批准为第四批省级非物质文化遗产项目代表性传承人。

沂山，位于山东省临朐县南部，是沂河、汶河、沭河、弥河的发源地，也是“龙山文化”的发源地。沂山古称“海岳”（见《明史》）、“神岳”（见《齐都赋》），又称东泰山、东镇，是泰沂山脉的东主峰。古人曾称赞其“嵬嶷磅礴，与岱埒尊，表东镇东方而萃秀，实齐东之巨镇也”，因此历史上又有“泰山为五岳之首，沂山为五镇之首”之说。

据《史记·封禅书》记载，黄帝最先登封东泰山（即沂山）；舜肇州封山，定沂山为重镇；禹时祭祀沂山；汉、隋、唐、宋、元、明、清，历代对沂山都有增封。唐代，沂山被封为“东安公”；到了宋代，沂山又被封为“东安王”；元代沂山被增封为“元德东安王”；朱元璋在他即位的第三年（1370年），以圣旨的形式诏封沂山为“东镇沂山之神”；到了清代雍正二年（1724年），沂山被清世宗封为“沂山佑民捍御之神”。

帝王将相封祭沂山，文人墨客为沂山题诗。到了清朝末年，东镇庙前的大小碑碣已经有360余方，它们形成了规模宏大的东镇碑林。这些碑林中有《宋太祖赵匡胤乾德三年御碑》《宋仁宗景祐御碑》《元二世铁木耳大德二年诏封沂山为东安王的蒙汉两文碑》《明洪武三年朱元璋诏封“沂山之神”御碑》《明永乐四年征伐安南黎仓父子犯边的祭告碑》《明成化年间户部尚书杨鼎的代祭碑》《明弘治进士户部尚书翁世资撰文的东镇庙寝碑》《明弘治进士陈凤梧赞咏沂山的手书行草诗刻》《明万历年间状元赵秉忠的观沂山瀑布草书诗刻》《清康熙帝手书“灵气所钟”御碑》《乾隆亲笔“大东陪岳”御碑》等。这些碑的撰文、书丹都是出自名家之手，它们不但记述了历代封建王朝致祭东镇的香火盛事，也记载了当时军事、政治和自然灾害等状况，对研究宋、元、明、清历史有重要参考价值。

帝王将相封祭沂山，源于对“岳镇海渎”的祭祀。对“岳镇海渎”的祭祀，又可以追溯到远古先民的原始崇拜。这是一个长期演变发展的过程，大体上经过了图腾崇拜、山形祭祀、山镇祭祀、封禅行典、岳镇海渎祭祀五个阶段。图腾崇拜和山形祭祀带有原始宗教色彩；从山形祭祀转变为山镇祭祀带有强烈的政治色彩；从山镇祭祀到封禅行典，融汇了丰富的儒家哲学思想；然而由神秘的封禅行典到岳镇海渎祭祀，则使古人对名山大川的崇拜走向了理性化、制度化。在“岳镇海渎”祭祀中，岳镇祭祀又是其中最为重要的部分，因为在那个时候，岳（镇）是皇（王）权和国家社稷的象征。“五岳”为“天”的代表，是仁德和尊严的象征；“五镇”是“地”的标志，是国土和统治的化身。

据史料记载，商周之前的东镇沂山祭祀时间是农历二月，祭祀之神是天帝；隋唐以后，朝廷祭山已不再祭祀天帝，而是从东方主生角度考虑，从立春开始祭祀。从民国开始，皇家祭祀沂山开始转变为民间祭祀。

每年农历四月初八，由沂山风景区管委会主持的东镇沂山祭祀活动，隆重而庄严。玉皇阁大殿内，天帝像身披红绸，祭台上红烛高烧，祭案上布满三牲、鸡（寓五谷丰登）、鱼（寓年年有余）、苹果（寓四季平安）、寿桃（寓长命百岁）和小麦、玉米、大豆、高粱、芝麻（此五类寓五谷丰登）等具有象征意义的供品。在大殿前竖起旗杆，杆头销金幡迎风飞舞。一名道长为执事官，四名道人为初献官或亚献官，他们各着职服，侍立在坛前。巳时（上午9时至11时），由主祭宣布祭祀仪式开始。随后大典之上香烟袅袅，鼓乐齐鸣（有钟、鼓、琴、笛、笙、锣、钹等）。主祭安排执事官请神、迎神、祭酒、拜神，朗诵祝文。四名初献官或亚献官吟唱乐章。祭祀东镇沂山的乐章是“东望迎神凝安”，其唱词是“盛德惟木，勾芒御神，沂岱淮海，厥功在民，爰熙坛坎，褒对庶神，于以歆格，灵贻具臻”；“升降同安”，其唱词是“绅襜兮，玉佩蕊兮，于我将事，神燕喜兮，帝命望祀，敢有不共？往返于位，肃肃雍雍”。除“东望迎神凝安”和“升降同安”外，后面的祭祀乐章依次是“奠玉币明安”“酌献成安”“送神宁安”“东方迎神凝安”“初献盥洗同安”“奠玉币明安”“东镇位”“亚终献酌献（四位并同）”“送神凝安”等篇章。这些乐章，其唱词大都是一些壮丽繁华的赞颂之词。

在祭祀乐章演唱完之后，自发参加祭祀的群众要依次焚纸，向天帝行三叩礼。叩拜动作要遵循道教礼仪，顺序依次是右手握左手拇指、打躬、右手放于跪垫，左手护丹田、双膝跪于跪垫上、左手压在右手上、叩头、左手护丹田起身、右手握左手拇指做阴阳状。

在祭祀当天，沂山东门的草山亭（宋太祖赵匡胤行遥参礼旧址）山集庙还会举行庙会，山集庙庙会与玉皇阁隆重的祭祀仪式遥相呼应。山货市、古玩市、饰品市、花卉根雕奇石市、特色小吃市等，琳琅满目，热闹异常。另外，当天戏班子也会在山口扎起戏台，从上午9时一直演到下午4时。

一直以来，东镇沂山的祭沂活动深受广大人民群众的喜爱。对东镇沂山祭祀礼仪的继承，离不开一代又一代人的努力。分管过沂山东镇庙、戏称自己当过东镇庙住持的张孝友以及他的守山“战友”们，是沂山的守护者。“山越青水越秀文物越金贵，我们的压力就越大。更何况沂山森林覆盖率已达98.6%，是国家4A级风景区，每天游人如梭，高峰时达2万余人，这都需要比以往更频繁地瞭望、巡查和守护。”在过去的很多年里，张孝友和其他守山人任劳任怨守护着沂山，他们像守护自己的孩子一样守护沂山，沂山上每一块碑刻的位置和内容，以及它们来自哪个田间地头，他们都非常清楚。

由于一代又一代守山人的努力，东镇沂山祭祀礼仪才得到更好地传承和发展。正像潍坊市临朐县图书馆副研究馆员王庆增所说：“五帝时期至清代是皇家祭祀，民国以来演变成了民间祭祀，两者都出自一个文化源头。出于文化寻根的考虑，我们作为中华儿女，也理应把一脉相连的沂山祭祀传统发扬光大。”

东岳大帝与碧霞元君信俗

2013年，泰安市的“东岳大帝与碧霞元君信俗”被山东省人民政府列入第三批省级非物质文化遗产名录。

东岳大帝与碧霞元君信仰的习俗发源于泰山，并以泰山为中心，辐射和影响全国各地。泰山被古人认为是生命起源的地方，受到一代代山民的敬仰。早期的泰山崇拜，随着社会制度的改变和文化的传播，逐渐演化成帝王的祭祀与封禅。据司马迁《史记·封禅书》考证，有多位古代帝王先后来到泰山进行祭祀、封禅，加之远古的东方崇拜，泰山演变出一个主管人生与死的东岳泰山神——东岳大帝。汉代歌谣“上泰山，见神人……驾蛟龙，乘浮云……”（《泰山镜铭》），说的就是东岳大帝。

伴随历代帝王的泰山封禅，泰山神的影响开始渗透到社会的各个层面。除了帝王将相，全国各地的普通百姓也都争相到泰山朝拜。唐玄宗于开元十三年（725年）封泰山神为“天齐王”，这一时期，不仅皇帝到泰山封禅，皇室的其他人也频繁祭祀泰山神，泰山神的信仰进一步扩大。宋真宗加封泰山神为“天齐仁圣王”，后又加封其为“天齐仁圣帝”，并钦定泰山神的生日为农历三月二十八，决定年年庆贺。唐宋以后，随着泰山神信仰在民间的影响日益深入，定期不断举行大型祭祀活动，形成了庙会。元世祖于至元二十八年（1291年）晋封泰山神为“天齐大生仁圣帝”。由于帝王的推崇，泰山神的地位更加显赫起来。明弘治十六年（1503年），《孝宗御制重修东岳庙记碑》记载：“东岳之庙今遍于天下，其在泰山者为专祀，历代所重。故庙之规制甲于他方，香火特盛。”当代著名作家汪曾祺《泰山片石》记载：“历代帝王对泰山神屡次加封，老百姓则称之为东岳大帝。全国各地几乎都有一座东岳庙，亦称泰山庙。我们县的泰山庙离我家很近……”从古代政府对泰山的重视、百姓对泰山的敬仰和古今文人的作品中，我们能看到人们对泰山以及东岳大帝的尊敬和崇拜。

碧霞元君又叫“泰山玉女”，在民间被称为“泰山奶奶”或“泰山娘娘”。根据清张尔岐《蒿庵闲话》记载，汉代仁圣帝宫殿前有金童玉女的雕像，随着时间的流逝，宫殿倒塌，金童玉女的雕像也倒了，金童像被风水侵蚀碎掉了，玉女像掉到了水池中，这个水池便被称作泰山玉女池。据说，宋真宗在泰山玉女池内洗手的时候，玉女像竟然浮出了水面，宋真宗认为是神仙显灵，于是下令疏浚该池，用白玉重雕玉女像，命有司建祠并更名为昭真祠，派遣使者进行祭神活动，号为“圣帝之女”，封其为“天仙玉女碧霞元君”，这就是碧霞元君的由来。

明代，昭真祠更名为灵应宫，后来又进行扩建，扩大规模，改名为碧霞宫。宋元以来，碧霞元君的影响甚至超过了泰山神，泰山娘娘庙会兴盛起来，每年三月十五，泰山娘娘生日，赶会的人甚至超过了三月二十八庙会的人数。明万历二十二年（1594年），王锡爵在《东岳碧霞宫碑》中说：“齐鲁道中，顶斋戒弥陀者声闻数千里，策敝足茧而犹不休，问之，曰：‘有事于碧霞。’问故，曰：‘元君能为众生造福如其愿。’”民间传说中的碧霞元君神通广大，人们相信这位女神能庇护众生，为信徒解答疑难，能保佑众生。在泰山有上、中、下三庙，在其他地方也建有许多“娘娘庙”。碧霞元君深受百姓爱戴，历经千年，香火却从未中断。

在泰安，信仰泰山神的主要表现方式是朝拜与进香。进香的人被称作

“香客”或“香官”；如果是有组织的一群人一起进香，就称他们为“香社”。香社一般由一个村或几个村的香客组成，人数或多或少，没有定数，组织者被称作“香首”“会首”或“善首”，一般由当地德高望重的人担任。

香社有一套完整的组织礼仪制度。一般先要商定进香的日期，准备香礼，如神袍、钟鼓、旗幡等。动身前要举行仪式，一是祈求一路平安，二是给东岳大帝或泰山娘娘先报个信。普通的进香是先烧上一炷信香，隆重一点的还要“演社”，即抬着东岳大帝圣驾或泰山娘娘圣驾，沿着街道烧香游行，以此告知人们进香的队伍就要出发了。进香途中，香会的队伍都要敲锣打鼓，伴着音乐前行，队伍还打着自己的旗子，每经过一个村庄便要鼓乐齐鸣，燃放鞭炮；到达泰山后，先礼泰山庙，后到碧霞元君祠献礼，《醒世姻缘传》等文学作品对此都有详尽的描写。

泰山还有很多记录进香的石碑，仅红门宫北就有进香石碑30余方，内容都是关于香客求神、建醮、进香、还愿等。著名的碑刻有《北斗圣会题名碑》，碑文在一开始就写道：“祈福延生修斋，顺百顺之康；辞演华封寿龄，推三祝之列。”所谓“祈福”即祈求神灵赐福；“延生”是祈求长寿的祭祀；“修斋”则是会集僧道徒，供应斋食。泰山至今保存的进香碑约有360处，立碑者南到福建省，北到黑龙江省，涵盖了全国20多个省市。

除了进香和朝拜外，泰安人民对东岳大帝和碧霞元君的信仰还演化出了更贴近生活的活动，那就是庙会。泰山的庙会不断发展，到现在，庙会增加了商贸、娱乐活动等新内容，服务于来自四面八方的朝拜者。因为碧霞元君的影响力不断扩大，所以东岳庙会的时间延长了，并增加了祭祀碧霞元君的活动。

今天我们所看到的庙会，除了正常的宗教活动以外，还有各种各样的经贸活动、旅游观光和文化娱乐活动。从独具魅力的民间曲艺到惊心动魄的游艺竞技，从多姿多彩的民间工艺到新颖时尚的旅游商品，从祈福纳祥的拜山仪式到古代帝王的封禅大典，东岳庙会的每个角落都充满泰山独特的地域文化特征，让置身庙会的游客每时每刻都能感受到多彩独特的文化气息。东岳大帝与碧霞元君信俗衍生出了越来越多的民俗活动，丰富着人们的日常生活与精神世界。

胶东饺子食俗

2013年，荣成市的“胶东饺子食俗”被山东省人民政府列入第三批省级非物质文化遗产名录。

俗话说“靠山吃山，靠海吃海”，有很多中国传统的民俗到了荣成，都带有一点“大海的味道”，其中最典型的例子就是逢年过节常吃的饺子。

馄饨和饺子都是北方面食文化谱系中最具代表性的食品，它们之间的关系悠久而又复杂。大约在秦汉时便有了馄饨，饺子是由馄饨发展而来的，将馄饨包成半月形就成了饺子。北齐颜之推《颜氏家训》里说“今之馄饨，形如偃月，天下通食也”，说明饺子这种偃月形馄饨，在当时已颇为流行。近几十年来，唐代的饺子实物在考古中屡次被发现，这说明在当时饺子已经广为流传。

据中国古代文献资料记载，因时代、地区、制作方法和馅料的不同，饺子有很多不同的称谓，如“角子”“角儿”“粉角”“扁食”“馄饨”“饺饵”“水煮饽饽”“水饺儿”，“角”是饺子的象形，“角”“交”“饺”谐音，“饺子”一名便由此而来。大约到明清时期，在整个北方吃饺子便已成为定俗。此时，饺子的称谓更趋多样化，除“角子”“扁食”“饺儿”

等前代既有称谓外，还有“水角儿”“水点心”“水点儿”“汤角儿”等叫法，因地域和制作方法不同而名称各异。

据有关史料记载，除夕之夜或大年初一吃饺子的习俗，早在明代便已开始流行，清代盛极一时。饺子的“更岁交子”之意，至迟在明清时期已基本形成，且是全民性习俗。

饺子先后流传到各地，在多个地区扎根并普及开来，形成了种类繁多的饺子“家族”，胶东海鲜饺子就是其中的一种。胶东地区背靠大海，有着十分丰富的海洋资源，胶东先民就地取材，按时令选择不同的海鲜，与蔬菜、猪肉配成馅料，制成颇具海洋风味的胶东海鲜饺子。

各种各样的海鲜，如鲅鱼、黄花鱼、海肠、海参、虾仁、贝丁等均可入馅，其中以鲅鱼馅饺子和鹰爪虾馅饺子为代表，其制作过程不是很复杂。要制作鲅鱼馅饺子，需要准备鲅鱼、酱油、清水、五花肉、生姜、大葱、白菜、韭菜、花生油、食盐、醋、香油、小麦粉等食材。准备好以后，第一步是处理鲅鱼。先将新鲜的鲅鱼清洗干净，去掉鱼头，剖开鱼腹，清除里面的内脏，再将鱼肉从鱼身上切下来，用菜刀剔除鱼刺。第二步是制作肉馅。先准备一碗兑了少许清水的酱油，一边剁馅儿一边将酱油洒在鱼肉馅儿上，这么做既可以给肉馅儿调味，又能起到使肉馅儿不沾刀的作用，还能去除鱼肉的腥味儿。剁鱼肉馅儿的时候，还要注意观察肉馅儿的细腻程度，一定要将鲅鱼肉剁成肉泥状态，这样，包出的饺子才能软硬适度。在鲅鱼肉馅儿里加入适量清水稀释，用手搅拌，可以让肉馅儿更加柔软，汁水更加饱满，烹制后口感更佳。下一步是将准备好的五花肉切成1厘米大小的肉块儿，切忌搅碎。搅碎后的五花肉油分就流失了，会影响饺子的口感和味道。然后将生姜切成姜末，大葱去除葱叶并切碎，一齐加入五花肉中，倒入适量酱油，用筷子搅拌之后，腌渍一段时间，腌渍时间不得少于20分钟。这样既可以使五花肉入味，又可以去除猪肉的腥味儿。在等待腌渍的时候可以准备配菜。将整颗白菜（以窖藏过的白菜为上）斩头去尾，只选用汁水饱满的中间部位，切成碎末，倒入些许花生油，保持白菜的鲜味儿。取适量新鲜韭菜（以春天第一刀韭菜为上），洗净后切成碎末，备用。然后将腌渍好的五花肉倒入鲅鱼馅儿中，也可以根据自己的口味加入适量食盐，顺时针搅拌。搅拌的时间越长，肉馅儿就越黏稠，越细腻，直到搅拌好为止，中途不能停下，这是整个制作过程中最辛苦的一个环节。搅拌得差不多的时候就可以加入之前切好的白菜末和韭菜末，接着顺时针搅动。搅拌完成后，在馅儿里加入少量醋与香油，搅匀。醋要适量，以免发涩。最后一步就是包饺子了。制作饺子皮也是有讲究的，要选用新磨的小麦粉，用凉水和成较为“筋道”的饺子面，用盆扣好，醒面。将醒好的面放在案板上不停搓揉，直至柔软发亮为止。然后把和好的面捏成大小均匀的“剂子”，压扁，用擀面杖擀成直径10厘米大小、中间略厚四周稍薄的圆形饺子皮，再包馅儿入内，将饺子皮边沿捏合，呈元宝形状。包饺子时，一家人围坐在桌前，一边看着电视节目，一边包着饺子，有说有笑，其乐融融。摆放包好的饺子时，要将饺子放在饺子帘上，从中间往外圈，有圈财之意。

鹰爪虾饺子同鲅鱼饺子制作步骤的区别主要是在饺子馅儿上。制作鹰爪虾饺子馅儿需要准备鹰爪虾、韭菜、白菜、猪肉、酱油、姜末、葱末等食材。先剥去虾皮。剥皮时手要轻、快、准，掐头去尾，把虾肉取出，既要避免浪费，又不能有一丝虾皮，必须干净。再去“虾线”，即取出虾肠。把剥好的虾仁，用指甲掐成1厘米大小的小段。进行这个步骤时绝不能用刀切，以防带入铁器之气，影响虾的鲜味儿。此外，虾段儿不能太碎或制成虾泥，这样拌到馅儿里，不仅失去了虾仁的鲜美味道，也不美观。下一步是准备配菜。将韭菜摘好后洗干净，切碎，放在盆里，不能盖住，否则会“闷气”，等包制前再放在盆里搅拌。同样，也将白菜洗净、切末。最后将处理完的虾肉和配菜一起放在容器里，加酱油、姜末、葱末煨上，这样能让肉菜更入味。

胶东海鲜饺子已经成为当地的一种文化符号，蕴含着浓厚的胶东沿海区域特点及民俗文化特点，是胶东人民心中乡情的最好体现。

“串黄河”风俗

2013年，文登市的“‘串黄河’风俗”被山东省人民政府列入第三批省级非物质文化遗产名录。

“串黄河”亦名“九曲黄河灯”“九曲黄河阵”“地灯”“平安灯”“九曲阵”“迷魂阵”等，是流传在文登境内的一种大型民间传统游戏习俗。关于它的来历，有着多种解释。

据说，它最早起源于道教的鼻祖——老子，而“九曲”实质上是道家阴阳太极图的变形。还有人说它是由古代战争中迷魂阵的图形演变而来的。此外，有一个更具传奇色彩的说法是，殷商末年，商纣王凶狠残忍、暴虐无道，极度宠信后妃妲己，不事朝政，大臣们不能忍受伴君如伴虎的日子，百姓也不堪沉重的赋税徭役，一时间，怨声载道。周武王决意让姜子牙领兵伐纣，一路上势如破竹，把商纣王的兵马打得节节败退。身为道教四大元帅之一的赵公明受好友闻太师的请求，出山率兵御敌。赵公明修道有成，法术高强，是在峨眉山罗浮洞中修炼的截教高人，手中持有法宝二十四颗定海神珠，姜子牙军队中阐教的仙人及将领们都不是他的对手，接连败下阵来。无奈之下，姜子牙只好请来陆压道君用法术将其暗杀。“三霄”（赵公明的三个妹妹：云霄、琼霄、碧霄）为替兄长报仇，依据黄河十八弯的迂回走势设下“九曲黄河阵”。此阵机巧灵动、迂回百转，还有重重机关，易守难攻。二郎神、金咤、木咤、哪咤等法术高强的仙人均被困阵中，无法脱身，面临险境。最后，姜子牙在老子、元始天尊、南极仙翁等仙人的协助下才得以破阵，“三霄”阵破人亡。后人特意把“九曲黄河阵”演变成游艺活动，供人们闲暇时娱乐与观赏。这一大型游戏活动从此在文登流传下来，成为当地一大习俗。

“串黄河”的表演地点多选择在宽敞的空地。它的阵势有很多种，如“九曲黄河阵”“黄河八卦阵”“六城黄河阵”等，阵势弯曲萦回，犹如迷宫。祁太秧歌《小观灯》，有关九曲黄河阵的唱词是：“叫声姐姐快快看，棍子上顶得灯一盏。按八卦摆成黄河阵，又想游来又不敢。进去容易出来难，这就是黄河九曲阵阵相连。”“九曲黄河阵”以19×19根草把为桩，桩端装一盏油灯，桩距1.6米或2.3米，等距竖立，用绳子界开，左三城，右三城，共12阵361盏灯，阵阵相通，阵前扎彩坊悬灯插旗。传统的“串黄河”活动先要由“灯官”巡视检查一番，待吉时一到，便号令全场点灯。然后“灯官”在祭坛前敬香、焚纸、拜祭，随后鸣枪三响，鼓乐齐奏，舞龙队、秧歌队、高跷队、跑旱船的、耍毛驴的、舞狮子的依次从入口入阵，载歌载舞地在灯海中盘旋回转，左进右出需两个多小时。如果不沿甬路行进或重新入串过阵，就得从拦截的绳子下过去，这叫作“钻狗洞”。“串黄河”活动进行到高潮时，场内外人山人海、锣鼓喧天、灯火通明，串阵队伍忽东忽西，忽南忽北，满场人流不息，但互不妨碍，气氛热烈，规模宏大，引人入胜。

据《文登文史资料》记载，1949年以前，境内大村如林村、葛家村、高村、坤龙邢家村、文登营等，多在农历正月十五晚上或二月二举行大规模的“串黄河”活动。但是，由于这项活动耗资费时，又必须有会摆阵势和善于组织指挥的人细细筹划，所以，这些村子都是每隔几年举办一次或者连办三年再停办一次，从没有年年都举行。1947年正月十五，举行了一场“串黄河”活动。当天晚上灯火一片，观众数万人，几十个表演队伍在黄河阵中来回穿行，使节日气氛达到高潮。

北邢家村时年87岁的邢德海，既会摆阵势又善于组织，他年轻时曾经历过两次“串黄河”。第一次大约在1936年至1937年间，当时他才10多岁，初次随父兄进阵表演。第二次是在1945年，就在村里土地庙前的空地上，邢老先生组织人力、物力并亲自表演。20世纪因为修水库，坤龙邢家村分为北邢家、中邢家、南邢家三个村。1962年正月十五晚，举行了一次“串黄河”活动。1993年至1994年，邢德海老人自己出资在本村空地上连续举办了两次“串黄河”活动，村民们的积极性也异常高，纷纷捐款捐物，以表示对活动的支持。1995年正月十五，又在中邢家村举办了一次大规模的“串黄河”活动，周围许多村的村民也都踊跃派表演队参加。邢老先生扎了一个老鼠坐轿的扮装，亲自披挂上阵，参加表演。1996年6月1日，应文登实验小学之邀，会组织“串黄河”的村民们在学校操场上扎了一次“串黄河”，全校师生与部分村民及学生家长共同体验了一次传统文化的盛宴。

“串黄河”这一大型民间传统秧歌游戏，蕴含着中华古老的文化传统，在曾经文艺活动缺乏的年代丰富了人们的精神文化生活，是值得我们永远传承下去的一种传统技艺。

宁津斗蟋习俗

2013年，宁津县的“宁津斗蟋习俗”被山东省人民政府列入第三批省级非物质文化遗产名录。

宁津县隶属山东省德州市，位于山东省西北部。中国蟋蟀文化历史悠久，源远流长，是具有浓厚中国特色的民间文化，从古代开始便流行在中国社会的每一个角落，而宁津县又是其中蟋蟀文化气息最为浓厚的地方。蟋蟀在中国分布极为广泛，而真正的斗蟋只产于黄河中下游和长江中下游地区，宁津斗蟋就是黄河中下游地区的典型代表，宁津也被誉为“中华蟋蟀第一县”。

宁津县盛产小麦、玉米、谷类、豆类、棉花、蔬菜、瓜果等各类农作物；宁津的土壤里富含钙质、铁、锰及各种无机盐、矿物质。丰富的食料资源和良好的土壤环境为蟋蟀的生长提供了得天独厚的自然条件，造就了宁津蟋蟀体质好、勇猛善斗的品性。

斗蟋之风始于唐宋，盛于明清。唐代斗蟋主要流行于宫廷、皇亲贵戚和豪富之家，而民间的普通百姓喜欢听蟋蟀的鸣声，常常将蟋蟀捉来放在小竹笼里玩赏。五代王仁裕《开元天宝遗事》记载：“每至秋时，宫中妃妾辈，皆以小金笼捉蟋蟀闭于笼中，置之枕函畔，夜听其声。庶民之家皆效之也。”这说明养蟋蟀已从宫廷流传到民间。

在玩赏、观察蟋蟀的过程中，人们逐渐发现雄蟋蟀具有好斗的特性，斗蟋之风由此逐渐兴起，皇室中许多王公大臣甚至整日沉迷于此，无心经营国事。南宋奸相贾似道将蟋蟀相斗看成“军国大事”，“乃至元军兵围襄阳，朝廷岌岌可危，他都充耳不闻……”（《宋史·贾似道传》）足见斗蟋之魅力。

明清两代是斗蟋最为盛行的时期。明宣宗特别喜欢斗蟋，他常常逼迫百姓向他进献好的蟋蟀，百姓如若不从，就会招来杀身之祸，人们都称他“蟋蟀皇帝”。那时候还有俗语说：“促织瞿瞿叫，宣德皇帝要。”《聊斋志异》中那篇脍炙人口的《促织》，就是据此写成的。在那时，还出现了斗蟋赌场。清代康熙年间的《宁津县志》记载，“民皆好斗蟋，怡养之趣，斗逐之乐，溢于言表，遂成风尚”，反映了宁津斗蟋的繁盛之景。

宁津蟋蟀闻名北方，是为历代帝王进贡斗蟋的有名产地，民间有很多颇有传奇色彩的传说。传说北宋末年，徽、钦二帝沉迷斗蟋，整日和王公大臣、嫔妃宫娥在宫廷中耍斗蟋蟀，不理朝政，最终被金兵灭国，徽、钦二帝也被俘虏，一路坐着囚车被押至幽州（今北京地区）。和二帝一起被押运的还有许多精致的宫廷物品。途中路过宁津的时候，一个精致的瓷罐突然破裂开来，有只七色的小虫跳了出来，振翅高歌。钦宗皇帝见此黯然泪下，悲凄地说道：“你们现在赶紧逃吧，等到再次出现盛世的时候，你们再出来拜帅称王。”果然，八百年后，宁津蟋蟀称霸了整个斗蟋市场。

在宁津，还流传着一个“宁津蟋蟀斗慈禧”的传说。清同治年间，慈禧太后酷爱斗蟋，北方地区又属宁津斗蟋质量最为上乘，慈禧太后便派人到那里寻找斗蟋珍品。但两个官吏为快速完成任务以讨慈禧太后的欢心，来到此地后大肆捕捉蟋蟀，态度粗暴，动辄对当地村民打骂奚落。当地人为了捉弄这些暴吏，给了他们几只个头大的雌蟋蟀。二人如获至宝，把几只雌蟋蟀带回京城献给慈禧太后。慈禧太后见到蟋蟀本来十分高兴，结果在斗蟋开始之后，才发现蟋蟀是雌的，根本不会斗。慈禧太后丢了脸面，勃然大怒，认为办差官吏是在影射她专权的事，便将二人打入了牢狱。

宁津斗蟋品种繁多，根据皮色特点可分为青、黑、紫、黄、红、白、三色、二色8大类200多个品种，其中以青虫为多，占斗蟋的70%。按照牙色特点划分，主要有红牙、黄牙、紫牙、花牙、墨牙、异形牙、黑头银翅7大类，其中大部分为红牙、黄牙，红、黄牙约占宁津蟋蟀总数的80%以上，其次为紫牙与花牙。宁津勇猛善斗、最负盛名的蟋蟀品种为红牙青，因曾多次在地方或者在全国比赛中荣获冠军而声名显赫。其次为红牙红线青、红纱青、白纱青、青金翅。此外，宁津的墨牙青、黑头银翅更是三秋超品，体形优美，勇猛善斗，战绩出色，数量虽少，但也时常被发现。

作为一项民间娱乐活动，捕、养、斗蟋在宁津由来已久，流传甚广，对当地人的生活产生了重要影响。每年立秋到白露这段时间，是当地老百姓捕捉蟋蟀的时节，晚上11点以后，家家户户都有人出门，在麦秸垛、玉米地、豆子地中捕捉蟋蟀。捕捉到蟋蟀之后，人们又根据蟋蟀种类的不同，将捉来的蟋蟀分出三六九等，悉心养护，对品相优良的蟋蟀更是观形听声，休闲赏玩，爱不释手。后来，赏玩蟋蟀又增添了斗蟋活动，大家邀请自己的亲朋好友，按蟋蟀个头的大小，将各自所养的蟋蟀放到地上的圆坑里或盆中，引它们进行咬斗、捉对厮杀，久而久之，斗养蟋蟀便成为传统习俗，流传至今。

宁津人很早就开始重视对斗蟋文化的研究。早在20世纪90年代初，就成立了宁津县蟋蟀研究会，并开始连续举办蟋蟀文化节。自1991年起，宁津县已经成功举办过九届蟋蟀文化节，在此期间组织了斗蟋邀请赛，活动内容的范围和规模都有了更大的发展，意义也更加广泛，特别是为丰富当地老百姓的精神文化生活发挥了重要作用，斗蟋成为当地百姓文化生活的重要组成部分，也成为宁津文化的一大亮点。

宁津斗蟋习俗逐步走进越来越多人的视野中，作为山东省非物质文化遗产，它需要我们提供更大力度的保护和发扬。

珠算文化

2016年，山东珠算协会的“珠算文化”被山东省人民政府列入第四批省级非物质文化遗产代表性项目名录。

珠算是以算盘为工具进行数字计算的一种方法，被誉为中国的第五大发明。2008年，它被国务院列入第二批国家级非物质文化遗产名录；2013年12月4日，被联合国教科文组织列入人类非物质文化遗产名录。

珠算历史悠久。190年，山东人刘洪发明了珠算。东汉徐岳（山东莱州人）在其所著的《数术记遗》中第一次记录了其师刘洪讲述的珠算，这是“珠算”一词第一次出现在现存典籍中。刘洪将历算与《乾象历》一同传给了杨伟、韩翊等人。珠算通过社会传承和教育传承等途径传播到周边地区并通行于全国。至唐宋，珠算日臻完善，逐渐替代了其他计算技术、方式和工具。元明时期，珠算得到了极大传播，进而兴盛起来，在计算领域独领风骚。从16世纪开始，中国珠算开始向周边国家传播，极大地推动了当地经济和文化的发展，尤其是对日本数学的发展起到了巨大的推动作用。到了清代，珠算应用于社会各行各业，影响到生活的方方面面，“不管三七二十一”“三下五除二”等珠算口诀也渐渐演绎为民间俗语。

清光绪二十九年（1903年）颁布的《奏定学堂章程》中规定，初小第四、第五学年和高小第二、第三、第四学年都要学习珠算，其目的“在使知日用之计算，与以自谋生计必需之知识，兼使精细其心思”。自此，珠算开始进入课堂，一直延续到20世纪末。

民国时期，中国民族工商业有所发展。国内市场扩大，商埠增加，金融汇兑、存款业务随之增加，这一系列的变化使社会计算工作日趋繁重。在这种形势下，珠算也得到了相应的发展。有人这样反映当时的情况：“20世纪以来，商业发展，大非畴昔可比……试观市侩酒佣，莫不手握珠盘，以为交易之利器。其用弥广，其法弥简，实为全球特色。西人犹且赞叹之，良有以也。”为了适应社会需要，各大财经院校及中小学均开设珠算课，不仅编出了优良的珠算教材，还提出了笔算珠算混合教学法。虽有些改革未能实现，但珠算教育始终不曾中断，其应用也越来越广泛。解放战争时期，解放军后勤人员为便于行军，将档珠固定于布带上，用时展开，行军时则卷起。新中国成立以后，珠算在经济领域继续发挥着重要作用。小学仍然开设珠算课，并编有珠算课本和教学参考书。后来“三算结合”的蓬勃发展对珠算的普及起到了很大推动作用。1963年11月，中国数学会在北京举行“珠算及辅助工具座谈会”，提出了珠算教学改革的意见，创办了油印刊物《珠算教学研究通讯》，对推动珠算事业的发展起了很大作用。1979年，中国珠算协会成立。从此，珠算教学、应用和学术研究均得到了快速发展。珠算再一次蓬勃发展起来。

作为珠算发明人刘洪的故乡，山东在珠算发展过程中的地位也不容忽视。1981年9月12日至9月15日，受承办首届全国珠算技术比赛大会的影响，山东省的珠算比赛不仅在官方，更在民间迅速展开，一股学习珠算的浪潮在齐鲁大地上迅速蔓延开来。在珠算受到山东人民广泛欢迎的同时，大量学者也在珠算和珠算史领域取得了不小的成绩。1982年6月，中国珠算史第二次学术讨论会预备会暨山东省首届珠算史研究会在蒙阴县召开，在此次会议上，山东省珠算史研究组组长靖玉树首次明确指出珠算由东汉蒙阴人刘洪发明，之后他又发表《关于算圣刘洪的数学水平及其所发明算盘的价值和贡献》等多篇论文，逐步确立了山东是珠算第一故乡的历史定位。1994年，由靖玉树主编的《中国历代算学集成》出版，使古算法得以传世，奠定了山东省算学研究在全国的地位。2003年，山东省承担了教育部、财政部珠心算脑机制研究项目，历时5年，经大量对比实验，完成了“珠心算训练开发儿童智能的脑机制研究”课题，揭示了珠心算训练对人脑各功能区的作用，从生物学层面对得出珠心算具有启智功能结论提供了最基础、最有说服力的支撑。这一结论为珠算在21世纪的蓬勃发展起到了巨大的推动作用。2010年4月，中国民间文艺家协会派出专家组深入蒙阴县考察，他们对该县算圣文化的保护与开发给予高度评价，正式命名蒙阴县为全国唯一的“中国算圣文化之乡”。2013年12月，珠算被联合国教科文组织列入人类非物质文化遗产名录之前，靖玉树将其收藏的我国现存唯一一本宋刻本《数术记遗》献给了国家，为确立珠算的发明人、发明年代提供了参考资料，为中国珠算申遗成功提供了最有说服力的证据。

珠算发展与社会发展是分不开的，与社会对计算速度的要求密切相关。在历史发展过程中，由于筹算的计算速度不及珠算的计算速度，再加上筹算计算时对空间位置大小的限制，珠算逐渐替代了筹算。珠算在人类史上是一项重大而有意义的发明，对人类社会的前进发展起到了不可磨灭的作用，是我国广大劳动人民智慧的结晶。它不仅具有极高的研究价值，还有丰富的现实意义，需要我们共同传承和保护。

山东煎饼习俗

2016年，山东省民俗学会的“山东煎饼习俗”被山东省人民政府列入第四批省级非物质文化遗产代表性项目名录。

煎饼是一种杂粮薄饼，由五谷杂粮磨成面糊，倒入烧热的鏊（ào）子，再用煎饼筢（pá）子摊平烙制而成。煎饼是山东泰沂山区最具代表性的特色食品，也是我国北方传统主食之一。山东煎饼已有两千多年的历史，莒县出土的铁鏊子表明，早在西汉时期泰沂山区就开始用鏊子摊制煎饼了。围绕山东煎饼的制作、食用而形成的一系列日常生产生活习俗、民间信仰习俗、节日习俗、民间传说故事及俗语、谚语、歇后语等民间传统文化习俗统称为山东煎饼习俗。

一、生产生活习俗

（一）山东煎饼的生产习俗

山东煎饼的核心流传区域是泰沂山区。山东煎饼以玉米、小麦、小米、大豆、高粱、地瓜等耐旱的农作物为主要原料。山东煎饼制作工具简易，主要包括鏊子、油擦子、舀勺、筢子、铲子等；其制作流程复杂，技术含量较高，主要分为淘洗粮食、粉碎粮食（拉糁子）、磨煎饼糊子、对半子、烧火摊制、储存等近十道工序，其中制作酸煎饼还有一道发酵煎饼糊子的程序。

制作煎饼又分为摊制、滚制、刮制等不同方式。制作一张煎饼花费时间较短但技术含量较高。比如，在用石磨磨糊子的过程中，推磨不能太快，添料要勤添、少添，以便磨出均匀细腻的糊子；发糊子采取传统的自然发酵法，根据温度掌握发酵时间，发酵时间要恰到好处；摊制煎饼的火候也很难把握，必须用秸秆、杂草等软柴火，火太大容易糊，火太小则影响制作进度，不好往下揭；摊制时手腕要十分灵活，要求在最短的时间内将煎饼糊子在鏊子上摊均匀，否则制作出来的煎饼厚薄不均。

（二）饮食习俗

煎饼由原粮制作而成，是绿色、健康的食品，且携带、食用、保存等都较为便捷，深受当地民众喜爱。关于山东煎饼的吃法，各地有各自的饮食习俗。最经典的吃法是煎饼卷大葱；也可以蔬菜、肉食、海鲜等卷食，比如猪头肉、牛肉渣、炸黄花鱼、炸黄鲫子鱼、海米等；此外，煎饼还可卷海带丝、小豆腐、各式咸菜，甚至是白糖、猪油、煮鸡蛋等。除此之外，煎饼还可以加入猪油、葱花、盐等用开水泡着吃；在凉了后的煎饼上撒上芝麻和盐用火烤着吃；将煎饼放至锅内馏着吃；将豆腐、粉条、韭菜等用油炒熟，然后将煎饼铺开，均匀摊馅儿后折成长方形，再在锅里加油将两面烙成金黄色做成塌煎饼吃。无论哪种吃法都风味绝佳，令人回味无穷。

（三）家族习俗

在农村，煎饼是日常饮食，因而制作煎饼也就成了日常生活的一部分。制作一次煎饼，从前期准备到后期储藏，需要全家人协作共同完成。挑水、淘洗粮、推磨等前期准备的体力活主要由家中男士完成，尤其是推磨，一般情况下是全家总动员；妇女主要负责摊制煎饼与后期储藏。在制作煎饼的过程中，全家要分工明确，团结协作，可以增进彼此之间的默契与情感，有利于家庭和睦美满。

在过去，摊制煎饼的好坏是衡量新媳妇称职与否的重要标准之一。因此，女孩子从小就跟着妈妈学习摊煎饼的各种技巧，等出嫁后在婆家能摊制好煎饼，以此为她赢得婆家人的认可和赞誉。

二、社会文化习俗

（一）节日习俗

每逢过年，临沂等地的民众都会置办大量煎饼。过年期间一般不烙煎饼，都在年前忙着烙煎饼来储备过年期间需要的食物。煎饼也是年礼的重要部分，出嫁的女儿会给娘家和婆家准备一些煎饼。当地有俗语“陪送不完的闺女，忙不完的年”，指的就是从腊月开始就准备忙着做煎饼，到了年关还是没有忙完。春节期间各家都要炸制各类菜品，一般都将煎饼铺在下面做衬，这样，既干净卫生，又不浪费油，浸满油的煎饼香喷喷的，更让人垂涎欲滴。这就是传统的过年习俗。

鲁西南地区流传着“二月二刮大风，拾柴火摊煎饼”的谚语。二月二这天，很多地方都要摊煎饼，据说是为了纪念为人间降雨而受责罚的龙王，这一天吃煎饼叫吃“龙鳞”，于是就有了二月二吃“龙鳞”的习俗。

（二）民间信仰习俗

煎饼补天习俗。明代诗人杨慎在《词品》中写道：“宋以正月二十三日天宰日，言女娲氏以是日补天。俗以煎饼置屋上，名曰补天。”这一民间习俗源于“天穿节”，把正月二十三定为天穿日，恰逢二十四节气中的“雨水”前后，在这一天用煎饼“补天”以求“雨顺”而五谷丰登。

在济宁等地流传着煎饼治头疼的习俗。以前每到打春前，用纸糊一头牛，里边放上煎饼，叫春牛。旁边挖个土坑，坑里竖一个竹筒，竹筒里放一些鸡毛，立春一到，阳气上升，鸡毛被阳气顶出竹筒。人们用木棍击打春牛，所以叫打春。大家都抢春牛肚子里的煎饼，说可治头疼病。

（三）语言习俗

有关山东煎饼的方言主要有：烙煎饼、铯煎饼、滚煎饼、刮煎饼、塌煎饼、馏煎饼、酱煎饼、翘边、油擦子、篪子、筢子、鏊子等。

关于山东煎饼的民谚、民谣大多与生活有关，比如高粱煎饼卷辣椒，越吃越上膘；麦子煎饼卷香油，越吃越瘦猴；麦子煎饼卷鸡蛋，不给俺吃俺不念（书）；吃煎饼，一张张，孬好粮食都出香等。

除此之外，还有关于煎饼的歇后语，如大拇指卷煎饼——自吃自、自咬自；巴掌上摊煎饼——巧手、好手；皇帝吃煎饼——君（均）摊等，这些无不体现着民间的智慧和情趣。

（四）民间传说

在民间流传着许多关于煎饼的传说，其中流传最广的有以下三种：

诸葛亮发明煎饼的说法。相传诸葛亮辅佐刘备之初，兵微将寡，常被曹兵追杀。有一次被围在沂河、沭河之间，锅灶尽失，而将士饥饿困乏，诸葛亮便让伙夫以水和面为浆，将金（铜锣）置火上，用木棍将米浆摊平，煎出香喷喷的薄饼，将士食后士气大振，杀出重围。当地人也习得此法做食，但铜锣昂贵，且易开裂，人们便以铁制成锣状的煎饼鏊。从此煎饼在沂蒙乃至山东大地上流传至今。

关于山东煎饼卷大葱还有一个爱情传说。相传在沂蒙山下，黄妹子和梁马二人情投意合，但因黄小妹狡黠刁钻、见钱眼开的继母阻拦而不能相守。黄母嫌贫爱富，背地里接受了富家人的钱财，让黄妹子嫁过去，可黄妹子不肯，于是黄母设下毒计，让梁马来黄家温习功课，许诺等他考取功名后便可以和黄妹子成亲。黄母对梁马说："书房和文房四宝，我都给你预备好了，你还需要什么东西吗？"梁马说："只要有书有笔，其他什么都不需要。"黄母一听喜出望外，就暗中吩咐家奴对梁马严加看管，不准送饭给梁马。梁马搬进书房后埋头苦读，一直到了傍晚也没人给他送饭。因家奴守门，他只好在书房里等，但久久不见有人送饭。梁马恍然大悟，意识到自己上了黄母的当：黄母正是要故意让梁马挨饿，直到他坚持不住，再让他逃跑，再诬陷他偷东西，以此败坏他的名声，从而让黄妹子对梁马死心。黄妹子知道后，又急又气。急中生智，烙了一叠很薄很薄的白饼，将饼切得方方正正，看起来就如同白纸一样，把大葱剥净剪叶去根，看起来就像笔，让丫鬟给梁马送去。家奴一看是一沓白纸和一捆笔，就放丫鬟进了院。梁马吃着"纸"和

"笔"，温习功课，身体非但没有瘦下去，反倒日渐精神起来。黄母知道后，便问他其中缘由。梁马骗她说是暗中有神仙相助，并说自己日后可中状元。黄母一听立马转变态度，对梁马好生相待。后来，梁马果然高中状元，把黄妹子也接到京城。这个美满的爱情故事从此传扬开来，煎饼卷大葱的吃法也自此在民间广为流传。

相传蒲松龄与山东煎饼也有一段故事。据说，在蒲松龄的家乡淄川，有一对以卖煎饼为生的母女。由于做的是小本生意，难以购置卷食来卖，娘俩只好把大葱剥净切段，再配以小菜，卷在煎饼中间卖给顾客，可买的人极少。蒲松龄路过煎饼铺时心生同情，便想帮助她们。不一会儿，蒲松龄便拿着一副对联走进母女的煎饼铺，并亲手帮她们贴到了门上。上联是"铛圆糊稀摊开大"，下联是"葱多酱少卷上长"，横批"越吃越短"。众人一看不禁齐声喝彩，人们纷纷掏钱购买煎饼，此后，母女俩的煎饼铺生意日益兴隆。

如今传统手工制作煎饼已逐渐被半机械化、机械化的生产取代，但在山东部分农村地区仍然保留着传统的手工煎饼制作技艺。山东煎饼习俗不断丰富、发展，已然形成了历史悠久、影响广泛、地域特色鲜明、文化内涵丰富的文化体系。同时，山东煎饼习俗对于研究泰沂地区的饮食文化、农耕方式、粮食加工制作、传统节日文化、民间信仰文化、民间文学、地方方言等具有极其重要的价值与意义。

东夷渔祖郎君庙会

2016年，青岛市城阳区的“东夷渔祖郎君庙会”被山东省人民政府列入第四批省级非物质文化遗产代表性项目名录。

城阳区隶属山东省青岛市，位于山东半岛南部，其下辖的韩家村里有个韩家民俗村，那里建有渔祖郎君（伏羲氏在东夷的称谓）庙，俗称“郎君庙”。据《中国渔业史》记载，炎黄时代，郎君来到少海（今胶州湾），教人们结网造船、出海捕鱼，受到当地人的敬仰，被尊为渔祖。当地人感念他的功绩，建庙纪念渔祖郎君，而建庙时间因过于久远已经无从考证。

清嘉庆年间，当地人对庙宇进行扩建并设立了神像。韩秉仁倡议重办东夷渔祖郎君庙会，庙会自此重新设立。到清同治年间，有胶州、即墨、海阳等外地客商来庙会上进行交易。庙会会址设在庙前相对开阔的场地上，每年清明节前一天为庙会日，庙会为期三天。庙会期间正值清明踏青时节，方圆几十里的人从四面八方云集而来，最远有从即墨、胶州、平度而来的香客和商贩。庙会上交易的商品有渔具、造船木材、铁锚、干鲜海产品、牲畜、农具、家具、粮食、果蔬及日用百货、地方小吃等，品种多样。清末，庙会街市货摊上有江浙的鱼篓、竹器，莱阳的叉、耙、扫帚和各种农具，还有平度的风箱，崂山的山货，本地各类海产品、土特产等。生意最红火的还要数沿街的酒馆了，因为远来香客和商贩都会在庙会开始前一两天赶到韩家村及附近村庄投亲访友，就为赶渔祖庙庙会，而没有亲朋的只能住在酒馆里。念私塾的学生、扛活的长短工们在庙会日和清明节皆放假一天。从清明前一天开始，渔祖郎君庙就香火缭绕，鞭炮声不绝于耳，说书卖艺的沿街设摊，胶州茂腔、即墨柳腔、板凳戏也相继登场。

1897年以后，渔祖郎君庙所处的阴岛（红岛）划归德占胶澳租界，比较安定，人们仍旧照常举办庙会，还有许多驻青岛的外国人光顾庙会，庙会得以延续和发展。1931年以后，社会相对安定，庙会平稳开展，道路建设加强，外地特产开始进入庙会。1937年以后，日本第二次占领青岛，战乱频繁，地方治安不靖，庙宇破败，赶庙会者寥寥无几，并时有游匪入市抢掠，庙会冷落，直至停办。

2000年，韩平德开始修复东夷渔祖郎君庙。此后，在每年清明节都会举办祭拜渔祖郎君活动，四方香客、商贾云集于此。渔祖郎君庙会已成为周边村庄和城镇居民旅游、参观、踏青、休闲的好去处。庙会周边交通便捷，置于经贸繁荣、文化兴盛、风光优美的氛围之中，并以韩家民俗村丰厚的文化积淀和海洋航海文化为依托，区位优势十分明显。

现在，韩家民俗村的东夷渔祖郎君庙会是中国沿海地区唯一的渔祖祭祀活动。每年清明时节，在出海前，当地的渔民都要为渔祖郎君氏举行隆重的祭祀活动，以表达对这位渔业祖神的崇敬，祈祷出海平安顺利、收获满仓。当地民众十分重视渔祖郎君庙会，他们会提前一个月就开始庙会的筹备工作，预定需要的各种祭祀物品。庙会的主持人和主祭人一般由韩家村的村支书或者村中德高望重的老者担任。其中，主持人主要负责庙会流程的制定、控制以及仪式内容的宣布，而主祭人则负责诵读祝文，带领民众进行行礼、敬酒、上香等仪式。等到清明节前后，随着一支极具地方特色的民俗巡游队伍现身韩家民俗村街头，东夷渔祖郎君庙会正式开始。巡游队伍由上百名当地的民间艺人组成，他们都身穿肥大的深色粗布衣服，脚上穿的鞋子是猪皮缝制的，猪毛清晰可见，这是当地的传统服饰，为展现渔民们冬天在船上作业时的场景。他们会向游客展现明清时期的渔家迎亲、高跷、赶驴、二鬼摔跤、杂技等活动，还原古代渔民出海捕鱼前的真实生活状态。接着，伴随着悠长的渔家号子，隆重的祭祀活动正式开始。祭祀仪式上，主祭人率队伍鸣号，献祭牲，请神祇入位，接着带领当地渔民行祭祀大礼，诵读祭文，行三拜九叩大礼。以海为傲、因海而兴的渔民们以此表达对渔祖的感激和尊崇，祈求这一年风调雨顺，务农之家能够五谷丰登，捕鱼为业的能够鱼虾满仓，身边的亲人朋友都能平平安安、健康幸福。祭祀仪式结束后，庙会上往往香客如云，其中大部分是附近的民众。商贩除本地的以外，还有从即墨、莱阳、平度等地辛苦赶来的。商品交易以当地特色的海鲜小吃为主，还有一些干鲜海产品、手工艺品、玩具、衣服等。每年庙会都有众多戏曲表演和杂要节目，例如，当地人十分喜爱的柳腔、茂腔等戏曲表演。在民俗村内，人们还可以体验骑马、坐轿、撒网、垂钓、荡秋千、划古帆船等活动，或者跟随渔民体验撒网打鱼，到渔盐展览馆和民俗博物馆看中国渔盐历史的演变，聆听老物件背后的故事，寻找老辈人的生活足迹等。

东夷渔祖郎君庙会起初是为了纪念渔祖郎君而兴起，后来逐渐融入了当地渔民们为求出海顺利对渔祖进行祭祀的元素，有着浓厚的中国沿海渔乡特色，是我国民间传统文化中不可缺少的组成部分。

博山正觉寺禅修茶道

2016年，淄博市博山区的“博山正觉寺禅修茶道”被山东省人民政府列入第四批省级非物质文化遗产代表性项目名录。

中国是茶的故乡，茶的发现和饮用历史悠久，在《神农本草经》中就有记载：“神农尝百草，日遇七十二毒，得茶而解之。”这说明中国很早就已经有了饮茶的习俗，并且在后世由茶衍生出了茶道和茶文化。茶文化兴起于中国，茶道出于修行者，茶道与禅修有着深厚渊源，而博山正觉寺作为禅修圣地，更是与茶道渊源颇深。

西汉时期，吴理真在四川蒙顶山种下七株茶树，开创了世界上人工种植茶叶的先河，他被尊称为“茶祖”。吴理真在种茶、泡茶、饮茶的过程中发现：种茶的辛勤劳动如同僧侣的苦行，泡茶时茶叶在沸水中上下翻飞寓意人生浮沉；茶味清淡，饮之却唇齿留香，如同佛家清苦修行，心中所怀皆是天下的大慈大悲。吴理真认为茶与禅有着密不可分的关系，于是他首创“佛茶一家”的说法，被后人尊称为“甘露大师”。

禅宗四祖道信大师倡导农业劳动和参禅悟道并重，僧人在潜心参禅的同时要自耕自种，自给自足，在劳作中修行和参禅悟道。因为禅寺多建在幽静的深山之中，僧侣的农业生产大多是植树造林，种地栽茶，于是僧人采茶、制茶、饮茶，相沿成习，几乎庙庙种茶，无僧不茶，僧侣们在茶园中行禅参道，进行修行。道信大师称僧人劳动为“出坡”，这一专有名词传到民间，在博山当地，至今仍然被安上村及附近的农民沿用着。

《晋书》记载：“僧人单道开坐禅，昼夜不卧，日服镇守药数丸，大如梧子，药有松蜜姜桂茯苓之气，时饮茶苏一二升而已。”在坐禅修定时，长时间静坐思考，容易使人困倦失神，僧人们就通过饮茶提神醒脑，辅助修行。南北朝时，梁武帝国师、如来禅的代表人物——宝志公禅师主持制定的《水陆法会仪轨》中，就有“香灯茶果”“茶烹香嫩”的字眼，这说明茶已经不单单是僧人们用于提神醒脑的饮品，而成为虔诚供养诸佛的必备供品。

由此可见，中国茶禅文化氛围浓厚，而禅修茶道文化发达的博山正觉寺，更是茶禅文化的代表性地区。

博山是一座风光秀美、历史悠久、人文荟萃、经济发达、文化底蕴深厚而又充满活力的魅力山城，素有“鲁中山水画廊”和“淄博的后花园”之美誉。除了地理环境清奇俊秀，博山的文化气息也十分浓厚，还是一座文化名城。博山因地扼齐鲁要冲，是齐鲁文化的交汇处，被称为“鲁中重镇”，拥有许多人文景观。

博山正觉寺始建于东晋，宋金年间重修，距今已有一千六百多年历史，曾是佛教禅宗的祖庭，如来禅的代表人物宝志公禅师在此出家、修道，祖师禅的三祖僧璨大师、四祖道信大师皆曾在此驻锡修行。后来，这里遭到严重毁坏，湮没于荒山中。2002年，仁炟法师来到此地，见到此处断壁残垣的景象十分心痛，于是便率领众人重建博山正觉寺。在此之前，博山正觉寺也经历了多次修缮。据志公塔及志公庙重修碑文记载，南北朝梁武帝年间重修一座志公宝塔，内塑金容圣像；元至正十年（1350年），重修寺庙佛殿；明嘉靖三十一年（1552年），合山僧俗弟子受志公祖师感应再次重修佛殿，并在志公宝塔前建了一所志公庙券石殿。

宝志公禅师是南北朝时期梁武帝的国师，被公认为是观世音菩萨的化身，至今博山区仍有“志公坪”“志公塔”等遗迹。据佛教仪轨和当地百姓传说，志公塔是安放宝志公禅师舍利之处，志公坪则是宝志公禅师的修行之地，博山正觉寺是全国为数不多的供奉宝志公禅师的寺院。

“冲茶旨在禅法，功夫为明自性。”禅宗临济宗第四十六代传人，博山正觉寺的住持仁炟法师，传承禅宗参禅悟道的修心方法，以丛林茶礼为基础，参考《禅林备用清规》《百丈清规》，发掘、整理而成“禅修茶道”。为了方便世人修习禅道，仁炟法师编著了12首禅修茶诗和《禅修茶道百句三字经》，诠释禅修茶道的十二道工序、每道工序的心法与修持要领，以及禅茶文化的传承与内涵。禅修茶道从博山正觉寺产生、传播，并发扬光大，寺中修禅的僧侣人人懂茶道，爱茶道。

发展到今天，禅修茶道已经成为集禅修、茶道、诗词、音乐、养生为一体的综合文化表现形式。作为禅修茶道的本源之地，博山正觉寺仍然保留着进行禅修茶道的传统，而且博山当地人在心思纷扰、难以平静的时候也喜欢通过禅修茶道平静心神，获得明心见性的体悟。在体悟禅修茶道时，人们要进行以下十二项工序：

一、燃灯焚香　参禅咏茶

二、煮水候汤　法海潮音

三、洗杯烫盏　荡涤尘垢

四、赏茶投茶　拈花一笑

五、观色闻香　色香密圆

六、冲水洗茶　放下桎梏

七、静心泡茶　涵盖乾坤

八、随缘分茶　分享慈悲

九、香凝茗露　普皆供养

十、小酌慢饮　品味参禅

十一、谢茶相约　善缘绵长

十二、禅茶一味　法性一如

借助茶具、茶叶、香、灯、水等主要工具和材料，在完成茶道仪轨的同时，将禅修的理念融入十二道工序的每一个动作之中，从而达到宁静身心、颐养性情、领悟禅的精神内涵、提升人生境界之目的。美妙深邃的禅理以茶为载体，形成独特的禅茶文化，吸引文人雅士，受到大众的追随和学习。

博山正觉寺中，上至长老、法师，下至每一位普通僧众，都十分重视禅修茶道文化，积极通过各种途径传播修禅茶道的文化，使茶禅文化不断壮大。禅修茶道的文化丰富了人们的精神生活，给生活在现代社会快节奏中的人们一个停下来、静下来的机会。博山正觉寺常年开设茶道讲习班，希望通过讲习班能让越来越多的人了解禅修茶道，喜爱禅修茶道，通过禅修茶道静心，修一颗淡泊宁静的慈悲之心。这也通过另外一种途径弘扬了佛法，造福了社会。

蓬莱阁庙会

2016年，蓬莱市的“蓬莱阁庙会”被山东省人民政府列入第四批省级非物质文化遗产代表性项目名录。

蓬莱市隶属山东省烟台市，至今已有两千一百多年的历史，是一座充满神话传说、令人心驰神往的历史文化名城。其境内被称为中国古代四大名楼之一的蓬莱阁驰名中外，蓬莱阁庙会便是随着蓬莱阁的建成而逐渐形成的。

蓬莱阁建筑群于宋嘉祐六年（1061年）开始建造，主要由天后宫与周围的龙王宫、三孙殿、弥陀寺、三清殿、吕祖殿、苏公祠、蓬莱阁等几座不同的祠庙殿堂、阁楼、亭坊组成。当地的神仙文化兴起于战国，至明清时期，郡志上记载的地方性神仙人物已多达数十位。这些都给蓬莱阁抹上了一层神秘的色彩，因而蓬莱自古就有“仙境”之称，而蓬莱阁庙会最初也是由对海神娘娘的崇拜而兴起的。海神娘娘，也称天后，即南方所说的“妈祖”。她生前好行善济世，常在海上救助遇险船民。她逝世以后，人们为她立祠祭祀，以示感念，并祈求她的佑护，妈祖信仰由此始兴，以福建莆田、台湾为最盛。明清以来，随着南北海上航运的开展，对妈祖的信仰逐步传到北方，妈祖也成为沿海渔民普遍崇信的海神之一。我国沿海地区建有大量妈祖庙，北方最具代表性的妈祖庙——天后宫，便位于蓬莱城北丹崖山巅蓬莱阁建筑群内。

蓬莱的老百姓，尤其是沿海的渔民，对海神娘娘有着无限敬仰。人们至今还传颂海神娘娘搏击风浪、勇救遇难船只的事迹，和她为民治病消灾、救弱扶危的美德。相传海神娘娘绕境巡乡，可驱逐恶魔，消除流行病和病虫害。正月十六是海神娘娘的生日，每年这一天，蓬莱都有请海神娘娘巡游的习俗，当地俗称“走百病”。其实，这只是借了地方上“耍十五、闹十六”的习惯，把元宵节延长一天，再造一个节日高潮，“生日”之说不过是附会的“借口”。蓬莱百姓从宋朝开始便把这一天当作节日庆祝，所以蓬莱人有“正月十六赶庙会”一说。

蓬莱阁庙会的早期形式仅是一种隆重的祈福活动，后来随着社会经济的发展，各地农村纷纷组织戏班、秧歌队到天后宫对面的戏楼献演俚俗戏剧、大秧歌，大量当地和蓬莱周边地区的人会来蓬莱阁赶庙会，给天后娘娘祝寿，祈求渔民平安，节日气氛十分浓郁。这一习俗从九百多年前一直延续至今，逐渐演变成“蓬莱阁庙会”。现在的蓬莱阁庙会已成为一项蓬莱人民不可或缺的满足生活需要和精神需求的民俗活动。

每年正月十六一大早，蓬莱阁内就早已游人如织，热闹非凡，处处都洋溢着浓浓的节日气氛。蓬莱阁全景广场上会举行隆重的祭拜祈福仪式，祈福仪式完全按照当地传统的风俗习惯进行。由于蓬莱阁庙会的盛名远播周边各县市，参加庙会仪式演出的胶东地区的各种戏班、秧歌队、文艺表演团体都早早来到广场提前做好准备。广场内锣鼓喧天，鞭炮长鸣，吸引游人驻足观看。蓬莱大杆号排在队伍之首，作为“开路先锋”拉开整个仪式的序幕。豪迈的大杆号乐曲表达了人们对新的一年的美好祝福和祈盼。紧接着，龙、狮、旱船、毛驴、腰鼓队、自由滑稽秧歌等民间艺术隆重登场。灵动的狮子时而争抢，时而嬉戏；飞腾的巨龙闪转腾挪，上下飞舞；形态各异的旱船、毛驴，夸张的服饰，惟妙惟肖的表演，可谓千姿百态、各具特色；蓬莱水城戚家军“鸳鸯阵、戚家拳”现场演练，赢得观众的热烈掌声。另有唱大戏的、玩猴盘蛇的、耍杂技的、吞刀吐火玩魔术的、拉洋片的等，五花八门，应有尽有。表演队伍中，有年逾古稀的老年秧歌爱好者，也有天真活泼的少年儿童，各类民间文艺表演夹杂其中，非常热闹。庙会成为活跃群众文化生活的场所，也使百姓领略到了原汁原味的地方民俗文化的魅力。

与此同时，天后宫、龙王宫等祠庙也按照传统礼仪进行祭拜、祈福。庙堂里钟鼓齐鸣，香烟缭绕。广大渔民到天后宫朝拜海神娘娘，祈求出海平安，满载而归；农民进龙王宫朝拜龙王爷，祈求今年风调雨顺，五谷丰登；信奉佛教的人们可去弥陀寺朝拜释迦牟尼，信奉道教的人们可以去蓬莱阁、三清殿，请求保佑全家幸福平安。因为庙会吸引了数以万计有着不同信仰的人们前来拜神许愿，所以在庙会期间，蓬莱阁上香火不绝，人流潮涌，各个殿内烟雾缭绕，灯烛通明。蓬莱阁戏楼前，人潮涌动，这里的吕剧演出、民乐演奏、歌舞表演等吸引人们驻足欣赏。

庙会当天，八乡百姓、外埠商贾，云集一处，熙熙攘攘，货棚摊点随地而设，百货奇物应有尽有；吆喝声此起彼落，买卖者各具姿态，生意十分红火。因为庙会的需要，人们结庐成市，形成了阁下古市一条街，后来慢慢形成了今日的小商品市场。蓬莱的著名地方风味和特色小吃齐聚此处，如蓬莱小面、芝麻糖、面鱼、卤驴肉、鲅鱼水饺等传统名吃当场表演，现做现卖，深受观众喜爱；各种特色工艺美术品，如丫腰烙画葫芦、彩绘球石、根雕等；儿童玩具，如风车、贝壳制品等，比比皆是。

如今除了传统节目，蓬莱阁庙会还增添了各种摄影展、春联作品展等现代展览。许多节目还与当地的民间传说相结合，为庙会增加了迷人的色彩和韵味。蓬莱阁庙会作为一种民俗文化，已深深地扎根在人们心中，在保持祈福活动的同时，逐渐融入了集市交易活动和娱乐性活动，现已成为科技交流、商品贸易和休闲娱乐的民俗文化盛会，被人们誉为“雅俗相济、商娱相融”。

蓬莱阁庙会的形成有着深刻的社会原因和历史原因，与当地人的信仰活动密切相关，它是伴随着民间信仰活动而发展起来的。蓬莱阁庙会集各种文化于一体，能够满足有不同信仰的群体，是一种具有浓厚地方特色的民俗活动，不仅丰富了当地群众的文化生活，而且对保护民间文化有重要作用。

毓璜顶庙会

2016年，烟台市的“毓璜顶庙会”被山东省人民政府列入第四批省级非物质文化遗产代表性项目名录。

庙会亦称“庙市”，是汉族民间宗教和岁时风俗，也是我国集市贸易形式之一。庙会的形成与发展和宗教活动有关，一般在寺庙的节日或规定的日期举行，多设在庙内及其附近。烟台市芝罘区中心地带的毓璜顶公园，至今仍定期举办一个具有六百多年历史的庙会——毓璜顶庙会。经过多年的发展变迁，毓璜顶庙会如今已变成一种群众广泛参与的文化经济形态的活动，百年延绵，盛极不衰。

起初，这里不叫毓璜顶。元代时，因此处的山顶建有玉皇庙，得名为“玉皇顶”。1890年，烟台雅士刘次垣游览玉皇顶时感叹：“异哉！玉皇顶之命名也，其毋乃亵尊严乎？况此山脉出塔顶，其势蜿蜒，气若争赴，遥而望之，如渴骥之奔泉，至此而一束。而其东，则群峰嵯峨，绵亘三五里。其西，则林峦层叠，峥嵘而突兀。左环右抱，犁然在目。独西山之郁然中处，直超尘而绝俗，此固我村之巨镇，实为菁华之气所钟毓。今即以玉皇之名更其文曰毓璜可乎？”至此，“玉皇顶”改为“毓璜顶”，并沿用至今。

据现存明清两朝的碑文记载，玉皇庙始建于元朝末年。相传，元末一位道人偶经此山，发现山顶上洞窟射出的金光直插蓝天。为探明原因，潜入洞窟，见一金蟾嘴巴张合，射出道道金光，道人大呼“真乃神山也”。于是他化缘集资，在山上修建三间庙堂，供奉道教中地位最高、职权最大的玉皇大帝，玉皇庙由此而始。明朝重修扩建，形成四合院式庙宇建筑。以后数百年间经不同时代多次重修增建。明万历二十三年（1595年），官绅刘惟业立会攒资对玉皇庙进行兴建，并在原三间庙堂的旧址上新建玉皇殿，增钟鼓二楼、东西厢房。玉皇庙在清咸丰、同治、光绪年间均有增修扩建，清光绪十九年（1893年）增修扩建的规模较大，遂形成由戏楼、山门、钟鼓二楼、玉皇殿、后殿、东西两厢、后花园、吕祖庙、向若亭、石牌坊等组成的建筑群。

早期的毓璜顶庙会起源于隆重的祈福活动。据《大明新建玉皇上帝庙辉煌记》记载：“每遇灾旱患，登顶（即今毓璜顶）祈祷无不灵应，故雨顺风调、民安物阜缘足。”自此毓璜顶之玉皇庙便成为胶东百姓进行神事活动的重要场所。正月初九是玉皇大帝神诞之日，自元代以来每逢正月初九，烟台百姓便自发来到玉皇庙进行祈福、朝拜等活动，逐渐形成了毓璜顶庙会。

毓璜顶庙会的“值年”活动传承至今。明清时期，芝罘有东门村、西门村、南门村、北门村等13个村，他们在福山县管辖下成立了自治会（亦称奇山社），13个村各举一名会首，轮流“执政”。每村一年，就叫“值年”。当年的交接工作就是在毓璜顶庙会期间进行的，地点就在玉皇庙内的后客厅（今王母殿）。会议期间除了议定13个村的大事，还要进行值年交接，即上一任会首把“权力”（账目）交给新任会首。

玉皇庙是烟台早期宗教文化的中心，堪称烟台地域宗教文化的活化石，蕴含着烟台特有的民俗文化价值。庙内供奉的玉皇大帝，是道教中的众神之王，在道教中拥有最大神权。正月初九是玉皇大帝的神诞之日，每到这一天，玉皇庙内的住持都会做道场，举行宗教仪式，祈求新的一年风调雨顺，周围百姓也会来此朝拜玉皇大帝，祈福求安，还愿谢神。现如今，每年庙会期间都会举办“祈福迎祥，戴福还家”大型民俗活动。

毓璜顶庙会中的娱乐活动也极为丰富。在玉皇庙前广场建有一座戏楼，是在原址基础上按原貌进行的复建，原有戏楼建于咸丰十一年（1861年），由社会工商界及百姓集资兴建，作为每年庙会演戏之用，是庙会的娱乐中心。庙会这天，戏台上的演出多为地方酬戏和义演，不需购票，备受百姓欢迎。现在的庙会仍然保留了在戏楼上唱大戏的习俗，每届庙会都有传统戏曲演出。正如著名侨胞曲拯民先生在《九四思忆童年》一文中写道：“玉皇庙既为十三村所支持，因此每届正月初九玉皇的生日戏台必有京戏演出，至少到十五日的元宵节为止。此时庙门大敞，供善男信女们进香。每年初九日各村的代表所组成的锣鼓队、秧歌队等在旗罗伞扇下，一路燃放鞭炮声中前来膜拜。此际山下热闹非凡，摊贩、说书、武术、魔术等杂耍统统出现。玉皇诞辰的节日最是地方的盛事。”

商品买卖也是毓璜顶庙会具有的重要功能。每逢毓璜顶庙会，当地及周边地区的商贩便聚集于此，买卖商品。赶庙会的百姓在朝拜许愿之后，既可观看演出，又可选购各种生活、劳作所需用品。据老人回忆，庙会时毓璜顶周边窄巷通道挤满了小商小贩，有卖糖的、卖玻璃球的、卖针头线脑的，物细而摊密；烙饼菜汤朝天锅、福山大面三鲜汤，地方小吃展览成市。其中有一种独特的习俗，每年庙会上都会有几个卖蜡木杆子的地摊，几乎每个赶庙会的人都要买上一根蜡木杆子。原本是为了登山作手杖，后来不知从何时起，扶杖登高可以保平安的说法兴起。

近几年，庙会以“弘扬传统民俗文化，打造精神文明品牌”为主题，邀请了海阳大秧歌、吴桥杂技、抬阁、胶东大鼓、八卦鼓舞、穿花舞、螳螂拳、太极拳、大杆号、皮影戏等进行展演。吕剧、京剧、杂技、锣鼓、杂耍、武术、秧歌等传统节目也是丰富多彩；一些新型的节目表演形式也融入庙会中，如魔术、街舞，吸引了更多的年轻人参与。此外，庙会期间还举办了CCTV-2《鉴宝》栏目专家组走进烟台毓璜顶大型民间寻宝赛宝活动、传统文化公益讲座、书画展览、摄影大赛、相亲会、猜谜、对对联等群众互动参与性较高的主题活动，为广大居民和游客奉上了一套精致、丰富的文化大餐。

如今的毓璜顶庙会已经成为当地的一大民俗盛事。来参加庙会的游客、商贩、演出团体，遍布山东半岛乃至全国各地，接待游客数量每年都创新高。更可贵的是，现在的毓璜顶庙会挖掘、整理了一大批几近湮没的民俗文化。毓璜顶庙会在传承胶东文化方面做出了巨大贡献，是弘扬传统民俗文化的一个重要载体。

寿光蔬菜生产习俗

2016年，寿光市的“寿光蔬菜生产习俗”被山东省人民政府列入第四批省级非物质文化遗产代表性项目名录。

寿光市隶属山东省潍坊市，位于山东省中北部。20世纪90年代，寿光市被国务院命名为“中国蔬菜之乡”，蔬菜种植影响全国。自2000年起，寿光市已经成功举办了十四届“寿光国际蔬菜科技博览会”。

寿光蔬菜生产历史悠久，夏、商、春秋时期便有记载。到北魏时期，寿光人贾思勰所著《齐民要术》有27篇记述农作物栽培技术，16篇专记述蔬菜培植、加工技艺。清康熙三十七年（1698年）《寿光县志》、民国时期《寿光县志》、1990版《寿光县志》等老书也记载了寿光蔬菜生产传承发展的情况。

寿光的蔬菜生产习俗包含整地、育种、种植、管理、收获、储藏、食用等，这一习俗是民众遵循自然规律，按二十四节气进行的。例如，春季有“二月二，灰打囤，黄瓜下地，祭灶神”，打囤、祭灶神，即从二月二开始与蔬菜生产有关的农事活动，祈求一年丰收；夏季有“五月中，种大葱”，“头伏萝卜二伏芥，三伏里头种白菜”；秋季有“秋分芹菜，白露种蒜”；冬季有“立冬出葱，小雪挤白菜”等。

寿光蔬菜品种繁多，其中比较具有代表性的是九巷韭黄、桂河芹菜、寿光鸡腿葱、浮桥青萝卜。其生产习俗各有特色，具体如下：

1. 九巷韭黄。分春播（3月下旬至4月中旬）和秋播（8月下旬至9月中旬）两种，种植上分为挑选优良种子与地块、整地作畦、韭黄栽培、田间管理、收获5个阶段。播种前需深翻约30厘米土层，暴晒7天左右；再整平作畦，播种浸泡处理过的种子，然后在上面盖一层薄细沙，接着用充分腐熟的有机肥料浇盖好。之后，适时追肥、浇水、除草。秋季前期水肥齐促，中期控制水肥，后期停水控长。韭菜长至5厘米时进行第一次培土，隔10天左右，割去上部青韭，再进行第二次培土；待韭苗长至10～16厘米时，覆盖草帘，并保持草帘内的湿度；当韭黄长至50厘米左右时，用专门镰刀收割出售。清康熙三十七年《寿光县志》有“春初早韭，若寿光九巷之韭，匪言春也。寒腊冰雪，便已登盘，甘脆鲜碧，远压粱肉”的记载。

民间谚语有“要想韭菜盛，要有灰来壅（施肥）”，“三月韭上街卖”，“韭菜黄瓜两头香”。《齐民要术·种葵》中也有“日中不剪韭”的记载。

2. 桂河芹菜。种植上，先整地作1米左右宽的育苗畦，床土由6份田土和4份腐熟好的有机肥配制而成。将浸泡好的种子播种后，搭盖草帘或遮阳网，以减少水分蒸发。幼苗长至1～2片真叶时，进行间苗和定苗，当株高10～20厘米、苗龄50～60天后，进行定植。定植畦亩施腐熟有机肥5 000～10 000千克，耕翻整平后作120厘米宽的畦，浇水后的第二天，用尖铲挖穴定植，并立即浇水。之后做好温度管理，适时追肥、浇水。追肥以炒豆粉、有机肥料为主。收获视市场需求和植株长势决定。收藏于窖池，窖池下挖70厘米，筑30厘米围墙，上面用竹条撑起并盖上草帘子，根据气温条件选择加减覆盖物或通风。经过60天左右的冬贮，桂河芹菜鲜黄酥脆，凉拌、热炒也是清香甜脆。

因管理精细，民间有“懒鬼莫作芹菜，作芹菜要勤快”的说法。

3. 寿光鸡腿葱。形似倒置的鸡腿，分春播和秋播两种。种植时先施用圈肥，然后耕地整平畦面，顺畦开浅沟，播种后覆盖细土。苗期要适时松土、清除杂草、追肥、浇水。秋播苗返青后或春播苗长出真叶时进行间苗，到6月中旬至7月初定植。定植时先南北向开定植沟，沟宜窄（25厘米左右），背宜宽，沟底施腐熟圈肥，并刨翻，使肥料掺入土中。定植一般用“水插法”，即定植沟内浇透水，待水浇完后趁湿插栽葱苗，这样假茎上下垂直不弯曲，产品美观。葱苗定植后要适时追肥（第一次追肥在开始旺盛生长时，以后每隔20～25天追肥1次）、培土（2次，时间在8月中下旬）、浇水（每次追肥培土后宜浇水2～3次），经保苗缓苗越夏、秋季旺长、假茎充实后适时收获。一般春季定植的，秋季可适时收获；冬贮大葱可于11月中下旬收获。

大葱收获后以冻藏效果最好。使整理好的葱捆处于-5～0℃的低温状态，以减慢其呼吸消耗和水分损失。大批量贮藏主要利用冬季自然低温，即在建筑物背阴场地排放葱捆（根朝下竖立），便于通风管理。冻结前葱捆敞露；冻结后，四周培土掩埋假茎，上部盖草苫防雨、防温度变化，使葱捆稳定在轻度冻结状态，最好带冻运输和上市。

生产习俗谚语有“七月中，种大葱”“七月种葱绿葱葱，八月种葱一场空”“深栽葱，浅种蒜”“冻不死的葱，旱不死的蒜”“淹不死的白菜，旱不死的葱”等。

4. 浮桥青萝卜。先选优质种植地，用腐熟圈肥作基肥，深耕、耙细、作平畦。8月中旬，开沟、选种播种、覆土、镇压。若天气干旱，可多次少量浇水，保持畦面湿润。苗出齐后进行第一次间苗，长至3～4片真叶时进行第二次间苗。定苗后追肥，浇水2～3次，以发挥肥效，促使叶子生长。之后，适时浅锄、追肥、浇水、中耕松土、除草保墒。在肉质根膨大前期，即叶子旺盛生长期，既要促进叶子旺盛生长，又要防止叶子徒长。秋分前2～3天，即肉质根膨大前期末和膨大盛期初，要进行一次大追肥。施肥后立即中耕松土，使土、肥混合，然后浇水。此后，植株进入肉质根膨大盛期，需注意均匀供水，避免土壤忽干忽湿，防止裂根。肉质根的尾部充分膨大呈圆形，说明肉质根已经长足，为收获期的标志。一般10月中下旬萝卜经几次霜后，品质变佳，故立冬前后为冬贮萝卜的适收期。收获后将萝卜根顶切去，置入深30厘米，宽100厘米的浅沟窖里，上面覆一层湿土，进行预冷、预贮。7 ~ 8天后再转入沟窖中贮藏。入窖宜在午后天气冷凉时，可摆一层萝卜，撒一层薄薄的、湿润的细土。一般可以摆4 ~ 5层，使窖内的萝卜高度达到60 ~ 80厘米。最上一层萝卜的上面，覆8 ~ 10厘米湿润的细土。以后，随着天气变冷，再分次覆土。

生产习俗谚语有“头伏萝卜二伏芥，三伏里头种白菜”“立冬（收）萝卜小雪（收）菜（白）”“萝卜不怕痒，越锄越肯长”“冬吃萝卜夏吃姜，不用医生开药方”“烟台苹果，莱阳梨，不如潍坊的萝卜皮”等。

寿光的蔬菜生产习俗与民众日常生活紧密相连。如当地置办喜宴，必须是“一鸡二鱼三凉菜，四喜丸子跟上来”。新年招待新女婿则“韭菜炒鸡蛋，外甥当年见”。儿女婚事，喜房内放两个脸盆，其中一个放麦子并插上葱，意“新房盆中插上葱，生个儿子当朝廷”。

寿光蔬菜生产习俗，蕴含着民众的生产智慧，由此衍生出来的蔬菜文化也丰富多彩。寿光蔬菜生产习俗，是当地民众在悠久的蔬菜生产实践中总结出来的，具有鲜明的地域特征，是中华民俗的重要组成部分。

青州宣卷

2016年，青州市的“青州宣卷”被山东省人民政府列入第四批省级非物质文化遗产代表性项目名录。

青州市历史悠久，文化昌盛，是中国古九州之一、中国丝绸之路的源头，以及东夷文化的发祥中心。悠久的历史和灿烂的文化孕育出众多非物质文化遗产，青州宣卷就是其中有名的代表。

佛教在两汉之际传入青州后，很快便在这块土地上生根、发芽、开花。据清光绪《益都县图志》载，青州最早的寺院宁福寺始建于西晋太安元年（302年），其故址在今青州市郑母镇倪家庄附近，地名塔儿坡。十六国时期，先后统治青州的后赵、前燕、前秦、南燕等国的君主崇信佛教，使佛教在青州境内得到了迅速发展。469年，青齐（指山东）入魏之后，宗教文化和艺术在这里得到了长足发展。在七级寺、龙兴寺、广福寺、兴国寺等寺院遗址上，有大量精美的佛教造像出土并流传下来。现在青州的龙兴寺是我国目前现存的唯一一座唐朝以前的大型寺院遗址。

据有关史料推断，青州宣卷是源自唐代的寺庙俗讲演唱活动。据史书记载，东晋义熙八年（412年），著名高僧法显西行天竺求法，整理大量经卷，从狮子国（今斯里兰卡）经海路返回祖国，在青州广郡牢山上岸，曾在青州龙兴寺整理佛经并进行俗讲，居住约一年。日本的圆仁和尚在唐开成五年（840年），在其所作的《入唐求法巡礼行记》中，记载唐代寺院中盛行一种俗讲。圆仁和尚也曾在青州龙兴寺暂居过。作为俗讲法师，他为青州俗讲演唱活动留下了珍贵丰富的资料。

山东民间宗教多出于佛教净土宗，南宋时称白莲宗，后称白莲教，历史上对山东及其相邻诸省影响最为广泛。白莲教派有其独特经卷，而各民间秘密宗教活动也有自己的独特经卷，它们旨在宣讲教义，这些经卷有宣卷、念卷、念佛、善书等名称。在宋代，寺院庙会中的“谈经”等说唱文艺，大部分都转移到了勾栏瓦舍，僧人们的“诵经”及“讲说因缘”与民间说唱相结合，脱离了宗教消灾祈福的内容，成为民众喜闻乐见的依托佛教讲故事的曲艺形式。

元明以来，宣卷这种曲艺形式在鲁中、鲁西南等地相当活跃。青州宣卷流行于明代。明永乐年间，青州一带农民起义军领袖唐赛儿，自称“佛母”，以白莲教之宣卷念佛形式组织起义。明中叶以后，民间宗教发展迅速，宝卷流传亦愈加普遍。明天启年间，巨野人徐洪儒发动农民起义，也是利用白莲教支派闻香教之经书宝卷发动的。显然，青州是民间教派活动频繁地区之一，各教派宣卷广泛流布于全省各地。民间秘密宗教的发展带动了青州宝卷的兴盛。康熙朝以后，清政府大规模镇压各地民间教团，查毁他们使用的经卷。据清政府档案记录，在山东地区查获的宝卷案例最多，其中就有青州宝卷。但是直到清末，宝卷在青州仍然十分盛行。

民国期间，在青州流行的各种宣卷活动，都叫“善书”。20世纪80年代前后至今，青州一带民间时常有信徒聚会演唱，主要分布于青州城区、黄楼镇、邵庄镇、庙子镇、王坟镇等。青州云门山庙会时间是农历三月三、九月九，庙会期间，信徒们聚集在山中，焚纸烧香参拜诸神后，分散于庙前庙后或各个山坡林间，席地围坐，演唱经卷，谓之“念佛”，人数动辄数千。朝山演唱者多为中老年妇女，年轻人亦有肩挑花篮边舞边歌者。各山坡间念佛唱曲声此起彼伏，日暮始歇。

青州宣卷表演形式多样，有坐堂唱的、群唱的、山会中担花篮（其实是担经）走唱的等，所用曲调多是民间小曲。

青州宣卷有的只唱不说，通篇一个句式。例如《佛家真言》唱词：

东天九门/中有始皇/出入三清/役运勾芒/上绕青霞/九千万重/左侍青腰/右卫神童/招执简籍/列表上宫/今日弟子/请陈所言/愿神愿仙/青绿簿中/上回灵驾/化形婴蒙/安治肝府/招致华光/坐致自然/神明交通/天地无穷/遨宴华房/安镇灵狱/参驾羽辇/十二飞龙/清扎玉文/核定仙名/身佩赤书/名参地堂/来将我房/二炁混合/灵辉流灌/面生金容/身得长生

全篇只有唱词没有说词。

有的宣卷是字句变格混用。例如《寿衣佛》：

西方路上一弦机，七十二个铜消息。九天仙女来织机，织成绸缎做寿衣。裁衣姐姐委实巧，也会裁来也会铰，也不肥来也不瘦，也不大来也不小。扣花姐姐委实巧，熨斗熨得光堂堂。钢针绒线拿在手，各样的花草都扣上；前身上俺扣上西江明月，后身上俺扣上海马朝阳。袖子上俺扣上银河两岸，肩膀上俺扣上织女牛郎。大襟上俺扣上鸳鸯戏水，底襟上俺扣上牡丹凤凰。袄缉上俺扣上金刚八卦，袄角上俺扣上托塔天王。袄领上俺扣上双龙入海，袄带上俺扣上花落天堂。这仙衣扣完毕献于老母，驾祥云上西天朝见玉皇。行善事脱轮回成佛作祖，封增给绣花女福寿绵长。

这叫作“佛”的宝卷，从语言上看古今杂陈，七字句、十字句变格混用。

有的是说唱结合。例如《北斗咒》唱词：

高上玉皇/紫微帝君/大周天界/细入微尘/何灾不灭/何福不臻/元皇正气/来合我省/天罡所指/昼夜常轮/俗君小人/好道求灵/愿见尊仪/求保长生/三台虚精/六淳曲生/生我养我/护我身形

唱后说词（单字吐说）：魁（kuí）、勺（旧读shuò）、圈（quān）、行（xíng）、魓（bì）、铺（pū）、魒（piāo）。

宣卷地点非常灵活，寺庙、家中、山中林间等地都可以。宣卷前，宣卷人还需要一定的仪式。先洗手、拈香、面对供着或墙上挂着的佛像磕头。然后，主宣人可以手敲木鱼，或敲打磬，或击法鼓，敲法钟。旁边还有多人附唱。也可以不用乐器直接说唱。主宣人需熟记宝卷内容，要有一定的口才，必须咬字准确。宝卷可以摊在桌上，也可以拿在手中，起到提醒作用。

青州宣卷真实记录了山东青州的风情和社会变迁，它是我们研究山东社会民俗史颇为珍贵的“信息库”。各种宝卷经文的演唱，逐渐吸收了不少民间技艺成分，具有民俗与民间艺术价值。青州宣卷劝人行善积德、孝敬长辈，对于净化社会风气、维护社会稳定有积极作用。

孙膑崇拜

2016年，昌邑市的“孙膑崇拜”被山东省人民政府列入第四批省级非物质文化遗产代表性项目名录。

昌邑市隶属山东省潍坊市，位于山东半岛西北部。孙膑（约前380—前320），原名宾，齐国人，战国中期兵家学派的代表人物，杰出的军事家，他是著名军事家孙武的后世子孙。孙膑从小便对行军打仗十分感兴趣，喜欢研究兵法，他继承发展了孙武、吴起等人的军事思想，形成了自己的一套军事理论。

孙膑青年时期与庞涓一起学习兵法，庞涓后来到了魏国，但心中一直暗暗嫉妒孙膑的才能，生怕孙膑超过自己，于是暗中派人把孙膑请到魏国，谋划着陷害孙膑。孙膑到了魏国之后，庞涓就捏造罪名诬陷他，致使孙膑受了膑刑和黥刑，想通过这样的方法将孙膑毁掉。但孙膑杰出的才能还是让一位齐国的使者发现了，齐国使者偷偷用车将孙膑载回齐国。孙膑到齐国以后，用计策帮齐国大将田忌赢得了赛马比赛，田忌认为此人是个难得的人才，便将他推荐给齐王，孙膑由此得到齐王的重用。在后来的桂陵之战中，孙膑表现出色，马陵之战中又采用“围魏救赵”的计策重创魏国，使其失去霸主的地位。孙膑因马陵之战一战成名，齐威王将都昌（今潍坊昌邑）赐予他，作为他的封地。乾隆七年（1742年）《昌邑县志》卷五《勋土》也有同样的记载。

由于宋元以来《乐毅图齐平话》《列国志传》《孙庞演义七国志全传》等关于孙膑的小说的流行，都昌民间对孙膑的信仰也逐渐兴起。

都昌在秦朝时设县，迄今已有两千多年的历史。昌邑市都昌街道东永安村是都昌街道重点历史文化村落，历史悠久，孙膑曾在东永安村西土埠上居住过。这里于明朝万历年间始建孙膑庙，纪念封地在此的军事家孙膑。

据孙膑庙前的碑文记载：清咸丰年间，有一群凶狠的流寇来到这里，烧、杀、抢、掠无恶不作，此地的百姓深受其害，村民们对这群流寇深恶痛绝。经过全村人的商议，决定主动出击，赶走流寇，以保护家园。于是，全村人聚集到当时有围墙的孙膑庙中，以此为据点，奋起反抗。这群流寇见孙膑庙久攻不下，就改用火攻，他们用烟熏的方法逼迫庙中村民投降。就在村民们几乎要放弃抗争时，天突然刮起了大风，把火和烟吹向相反的方向，将流寇赶跑了，村民和孙膑庙得以保存下来。村民们一致认为是孙膑保佑了他们，从此以后，村民对孙膑的崇拜更加虔诚了。

满怀着对孙膑的崇拜，人们开展了一系列以孙膑为中心的民俗活动。正月十四是孙膑的诞辰，东永安村自明朝万历年间始建孙膑庙起，就将每年正月十四定为孙膑庙会，以此来纪念这位卓越的军事英雄。相传，孙膑每次取胜时，总是坐在由一头凶猛高大、威力无比的独角大牛拉的战车上，于是每年孙膑庙会这一天，都要举行“烧大牛”民间祭奠活动，至今已有四百多年历史。每年的孙膑庙会都有很多人，还有来自各地的民间文艺团队，给当地旅游增加了浓浓的文化氛围。

“烧大牛”活动是孙膑崇拜系列活动中最具有特色的一项活动，一般来说，这项民俗活动从开始到结束有五项工作需要完成：

首先，是“扎大牛”。每年正月初六，东永安村的人们便怀着无比虔诚的心情开始准备，他们用当地产的珠子、棉槐条、葵花秆、高粱秸等质地软硬适中的植物秸秆开始扎制老牛的框架。到正月十二，老牛框架扎好后，妇女们用黄色彩纸剪制牛毛，并用各色彩纸剪制成牛鞍、大刀、铃铛等装饰品，粘到老牛身上，整个扎制过程需要140多道工序，扎制好的老牛高5米，长10米，独角长1.8米，威武壮观，神气十足。

其次，便是“游大牛”的活动。正月十四早上8时，村民们就在孙膑庙前燃放鞭炮，大牛就在鞭炮声中“起驾”，由人群簇拥着开始游行。整个“游大牛”的队伍浩浩荡荡，前面由鞭炮队开道，后面是锣鼓队、秧歌队、高跷队，再往后是由20多位青壮年组成的抬大牛队伍，最后面的是乡民。游行的线路是：沿着村委东邻的南北街道至十字路口，再拐至西侧，最后停放在孙膑庙西的空场上。一路上锣鼓喧天，鞭炮齐鸣，热闹非凡。

大牛游行完毕，开始第三阶段的活动——“祭大牛”。这项活动一般在上午10时左右开始，人们在空场上摆好供品，给孙膑烧纸、烧香，并磕头祈愿。与此同时，村民自发组织的扭秧歌、舞龙、打腰鼓、唱吕剧等活动，也开始上演。演出现场，肃穆的孙膑庙、威武的大牛和庙前空地上热闹非凡的文艺表演相映成趣。

各项祭拜活动结束后，便开始“摸大牛”。在场的人蜂拥而上，争相“摸大牛”，乞求神牛将疾病带走。村民们祖祖辈辈流传着这样的俗语：“摸摸老牛头，吃穿不用愁；摸摸老牛腚，到老没有病。”“摸摸牛角不生痘，摸摸牛鞍不生癍。”村民们相信，在正月十四这天“摸大牛”，能够祛除百病，给家里带来一整年的好运。

最后一项活动是“烧大牛”。“烧大牛”又称“发牛”，一般在中午11时至12时之间举行。早在“发牛”之前，一些虔诚的村民就已经跪在圣物前方，虔诚地唱着神歌，兴奋与期待之情溢于言表。时间一到，村民便将大牛抬至早已准备好的香纸堆上，口念“孙老爷”名号，嘱咐老牛莫要“惊驾”，直到村中的组织者高喊一声“发”，牛身迅即被点燃，霎时火光冲天，烟雾缭绕，精心扎制的大牛最终燃烧为青烟，袅袅升天。村民认为，只有“大牛”焚烧升天，才能将人们的虔诚之心和所要表达的愿望传达给孙膑。

孙膑崇拜还包含传说故事、扎制技艺、艺术表演等内容。因孙膑崇拜而兴起的一系列民俗活动，拉近了周边村落的关系，丰富了当地人的精神生活，形成当地特有的一种文化。应将这一民俗活动传承下去，并不断进行创新和发展。

峄山会

2016年，邹城市的“峄山会”被山东省人民政府列入第四批省级非物质文化遗产代表性项目名录。

邹城市位于山东省南部，早在新石器时代，这里便有先民繁衍生息；春秋战国时期，它成为邹国的国都，同鲁国并称为“邹鲁圣地”，是当时的文化繁盛之地。邹城是孟子的故乡，素有“文化发祥之地，孔孟桑梓之乡”的美誉。在这样一座历史文化名城，自然少不了民俗文化盛事，峄山脚下的峄山会，正是极负盛名的一项。

峄山位于邹城市东南方向约12公里处，海拔550米，被誉为“邹鲁秀灵，岱南奇观”。古往今来，峄山经过多次开发，形成了四大奇观——二十四景、三十六洞天、二百二十八庙宇、数百楹宫殿庵观。如此胜景，自然吸引了远近游人、香客前来观光。

峄山会便设在峄山的脚下，在每年农历二月二举行，一般延续3~5天，长时达7天。山会的管理机构叫“行会”，经纪人成交或设摊叫“报行”。到会的商品按类别划片分辖区场地，设牛马市、家具农具市、黑棚（包子棚）、白棚（卖布匹的）等。峄山会以山前为中心，东起马家沟，西至刘家沟，方圆五六里。它是当地民间影响较大、最具规模的古会。届时，近至周围诸县，远至附近各省都有来赶会的人，有求神拜佛的，有许愿还愿的，有买物卖物的，还有说书唱戏、玩杂耍的。一般赶会的人会先上山进香，然后再下山听戏，最后买一些必需品。商品交易在第二天或者第三天进入高峰，参会的人数不胜数。

峄山会的起源与当地最早开始的祭祀活动有关。具体起源没有明确记载，但有两种传说。一是后汉刘荟在其编纂的《邹山记》中记载，二月二为龙抬头之日，人们祈祷风调雨顺，一年好景，齐集于峄山，进香朝拜。二是公元前615年二月二，“知命之君”邾文公在峄山之南立国，因此二月二是庆贺之日，每年的这一天都有活动，后来逐步演变为峄山会。

在以后的发展中，峄山会的功能不再仅限于祭祀祈福，增加了许多新的内容。每年二月二，峄山上会汇聚许多香客，较为特殊的是以村庄为单位组织的“香社”。所谓“香社”，就是由村里的长老或头人组织的文艺团体。一般从本村选拔能歌善舞的青年，按照农村风俗习惯排练“龙灯”“高跷”“花船”等文艺节目。香社按户头（或人口）收缴部分钱粮，供集体开支，家境殷实的人家会多交一些。香社时间一般从农历正月初一到二月二。赶会那天，香社挑着“××香社”“××进香团”等字样的彩旗，敲着锣鼓，奔往峄山，途中经过村庄或人群比较集中的地方还要燃放鞭炮。进山后，要到龙庙前进香朝拜，演唱文艺节目，四周的观众喝彩声越热烈，表演者表演越卖力。

个体香客有求子求孙的，有求祛病免灾的，有求神问卜的。他们会将香放进香炉点燃，虔诚地跪拜祈求。峄山周围的村民，有不少是来此求子的，有的祖孙三代都来“求神得子”。在峄山会当天，他们都要梳洗打扮，带上火纸、香烛，临行前在家中燃一炷香，以求祖先庇佑，沿途默默祈祷，祈求赐子赐福；更有虔诚者上山时每一个台阶都要磕一个头。进庙后有道人做证，焚香磕头，自报姓名、家住何方，并于次年某月某日再行“还愿”礼。接着，请道人取“石子”（拾子）或泥娃娃。许愿者接过“石子”，用事先准备好的红头绳（或红布）系住该“石子”，放入怀里返回家中，途中嘴里还念叨着“孩子回家”，“孩子回家”，到家后把“石子”放在床上。如若事后果真有了子孙，许愿者会带上供品到山上还愿。有的生子后，还会缝制一个“长命锁”，即用七色丝线缝制成元宝形“长命百岁锁”挂在幼儿胸前。按照当地习俗，在山上“拴来”的孩子终生不能登峄山，以免被仙人留住。

如今，峄山会已发展成集香火、骡马等于一体的文化物资交流会。交流会上有各种各样的小吃，还有各种特色文化商品，品种繁多。据明万历四年（1576年）六月白云宫一刻石记载，峄山上下有商号、堂号、店铺达38家。据史料记载，明末清初，此处的山西会馆一度垄断了峄山的市场，经营上百个品种的商品。

峄山会上的特色小吃颇具文化特色。其中，以八花宝粥与醉枣最知名。八花宝粥始于唐宋，盛于元明清，峄山街上的乔家老粥馆、齐家粥店卖八花宝粥，生意兴隆。所谓“八宝花粥”，指的是以峄山盛产的豇豆、绿豆、红白小豆、糯米、红枣泥、花生糁、黄扁豆、西瓜仁八种土特产为原料，先后适时下锅，取甘露泉水，文火烧煮细熬，八宝力求开花、分瓣、纵笑、绽开。出锅后清香适口，美味异常，老幼皆宜，常称“忘姓粥”，意即此粥美味到喝了后会一时忘记自己的姓名。醉枣之“醉”，源于峄山的一种特色老酒——天福甘露，它是以峄山甘露池中的水酿制的老酒。相传，邾国第十八世国君邾庄公饮之，赞不绝口，命以“天福甘露”。醉枣即为酒枣，取新鲜未落地的长枣，用筷子夹入“天福甘露”酒中浸泡数日，取出后放入瓷罐或陶罐里，封贮于室内阴凉处，备在年关大节食用或峄山会上出售。该枣鲜脆可口，酒香扑鼻，原色不减，有增进食欲之功效。此外，知名的美食还有金凤朝阳（山鸡）、白元大仙（白野兔）、横卧将军（螃蟹）等。

峄山会在当地居民的生产生活中留下了深深烙印，在中华土地上闪耀着独属于邹城峄山的那份光色。

泰山豆腐宴食俗

2016年，泰安市的“泰山豆腐宴食俗”被山东省人民政府列入第四批省级非物质文化遗产代表性项目名录。

泰山豆腐宴历史悠久，它伴随着古帝王在泰山的封禅祭祀活动而产生。帝王为答谢上天的授命之恩登临泰山，为表诚心封禅前必“沐浴更衣，素食洁心”，泰山豆腐这一寻常百姓食品也因此得以进入帝王的御膳中。

泰山豆腐选用优质大豆为原料，采用手工石磨工艺配以泰山泉水加工而成，其色白如玉，嫩而不散，故有“神豆腐”之称，并与泰山的黄芽白菜、泰山泉水并称为“泰山三美”。用其制作的泰山豆腐宴席更是帝王封禅活动中不可缺少的组成部分，并伴随着帝王的封禅祭祀活动而流传至今。

自汉武帝开始，豆腐便是封禅饮食中重要的成分，宋代达到了繁荣时期，明清臻至鼎盛，豆腐宴已成为泰山文化不可分割的一部分。泰山豆腐宴菜品种类丰富，讲究营养与美食、菜品与文化的搭配。十二道主菜、百余道行菜反映出帝王饮食的习性，如“吉祥纳福”便是在继承康熙年间宫廷御菜“布袋鸡”制作工艺的基础上，融入素食文化演变而来；“福气滚滚”来源于传统鲁菜“干炸豆腐丸”，当年乾隆皇帝品尝此菜后，大为赞赏并取名

“龙眼金球”。由此可见，泰山豆腐宴是皇家御膳文化与当地传统饮食的完美融合。泰山豆腐宴在历代传承过程中不断吸取了豆腐菜品制作工艺，并融入了泰山文化、封禅文化、民俗文化，逐渐成为独具当地特色的宴席。乾隆年间修订的《泰安县志》曾记述：“凌晨街街梆子响，晚间户户豆腐香，泰城家里豆腐坊。”由此可见，当时家家户户做豆腐已是一种生活常态。

泰山豆腐宴系山东鲁菜的代表菜系之一，以豆腐为主的泰山豆腐宴大体经历了三个发展阶段：

第一阶段是萌芽融入期。帝王在封禅活动时必须食素食，以表敬天的诚心，故当地的山珍野菜曾一度成为封禅御膳的主要组成部分。豆腐传入泰山是在元封五年（前106年）三月，汉武帝南巡还至泰山，于明堂祭高祖，祭品中除了牛羊豕三牲、玉帛外，还有“黎祁”，也就是豆腐。由于口感爽嫩、营养丰富，豆腐逐渐被引入封禅御膳中。

第二阶段为发展期。豆腐可因加工、烹饪技法的不同而制作出不同口味、不同形状的菜肴。自唐宋时期，豆腐便成为帝王封禅御膳中的主要菜品；宋代为快速发展期，当时泰城的豆腐加工作坊盛极一时，但此时仅仅是豆腐菜肴，并未成为真正的系统宴席。

第三阶段为重要发展阶段，此阶段以明清时期为代表。豆腐的大量加工也促进了对豆腐加工技艺的改革，豆腐菜也渐渐地由原来的“煎炒烹炸”技法，发展成为以豆腐为主料利用烹饪手法融入当地文化的“文化大菜”，出现了以“豆腐素鸡”“豆腐素鱼”等为代表的特色菜肴，为豆腐菜肴转向豆腐宴席奠定了坚实的基础。到清代，豆腐宴已经成熟。民国时期及新中国成立初期，豆腐菜肴的制作方法散落民间，豆腐宴也成了泰山饮食文化在当时文化空间中的重要代表。

泰山豆腐宴受泰山封禅文化的影响，在制作上讲究素菜荤食，以体现帝王食素食以诚心敬天的思想；在工艺手法上，蒸、炸、煎、炒、扒、烩、汤样样俱全；上菜讲究四美碟、四配碟、九主菜两两搭配，能够达到“吃鱼不见鱼，吃鸡不见鸡，只享其味不见其物”的境界。上菜程序为先美碟、后配碟，然后上主菜及各类小吃。在上菜过程中伴有讲解人员，会介绍菜品的历史渊源及文化内涵，以体现当地文化帝王御膳的风格。

泰山豆腐宴的菜品在保留传统工艺的基础上加以改进，形成的主要菜品有：外形为太极形，以黑海苔与白豆腐来体现阴阳，寓意和谐的“太极福寿羹”；外形为童子鸡，内填豆腐、海参、虾仁及豆类等制成的“吉祥纳福”，此菜品展现了康熙皇帝六次南巡、三至泰山、两登岳顶时食素静心的原则；用蜂窝豆腐，下衬牛肉体现泰山的厚重感，并加以玉皇草来滋阴壮阳、健脾益气的“玉皇赐福”；选用鲈鱼、豆腐、胡萝卜、香菇、黄精制成一鱼两吃的“麟鳞豆花鱼”，此菜品依据宋真宗登封泰山时平息民怨、封禅泰山而制作；在“九转大肠”基础上演变而来，展现泰山文化中的宗教文化特色的“九转福肠”；被称为“龙眼金珠”的“福气滚滚来”，用泰山三美（白菜、豆腐、水）煲成的“泰山三美汤”，以及被誉为“神豆腐”的“洞天福地”等400余道菜品。

泰山豆腐宴特色鲜明，是历代帝王登封泰山时御用豆腐菜品之精华，其菜品展现了几千年封禅文化和民俗文化的融合，体现了在传统饮食文化中对福文化的传承与发展。如今，将古代帝王来泰山封禅的豆腐宴搬上大众餐桌，不仅丰富了泰山的美食文化，而且体现了老百姓对传统文化的吸收与传承。人们用“豆腐”寓意“都福”，寄托了人们对于美好生活的追求和幸福人生的期冀。

泰山玉习俗

2016年，泰安市岱岳区的“泰山玉习俗”被山东省人民政府列入第四批省级非物质文化遗产代表性项目名录。

泰山玉吸纳数十亿年的日月精华，结合泰山孕育数千年的历史文化，集国山的尊贵与国石的灵气于一身，被国内专家称为国玉。如今，泰山玉石以其独有的幽深墨绿、细腻的质地受到广大玉石收藏者的青睐。

泰山玉的历史源远流长，最早可以追溯到新石器时代。那时，汶河流域的先民就已经用泰山玉石制作碧玉铲、臂环、佩饰等艺术品了。《尚书·禹贡》篇记载，在夏朝时，“泰山怪石”即是进献给大禹的贡品，《山海经·东山经》里也有“泰山其上多玉，其下多金，环水中多水玉”的记载。曹植的诗对泰山玉有明确记载：“驱车掸怒骂，东到奉高城。神哉彼泰山，五岳专其名……上有涌澧泉，玉石扬华英……”五代时期，道书《福地记》记载：“泰山多芝草、玉石。”直到当代人撰写的《五岳志》还有“泰山方圆四十四，多芝美玉石”的记载。

在秦汉之前，泰山玉十分受民众的欢迎，它们甚至被当作“镇山石”“辟邪石”来出售。秦始皇、汉武帝等帝王到泰山封禅，他们都对峰顶的立石顶礼膜拜，玉器是封禅典礼中的一个重要道具。唐宋以后，泰山玉石开始在民间流行，泰山石作为护身符，此时已经成为人们的精神寄托。人们深信泰山石可赈灾厌殃，保人平安。泰山石敢当风俗的影响至东亚，日本京都民族博物馆便收藏有冲绳出土的泰山石敢当制石。

正所谓“名山出名玉”，泰山玉贵在“泰山”二字，蕴含“平安吉祥”的非凡寓意和祝福，被赋予了保平安、助家兴之意，被尊为镇宅玉、吉祥玉、辟邪玉、敢当玉、平安玉，正所谓“园无石不秀，厅无石不华，居无石不安，人无石不美”。泰山玉在民众中广泛流传，收藏泰山玉成了一种习尚。

天下奇石数不尽，唯有泰山石敢当。在泰山脚下，家家户户的民宅墙上都镶嵌着一尊“保护神”——泰山石敢当，“一石安则全家安”的信崇意识已深入人心。为祈福平安，来泰山观光的游客回家时也不忘请一尊泰山石敢当。

玉石自古就有入药的先例，对于治疗疾病和保身健体具有极好的作用。佩戴泰山玉，不仅美观，而且有益于健康。无论是从自然气场角度还是科学医疗角度，都不能忽视其对人体保健的作用。据科学验证得知，泰山玉中含有许多人体所需的微量元素。经常佩戴和使用泰山玉，能使这些有益的元素透过皮肤进入人体，从而平衡人体阴阳气血的失调情况，有益于促进人的身体健康。这些微量元素不但能维持人体的正常生理需求，它们在人体中含量的多少也会影响人的智力发育等。此外，泰山玉石具有一定的磁场效应，有助于加快血液循环和提升新陈代谢，提高人的免疫力。由泰山玉石制成的容器，有润心肺、助生喉、健脑提神以及延年益寿等诸多功效。

由于泰山玉矿物颗粒细小，分布均匀，结构致密，比较适合打磨抛光，且易于钻、锯、切磨、雕琢等，是制作较好的观赏石、雕刻工艺品或饰品的玉质矿物原料。泰山玉石色泽凝重、典雅，与泰山石敢当的阳刚之气一脉相承，故泰山玉不仅具有极高的艺术价值，还具有较为深厚的精神文化内涵。

泰山玉深厚的文化底蕴，使泰山玉石雕刻业长盛不衰。泰山玉石雕刻技艺很好地继承了中国传统玉雕的技法和特点，吸收百家之长，同时又大胆创新，站在弘扬泰山文化的高度，将泰山的文化、风俗、风景融入其中，成为一部玉雕版的“泰山百科全书”。近年来，随着泰山玉石的保护与开发，泰山玉石雕刻而成的作品得到了社会各界的广泛认可，泰山玉精品已经成为现代玉雕工艺高水平的代表之一，获得了广阔的市场，不仅在泰安占得了一席之地，并成功销往全国各大城市。与此同时，它也将泰山博大精深的文化传播到了四面八方。

从新石器时代起，泰山玉就广受华夏儿女的喜爱。泰山墨玉质地细腻，色黑而晶莹，气质儒雅，温和内敛，被认为是君子的象征与贤士的代表。泰山与儒家有着极大的渊源，使泰山玉同时又拥有儒家气息。用泰山玉石制成的孔子像频繁地出现在我国领导人与各国友人往来的礼品中，北京天安门广场的许多建筑也特意选用泰山石做基石。我国驻美大使馆新馆奠基，其奠基玉石来自泰山。北京奥林匹克森林公园主山上，一块高5.7米、重达63吨的泰山景观玉石矗立在主峰上，这块巨石成为奥林匹克森林公园标志性景观之一，并被命名为“天境”，就是取“稳如泰山，安如泰山”之寓意。

随着人们的普遍重视，泰山玉的价值也逐渐展现出来。2010年4月10日，上海世博会特许商品“泰山玉·世博徽宝”“泰山玉·中国馆”在北京和上海两地同步首发。“泰山玉·世博徽宝”“泰山玉·中国馆”凝聚了浓厚的中国元素，表达了中国文化的精神气质与神韵，极具观赏与收藏价值，也掀起了泰山玉的收藏热潮。

泰山玉石宁折不弯、坚贞不屈的高尚情操，激励着中华儿女为民族大业奋斗不息。人们对泰山怀着无限敬仰，并且歌颂泰山石，借泰山石寄托自己美好的希冀与愿望。

泰山祭祀习俗

2016年，泰安市的“泰山祭祀习俗”被山东省人民政府列入第四批省级非物质文化遗产代表性项目名录。

泰山自古就享有盛誉，被人们称为“神山”“圣山”。“泰山祭祀习俗”从人对大自然的敬畏、祈求、景仰、朝拜、融合出发，以柴望、封禅、朝山进香为形式，融政治与信仰于一体。它对于中华民族精神的形成与发展有着深远的影响，是泰安市最重要的非物质文化遗产之一。

在中国的早期典籍《尚书》中，便有关于泰山祭祀的记述。如《尚书·舜典》说：“岁二月，东巡狩，至于岱宗，柴。望秩于山川。”所谓“柴”，指的是燔柴祭天；所谓“望”，则是指望祭山川。舜的岱宗“柴望”以及古籍中的相关记载表明，泰山不仅在东夷文化发展中占有重要地位，而且对东夷各部落的形成也产生过重要影响。泰山不仅是先民们崇拜的对象，已经成为一种文化象征。

远古时期的泰山祭祀，是先民对大自然的敬畏、崇拜和祈求。他们在天地之间寻找适合自己生存的空间及生活方式，并利用自然条件谋求发展。大汶口文化的形成为泰山崇拜和祭祀创造了物质条件。在先民的心目中，他们既可以借助大山躲避洪水灾难，又可以从大山中获得所需要的生活、生产资源。人们敬畏大山、崇拜大山，并需要凭借一定的形式来加强对大自然的认知，从而表达对大自然的敬畏与崇拜。原始的祭祀也由此产生。先秦至唐宋时期的泰山祭祀，是昭示帝王受命于天、取得显赫业绩的政治大典。

泰山封禅的具体仪式富有象征性，班固曾对此有所解释："故升封者，增高也；下禅梁父之基，广厚也；刻石记号者，著己之功绩以自效也。天以高为尊，地以厚为德，故增泰山之高以报天，附梁父之址以报地，明天地之所命，功成事遂，有益于天地，若高者加高，厚者加厚矣。"封禅还包含更为深层的意思：协调人神之间的关系，最终实现精神意志与外在行为的和谐统一。夏、商、周以来，泰山逐渐被视为权力的象征，祭祀泰山之权也为帝王所独有。这种象征政权的祭祀，在战国时期形成封禅之说。此后，泰山也成为皇权的象征，也就是说，泰山封禅昭示的是君权神授的正统性、合理性。秦始皇于二十八年（前219年）巡行东方，先到峄山行祭礼，刻石颂秦功业。同时召集齐、鲁两地的儒生稽考封禅礼仪，众儒生各持己见。秦始皇就自行修订礼制，整修山道，从泰山的阳面登山，在泰山山顶行登封礼，并立石颂德。此后，共有12位帝王来泰山封禅与祭祀。

明清及至近代，泰山封禅祭祀由祭天地演变为祭泰山神——东岳大帝和碧霞元君，泰山祭祀习俗逐步从宫廷走向民间，逐渐走向世俗化、普遍化、多元化。明清之际，带有强烈政治色彩的封禅大典发生了重大变化，明太祖主张不再进行"封禅"，而只是举办祭祀活动。此后，帝王的泰山祭祀变得世俗化，世俗的祭祀逐渐转向宗教化。

泰山祭祀习俗与泰山信仰诉求从北方传播到南方，从汉族地区传播到少数民族地区，从国内传到国外。泰山祭祀在唐代就已漂洋过海传到国外，至今日本、韩国、马来西亚、菲律宾、印度和海外华裔居住的地方都有泰山神、碧霞元君和泰山石敢当信俗，可见其影响深远。

在泰山封禅与祭祀习俗传承发展的过程中，非物质形态与物质形态相互结合，民间传说、表演、庙会及戏曲等，与泰山上的秦石、汉柏、唐摩崖、双束碑、碧霞祠、岱庙、泰山三宝等文物古建筑、祭器共存，相互印证，积淀成博大精深的泰山文化。大型实景山水演出《中华封禅大典》自2010年公演以来，受到人们的欢迎；泰山东岳庙会也已形成定制，影响力不断扩大；仿宋封禅表演常年在岱庙演出，深受海内外游客的欢迎与喜爱。

成山祭日

2016年，荣成市的“成山祭日”被山东省人民政府列入第四批省级非物质文化遗产代表性项目名录。

成山祭日，是指荣成市成山头区域的人们因对太阳的尊崇而形成的祭祀活动，它是当地人们对上古的“八主”（天、地、兵、阴、阳、月、日、四时）尊崇所形成的祭祀文化的传承与延续。

成山头，古称“朝舞”，意为“朝日而舞”，是中国最早看到海上日出的地方。这里一面接陆，三面环海，群峰苍翠，峭壁巍然，气势恢宏万千，是不可多得的旅游胜地。这种独特的地理环境孕育出了独特的神话崇拜。

成山是中国祭日文化的重要发祥地，对太阳的祭祀活动，表达了成山人民对日神的虔诚信仰和对生活的美好祈愿。这种祭祀仪式由来已久，已经延续两千余年。其起源最早可追溯到战国时期。那时，百家争鸣，各个流派争相探讨宇宙、世界的起源问题。在这样的文化背景下，齐国（成山古属齐国）的思想家借着当地早已存在的自然崇拜信仰，将当地的自然信仰排列组合，归类出“天”“地”“兵”“阴”“阳”“月”“日”“四时”八种神的信仰模式。这八种神各有各的祭祀地点与形式，其中，第七位便是“日神”，亦称“日主”，它的祭祀地点，就是如今的成山头。《史记》记载：“成山斗入海，最居齐东北隅，以迎日出云。”意思是说，成山头陡立在海边，在古齐国的东北端，因为是最先迎接海上日出之地而闻名。

到了秦汉时期，此地的日神祭祀依然十分兴盛。1979年和1982年在成山头始皇庙前曾先后出土过两批玉器。据研究考证，第一批玉器为汉武帝在此地祭祀日神所埋献的；第二批则是更早的秦始皇来此祭日所埋献。埋献玉圭、玉璧的做法均为秦汉时期举行国家祭日的最高礼仪。

根据史料记载，秦始皇曾四次东巡，两次行至成山。第一次到成山的目的有二。其一，齐国是战国七雄之一，最后被灭，秦始皇初并天下，对齐国存有戒心，故效仿尧、舜巡访民间，“以示强威，服海内”，宣示自己“功过三皇，德高五帝”。为炫耀秦朝的强盛和皇帝的尊严，秦始皇以六百黄门郎中、六千虎贲军、六万精锐秦兵作护卫，以此震慑齐国的残存势力。其二，祭祀日主。成山头是秦国的东方极地，当时被称为“秦东门”。信奉天命的秦始皇在泰山封禅祭天拜地后，又巡至成山头，祭拜日主。此次巡视，留下了“秦桥遗迹”“秦代立石”“射鲛台”以及秦丞相李斯手书的“天尽头秦东门”石标等历史遗迹。所谓“石标”即“石表”，是封疆定界的“国界碑”，民间称“法碑石”。公元前210年，秦始皇在丞相李斯和少子胡亥的陪同下再次出巡，“自琅琊至荣成山”。这次出巡的目的是要到海上仙山寻采长生不老之药，以益身延寿。根据《史记·秦始皇记》的记载，齐国人徐福等人上书给秦始皇，称海中有三神山，名曰蓬莱、方丈、瀛洲，是仙人居住的地方，仙山上有长生不老之药。徐福还欺骗秦始皇，说：仙药采到了，可周围有大量鲛人巡守，带去的人被鲛人咬伤，只有射杀鲛人才能得到仙药。秦始皇误信了他的话，便开始第二次东巡。秦始皇东巡成山时，在成山头西侧建了一座行宫，名曰“始皇宫”，后来因年久失修而坍塌，后人在始皇宫的遗址上建了一座庙，此庙是我国现存的唯一一座“始皇庙”。

西汉时，汉武帝也曾登临成山。其中一次，汉武帝率领文武百官从长安出发，途经泰山，一路东巡，直至成山头，被“成山头日出”的宏伟景观震撼。于是大祭日神，并作“日主祠”，以感日神恩泽。现今，成山头还存留着武帝拜日的拜日台，海岸边有汉武帝率群臣拜日的塑像。

到了宋、元、明、清时期，对太阳的崇拜虽然有所衰落，但从长安城所建的天坛、日坛、地坛、月坛看，拜日作为一种文化习俗在多个地方被保留下来。尤其是成山的太阳祭祀活动，在民间得以传承弘扬并延续至今。只是由最初的国家大祭，演变为民间祭祀，但仍设祭坛，制定严格的日程、仪式方案和祭品等。

再后来，成山祭日这一民俗产生了民俗传承人，起初是家族传承，后来则出现师徒传承。据现存史料记载，最初代表性的传承人是清代初期的田万顷。经过几代的传承，如今的代表传承人是年逾古稀的第七代传承人——田文沪。田文沪出生于成山渔家，祖祖辈辈以捕鱼为业，与村中同龄人一样，他从小就跟着祖辈参加成山的祭日活动。他对成山祭日这一历史民俗文化有着深刻感受，又因其注重研究、保护与传承这一民俗，2014年，他被批准为市级非物质文化遗产代表性传承人。

随着现代社会经济的发展，祭日、祭海等祈福、祈愿行为逐步融合。无论是古代帝王的国家祭祀，还是如今的民间祭祀，都有明确的仪式步骤。首先要设立祭坛，在供桌上摆上太牢（牛、羊、豕三牲全备谓之太牢）、少牢（只有羊、豕，没有牛，称少牢）、生鲜果品等；其次，要确定详细的仪式方案，由德高望重的长者主持，行礼，拜日，宣读拜日颂词；再次，进行歌舞表演，以示歌舞升平、国泰民安；最后，是祭日欢度，家家户户杀猪宰羊庆贺节日、祈佑福祉。

成山祭日，作为一种历史悠久的民俗文化，体现了中华儿女崇尚美好、奋进向上的理想追求；是维系区域团结、促进社会和谐的重要媒介。保护、传承与弘扬这一民俗，将会对传统文化的传承与发展产生不可忽视的重要影响。

中元节习俗

2016年，莱芜市莱城区（今济南市莱芜区）的“中元节习俗”被山东省人民政府列入第四批省级非物质文化遗产代表性项目名录。

每年农历七月十五，莱芜地区的人们会欢度当地的传统节日——中元节。中元节俗称“七月十五”“孝子节”“团圆节”“鬼节”“过半年”“祭祖”“瓜节”等。中元节习俗的代表性村落为张公清村。明洪武三年（1370年），张氏由河北枣强县迁此建村，因耿公清村东有铁矿坑，邻村都以“矿坑”名村，张姓也将村名改为张矿坑，后演变成张公清。村内现存明洪武年间修建的“张氏家祠”。

莱芜地区的中元节习俗起源于清代乾隆年间，迄今已有二百七十多年的历史。据《莱芜县志》记载：清高宗乾隆十三年（1748年），民间暴发瘟疫，无数乡民死亡。张公清村张丙毅在山西洪洞任城隍，为救故乡乡民，他受莱芜仙人安期生指点，用祭祀祖先的方式驱赶瘟神。后来，这种祖先祭祀逐渐演变成一种区域性的地方习俗。清嘉庆年间，习俗活动得以发展，张公清村张氏家族在家祠设家堂，摆瓜果酒肴供奉祖先，形成了祭祀规模。到了同治年间，李筌因氏族间“中元节”祭祀活动变革，决定在家中举办家庭祭祀祖先活动。他把家人组织起来，在正房内摆好供桌，挂上请人绘制的家堂轴子，亲自到村外焚香请祖先回家接受香火。自此，中元节家庭祭祀活动传承发展起来，李筌也就成了现今的中元节祭祀习俗的第一代传承人。

第二代传承人李海安继承和发扬了习俗活动的家庭祭祀，肩负起了祭祀祖先、教育后代的责任。此时的家庭祭祀活动已趋于完善，供奉祖先的仪式越来越讲究，酒菜面食不断翻新。第三代传承人李自修处在时局动荡的年代，虽中元节习俗祭祀仪式时简时繁，但从无中断。第四代传承人李洪俊肩负起了传承习俗、教育子孙的重任，在战乱时期，他以简朴的瓜祭形式来祭祀祖先，将祖先的感人故事讲述给后代，目的是让子孙懂得感恩祖辈。到如今，已是第五代传承人李乃东，他着手研究习俗的历史渊源、孝德文化的传承发展及节俗意义，整理出了10余万字的习俗资料。

如今，莱城的中元节习俗还传承着“请家堂”“祭祀”“送家堂”的仪式步骤。

“请家堂”说的是农历七月十五的早晨，当地人会打扫庭院，摆设供桌，在墙上挂上家堂轴，在供桌下放一个脸盆，用来装祭奠用的茶酒和烧纸。男主人为主祭人，负责写祖先牌位，布置祭祀工具和用品。祖先牌位分彩、素两种。将一张黄表纸叠成长方形，上端折成三角形，把上三辈的先人名讳、夫人姓氏，按照左男右女的次序分别写在上面，成为“祖先牌位”。安放牌位要主次分明，中间为“高祖”，“曾祖”“先考”由中往两边分，也可自左往右从大到小依次排列。女主人带领女眷用金银纸叠制元宝锞子，以备祭祀用。特别需要注意的是，有身孕的妇女和刚刚生育的妇女不能参加祭祀活动。

上午10时，摆好牌位、茶、碗、盅、筷，主祭人携子焚香，提着酒壶到村外大道上迎请祖先。请祖先一般选在村头大路边，堆土成香炉，倒满一盅酒，面朝路前，捧香作揖，祈祷道：“列祖列宗，各位老人请跟我回家坐席吧！”将一炷香插在土堆香炉中，把酒浇在地上，跪在地上磕三个头。然后带着其他香（俗称“信香”）回家。到家门口，先将手中一炷香插于大门边框左边，用木棒（棍）拦在门口，俗称“拦门棍”。拦门棍说法有二：一是祖先进门后，防外鬼进入；二是祖先已进家，非本族人不得进入。家族以外的人如有要事进门，必须到家堂桌前磕头。院内各房门也插香，用木棍拦在门口。插完家仙、灶王供桌，最后三炷香插在家堂桌的香炉内。全家人要在家堂桌前磕头，男在前、女在后，表示欢迎祖先回家赴席。请家堂仪式完成，接下来便是祭祀活动。

“祭祀”指的是主祭人按照传统的祭祀方式祭祀到家的祖先的行为。首先，摆放茶点。将点心摆放在碟中，主要有糕果、饼干、口苏、蜜食等。将供桌牌位前的茶碗倒满茶，按供奉祖先辈分的大小献茶。习俗讲究茶要七分满，酒要八分满。要摆放新鲜水果，水果以西瓜为主，将西瓜切成莲花瓣状一分为二，瓜形似莲花座，象征吉祥如意、家庭团圆、日子红火；再摆上苹果、香蕉、葡萄，忌用桃、梨。桃有辟邪的功能，供桃祖先可能不敢落座；“梨”与“离”同音，供梨是怕祖先与后人生分。

再摆供菜。菜数为单，三、五、七、九不等，必不可少的主菜有鸡、鲤鱼、肉丸子、豆腐、芹菜等。肉菜上边放一点菠菜，俗称“菜财头”。七月十五的家堂与春节家堂不同之处在于不上三牲——生鸡、生鱼和生肉。菜要从中间往两边摆，因中间是高祖（从左到右的除外）。忌用狗肉，民俗有“狗肉不上席”一说。韭菜、大葱、洋葱等有异味的菜蔬亦忌用。供白菜要用红纸包，或者放点胡萝卜，寓意红红火火。摆放好供菜，再将酒盅倒上酒，主祭人高兴地为子女一一讲解牌位上的祖先，尤其是有过骄人功绩、为家乡做过贡献，在乡民中有良好口碑或勤劳耕读的先辈的事迹，以此鼓励子孙。全家人聚在一起畅所欲言。午饭时，要在供桌上摆放馒头，还要敬酒、敬茶。敬酒、敬茶时，主祭人要虔诚地说：“请老人家吃饱喝足！”然后，一家人在家堂桌前共进午餐。

下午5时左右，准备“送家堂”。主祭人亲自或吩咐儿子打纸（用木制钱模具打印花钱，俗称“纸窝子”）、花纸（将打好花钱的烧纸划开，按刀叠好备用）；女主人煮好肉馅水饺（春节用素馅），用茶碗装盛，一个牌位前放一碗，每碗放两个水饺。“送家堂”时，要将牌位前摆放的酒、茶、水饺一一浇奠（倒在桌下的盆中，意为向先人敬酒、敬茶），把牌位由“高祖”到“先考”按顺序收起，放在簸箕或传盘中，带上烧纸、酒、茶、水饺汤、鞭炮，主祭人在前，手里拿着从香炉中取的香，全家老少一起到村外的大道上送家堂。出门时要将拦门棍拿开，传说不拿开挡门的木棍，祖先出不去。

“送家堂”也会选村外的大道边，先用沙土堆一个香炉，把手中的燃香插在上面，将高祖牌位放在前面，按大小依次排成一条线，每刀烧纸上放一个牌位，用一炷香压住，将烧纸、牌位画半个圆圈，俗称“圈钱”。点燃烧纸，烧完后用酒、茶、水饺汤从半圆圈口浇过去，主祭人面朝路前方，虔诚地说：“请老人家一路走好！”全家人磕头，再燃放鞭炮，“送家堂”祭祀礼结束。

农历七月十五这天，莱芜人从四面八方回到老家，举办传统的“请家堂”仪式，全家老幼欢聚一堂。中元节习俗在两百余年的流传中，虽经战火离乱，也未曾断绝。中元节习俗的传承与发展，极具敬祖爱老的教育意义，也有助于形成和谐共处的良好道德风尚。

珠算文化（蒙阴）

2016年，蒙阴县的“珠算文化”被山东省人民政府列入第四批省级非物质文化遗产代表性项目名录。

蒙阴县隶属山东省临沂市，是珠算首创者刘洪的故乡。经考证，刘洪是东汉光武帝刘秀的侄子鲁王刘兴的六世孙，他天性喜爱悠闲宁静的生活，厌恶钩心斗角、玩弄权术。为了避世，他来到了鲁王领地的泰山郡龙眼官庄隐居，龙眼官庄就是今天蒙阴县蒙阴街道召子官庄村，刘洪故居的遗址就在蒙阴县蒙阴街道石子官庄村西200米处。

珠算是用算盘作为工具进行运算的一种运算方法，《数术记遗》记载：“珠算，控带四时，经纬三才。刻板为三分，其上下二分以停游珠，中间一分以定算位，位各五珠，上一珠与下四珠色别，其上别色之珠当五，其下四珠，珠各当一。”珠算的发明，使人们的计算能力得到了极大的飞跃，珠算也成为中国四大发明之外的第五大发明。

“珠算”最早见于东汉徐岳所著《数术记遗》一书，徐岳在书中说：“刘会稽，博学多闻，偏于数学……隶首注术，仍有多种，其一珠算。”文中所说的刘会稽就是刘洪，经过学者多方论证，刘洪就是珠算的首创者。

190年，刘洪发明算盘，创造出珠算这种计算方法，随后传给徐岳和郑玄；从196年开始，刘洪广收门徒，传授历算技艺，将珠算的技艺和天文著作《乾象历》一同传授给杨伟、韩翊等人，又由其弟子代代相传，通过这样的方式传承至后世。除了计算方法，刘洪发明的计算工具算盘对推动计算方法的进步做出了很大贡献。刘洪发明的算盘综合继承了筹算五升十进、集散式计算方法和位置制的优点，又克服了筹算纵横计数与置筹不便的缺点，是电子计算机出现之前非常先进的计算工具。

蒙阴作为珠算创造者刘洪的故乡，从古至今一直有着非常浓厚的珠算文化氛围，当地老百姓对珠算颇为了解，并引以为豪。

1994年，由山东电影电视剧制作中心拍摄的8集电视连续剧《算圣》在北京举行了首映式，这部电视剧是第一部描写刘洪发明算盘历程的文艺作品。不久，这部电视剧就在中央电视台播出，并连播3次，引起了很大反响，蒙阴的珠算通过电视剧这种大众传媒的传播，走进了老百姓的视野。2010年4月，中国民间文艺家协会派出专家组深入蒙阴县进行考察，他们对蒙阴县“算圣文化”的保护与开发给予了很高的评价，不久即正式命名蒙阴县为全国唯一的“中国算圣文化之乡”。2010年5月，世界博览会在上海隆重举办，每个参展地区都展出了本地区最具有代表性的文化，其中的山东厅一共布展了四个展柜，第三个展柜就展示了刘洪发明的珠算法和算盘。2013年12月4日，联合国教科文组织保护非物质文化遗产政府间委员会第八次会议在阿塞拜疆的巴库举行，会上通过决议，正式将中国珠算项目列入人类非物质文化遗产代表作名录，并特意介绍说：“珠算是中国古代的重大发明，伴随中国人经历了一千八百多年的漫长岁月。它以简便的计算工具和独特的数理内涵，被誉为‘世界上最古老的计算机’。”

珠算文化所蕴含的科学方法和程式化、机械化的思维方式，也推动了车舟制造、桥梁建筑、航海等的创造与发明，对商业、军事产生了深远影响。珠算的诸多元素作为象征符号还常常出现在语言、文学、建筑、绘画、雕刻等领域，对人们生活的方方面面都产生了重要影响。2007年，英国《独立报》、印度《印度时报》对改变世界的发明创造进行排名，都把中国珠算排在了第一位。

现在越来越多的人愿意了解并学习珠算文化，更有许多家长鼓励自己孩子从小学习珠算，以此提高孩子的反应能力、记忆力、反应速度，珠算与人们的日常生活越来越近，珠算文化也被越来越多的人熟知。

胶东花饽饽习俗（栖霞）

2016年，栖霞市的“胶东花饽饽习俗”被山东省人民政府列入第四批省级非物质文化遗产扩展名录。

栖霞市隶属山东省烟台市，位于山东省东北部。栖霞花饽饽是当地农家妇女根据地域文化特点，结合节日和生活习俗而创造的一种传统民间艺术。

栖霞花饽饽早在汉代就已经有了雏形，但是当时的花饽饽只将面团制成了一定的形象。宋代吴自牧《梦粱录》中曾记载，花饽饽用在春节、中秋节、端午节以及结婚祝寿等喜庆日子。到了明代，花饽饽技艺不断提高，这时的栖霞花饽饽多用于春节、元宵节、清明节、中秋节、小年等节日。后来，延伸至婚丧嫁娶等事项；再后来，为表现仪式的隆重，这种代表着美好祝福的花饽饽便越来越多地出现在普通百姓的神龛前、供桌上。到了近代，受牟氏望族的影响，栖霞花饽饽的内容和形式在传统面塑的基础上，将古今百姓生活的点滴趣味融入其中，推陈出新，表现手段和表现技巧日臻成熟完善。经过几千年的传承与经营，栖霞花饽饽习俗已深入人们的日常生活，形成了自己独有的特色。

栖霞人以面粉为加工对象，用刀、剪、笔、刷子、竹条以及一些自己顺手、习惯使用的自制工具制作花饽饽。主要分为两类：一类是熟制花饽饽，主要有“和面—发面—揉面—捏型—雕刻—锅蒸—上色”等工序；一类是生制花饽饽，主要经过“和面—揉面—捏型（兑色）—黏合—风干”等工序。

在不同的节日里，栖霞人会制作不同的花饽饽，题材丰富，表现形式多种多样。这些花饽饽有不同的造型、色彩，寄托着人们祈求幸福生活的美好愿望，蕴含着人们朴素的审美观和传统的图腾信仰。

春节是我国的传统佳节，每逢这个时候，人们会做一种叫作“圣虫”的花饽饽。“圣虫”是春节期间人们用来供奉的花饽饽。其形状像龙，通体有刺，龙嘴里含一枚铜钱，寓意招财进宝。大多数人将“圣虫”放入盛面的缸里，寓意来年有吃不完的粮食。此外，以龙威镇住各类害虫，不使主人家的粮食遭受损失。

到了正月十五，栖霞家家户户开始制作各种各样的豆面灯。豆面灯是以水、花生油和豆面按照一定的比例混合揉匀后捏制而成，其形状为8~10厘米高的圆柱形，上面是一个大小合适的“小碗”。栖霞人对豆面灯颇为讲究，十二个月要捏制十二个豆面灯，一月的豆面灯小碗上只有一个折，二月豆面灯小碗上有两个折，依次类推。正月十五这天晚上，在十二个豆面灯的灯碗内都放上棉花芯，倒上花生油点着，哪个月的豆面灯亮的时间长，就说明当年哪个月的生活顺顺当当、红红火火；还有的是看流下的灯油形成的模样像什么庄稼，预示来年什么庄稼能够丰收。除了十二月灯，人们还会做“看场佬”灯，点燃灯芯后男主人持灯照照家里院落四处，意为看家护院保平安。点完的豆面灯不能扔掉，第二天还可以切片烹饪食用，口味独特。人们在自己欢度节日的同时，也不忘逝去的亲人，通常会做圆形的或是柱形的豆面灯，将其点燃，用来为逝去的人照亮前行的路。

到了清明节，家家户户都要给孩子专门做一种叫“饽饽鸡”的花饽饽，家境好的人家还要给孩子煮上几个鸡蛋。事实上“饽饽鸡”的形状更像燕子，早时叫“饽饽燕”，只是在长期的传承过程中被人们叫成了“饽饽鸡”，也有称其为“疙瘩燕”的，寓意是孩子们吃了“饽饽鸡”，就会身体健康。

“七月七”吃巧果也是栖霞的传统民俗。巧果是花饽饽的一种，最常见的是鱼形，亦有荷包、福禄寿喜、长命富贵、各种小动物、石榴、莲花、莲蓬等图案。这些造型各异的巧果大都是用模子刻出来的。做巧果时，将面团放入模子中压制好后，再放入锅中烙制，造型各异的巧果就做好了。然后用线串起来，找一根玉米秸作把手。孩子们手提一串巧果，聚到一起互相炫耀，看谁的花样多、数量多。七月七是乞巧节，在这一天吃巧果，预示着孩子们会心灵手巧。

除了节日期间的这些花饽饽之外，还有结婚花饽饽，过满月、百岁花饽饽，上梁、贺寿花饽饽等。

结婚花饽饽工艺最为复杂，其大小一般超过铜盆（脸盆）口的直径，做好后都要放在铜盆上由新娘带到新郎家，因而也叫“铜盆饽饽”。它是在传统婚嫁风俗习惯中长久形成的具有代表性的地方文化。其形体大，直径50～60厘米，高40～50厘米，底座是莲花瓣，上面精塑十二生肖造型，有龙凤（龙凤呈祥）、葫芦、金鱼（金玉满堂）、鸳鸯（比翼双飞）。点缀的组件多达20个。花饽饽经过细加点缀，造型生动，形成强烈的艺术效果，寄托了亲人的祝福，增强了喜庆的气氛，丰富了民间婚俗的内容。这种精美的铜盆饽饽是由新娘家中送亲的客人在结婚当日带到新郎家。送亲队伍到了新郎的村子，新郎家中专门迎亲的两人就会迎上来接过铜盆饽饽，将它们拿回新郎家中，摆放在显眼的位置，给来贺喜的宾朋欣赏。做得好看的饽饽会受到宾朋们的一致赞许，新娘也会感到很有面子。因此，新娘的娘家人都会下大力气做一个精美的铜盆饽饽，手艺差的往往会找人帮忙。好看的铜盆饽饽，新郎的家人一般都不舍得马上食用，会摆上一段时间再吃。

过满月也颇为讲究。满月花饽饽的主要形式为“虎头”“佛手”“百岁儿”“牛蹄”等，表达大人们对孩子的真情祝福和热切期盼。百岁花饽饽是妇女生孩子满百天，由姥姥家送百岁花饽饽，主要形式为“长穗（岁）”“糖包”“糖帽”“挂花”“虎头”等，寓意老人盼望外孙健康成长。

上梁花饽饽。盖新房上大梁，是农村比较重大的活动之一。这天正午，新房的主人都要举行“上梁大吉”仪式，女主人会做一些小巧精致的花饽饽，主要有“龙凤呈祥”“狮子把门”“宝葫芦”等形式，寓意蟠龙抬头，凤落宝地，家业兴旺。在举行仪式的时候，由木匠和瓦匠将花饽饽用“斗”盛着，嘴里念叨顺口溜表示祝福，在屋顶扬给前来看热闹的观众。观众会在下面争抢，抢到花饽饽的人会沾到房主的福气。

贺寿花饽饽是晚辈在家中长辈年至花甲之时，为祝寿庆贺而做的大寿桃，以祝愿长辈健康长寿，表达对长辈的孝敬之心。

还有一种日常花饽饽。这是最为常见的花饽饽，不论什么节日都可以做。这种花饽饽呈半圆形，有的还要在上面捏出一个凸起。制作时，先做成普通的饽饽，放在一边，然后再进行装饰，根据个人的喜好，制作梅、兰、竹、菊，花、鸟等饰物，将它们粘贴在上面。据老艺人讲，装饰的面不能发酵，要用生（凉）面才行。这样，蒸熟后饽饽才不会变形。饽饽蒸好等凉了以后，再用毛笔根据需要上色，颜色以粉红、黄、绿为主。

栖霞花饽饽继承了先人钟爱花鸟鱼虫的传统，同时，还将古今百姓生活的点滴趣味融入其中，使其更具生动性、趣味化，观其形便可了解栖霞风情。千百年来，栖霞花饽饽渐渐地融入了百姓的日常生活，以其浓郁的乡土气息，在民间艺苑中熠熠生辉。

胶东花饽饽习俗（莱州）

2016年，莱州市的“胶东花饽饽习俗”被山东省人民政府列入第四批省级非物质文化遗产扩展名录。

花饽饽习俗真正始自何时已不可考，但从新疆吐鲁番阿斯塔那唐墓出土的面制人俑和小猪来推断，距今至少已有一千三百多年。《东京梦华录》中对捏面人有过记载：“以油面糖蜜造如笑靥儿。”那时的面人都是能吃的，谓之“果食”。关于捏面人，民间还有一个传说。相传三国时期诸葛亮征伐南蛮，在渡芦江时忽狂风大作，机智的诸葛亮便命随从用面料制成人头与牲畜的模样，以此来祭拜江神。说也奇怪，江面果真平静下来，队伍安然渡江并顺利平定南蛮。从此以后，凡是从事花饽饽制作的人都供奉诸葛亮为祖师爷。

莱州花饽饽起源于乡俗节日祭祀所需的面食供品。花饽饽可分为沿海渔村花饽饽和平原山区花饽饽两类。沿海渔村多制作一些带有鱼精、虾精、蛤蜊精形象的花饽饽，即用面做一个古装男女，背后或脚下附一鱼或蛤蜊的花饽饽；平原山区的花饽饽多做一些圣虫、寿桃、戏剧人物等形象。

莱州花饽饽是用小麦面粉制成的，造型除小型人物之外，还有各种动物及花卉，花样很多。明清时期，这种花饽饽多用于春节、元宵节、清明节、中秋节等节日；后来，延伸至婚丧嫁娶等事；再后来，这种代表美好祝福的花饽饽便越来越多地出现在各家各户的神龛前、供桌上，表示仪式的隆重。据《莱州市志》记载，莱州花饽饽已有六百多年的历史，曾是当地的四大贡品之一。明朝初期，掖县（即现在的莱州）就有花饽饽作坊，从事专业生产。后经历代花饽饽艺人的探索和创新，莱州花饽饽的品种不断增加，技艺得到显著提高。

于是，莱州花饽饽就成为人们在节日里活跃气氛、展现自家手艺的民间艺术品。每逢春节，当地多数乡镇都会举办花饽饽展，上千人参与这一比赛，还出现了花饽饽专业户。1986年，烟台艺术节展出莱州花饽饽140多件；朱桥镇张村杨克太1987年做的圣虫花饽饽，参加了在上海举办的中国文化部（现改名为中国文化和旅游部）主办的“中国民间一绝”展；1988年，10多件莱州花饽饽被山东省美术馆收藏，有朱由沈占民的《双狮》、西北隅刘夕蕴的《福首喜鹊》等。

莱州花饽饽，同全国其他各地的花饽饽都是中国特有的民间艺术品，但莱州花饽饽又因其独有的特征，有别于其他品种。

一是莱州花饽饽历经完善，逐步形成了造型圆浑、敦厚、生动、流畅而张扬的艺术风格。

二是莱州花饽饽体裁多取自动物、花、鸟、鱼、虫、传统神话中的人物及情节，最具代表性的为“年年有余”“鸳鸯”等。

三是莱州花饽饽为家庭作坊生产，因每家的兴趣、爱好角度有所差异，形成了不同的制作风格，使得莱州花饽饽的种类丰富多彩。

四是当地原料充盈、做法简单，出货快。“家家有巧工，户户出精品。”

五是主要传承方式为父传子、师收徒。

六是易操作、原料普遍、价格低、销路广。

花饽饽的制作。通常是先在精面粉中加入适量的白糖，再和好面团，然后经过揉、搓、选、捻，塑出基本形态，再用简单的工具进行提、点、剪，使其特点突出，气韵生动，蒸熟后，涂上颜色。大一些的花饽饽在蒸的时候要把各部分单独蒸熟，涂上色再组合，安放在主体上的一些特别细腻精巧的人物、花、字，要用实面完成，其余部分用发面做成。具体制作步骤如下：

一是“和”。将莱州优质小麦粉、水、酵母按比例掺和在一起搅拌，使和出的面团均匀、筋道、光滑、软硬适宜，不粘手、不粘案板。

二是“揉”。即揉面，其目的就是要使各种原材料混合均匀，使面粉中的蛋白质充分吸收水分，形成有弹性的面筋网络，增加面团筋力，使面团光滑、柔润。

三是“搓”。将揉好的面团根据自己想做的模样搓出花饽饽的大体形状。

四是“捏”。即捏面人，在现有基础上用手进行细化，“文的胸、武的肚、老人的背脊、美女的腰”。

五是“剪”。使用刀、篦、针等工具，对花饽饽进行切、点等精细加工，使制成的花饽饽形象逼真，栩栩如生，造型饱满、生动。

六是“描”。塑造的形象可用油画颜料、国画色、水彩、水粉等颜料上色。为了使各种形象的花饽饽看起来颜色鲜亮，有时也会用荧光色上色，形成了莱州花饽饽色彩鲜艳、艳而不俗的特点。

跟剪纸一样，莱州的花饽饽讲究的是线条的柔美，多纤细轻盈。花饽饽上的鸟雀之羽，无论是描摹的或是刀剪的，都有风吹可动之感。加上莱州花饽饽口感清香甜软，色、香、味、形俱全，深受人们的欢迎。

莱州花饽饽的体裁内容来自人类生活的各个方面，是莱州人民在长期的劳动实践中创作出来的艺术精华；表达了他们对美的渴求；是经历代艺人创造出来的艺术之花；是中华民族传统习俗中的瑰宝。因此，我们应将其继承、发展下去，不断为其注入创新元素，永葆其活力。

胶东花饽饽习俗（牟平）

2016年，烟台市牟平区的“胶东花饽饽习俗”被山东省人民政府列入第四批省级非物质文化遗产代表性项目名录。

整个黄河流域都流传着制作面人的习俗，但各地称呼不同。牟平地区独具特色，俗称“大饽饽”“枣饽饽”“大桃”等。牟平花饽饽至今已有三百多年的历史，是胶东妇女根据牟平地域特色、节日和生活习俗而创造的一种艺术样式，具有鲜明的艺术特色和生活情趣。牟平花饽饽主要分布在牟平王格庄镇、姜格庄镇、龙泉镇等乡镇及周边地区。

每逢岁末，胶东妇女都要蒸制许多大枣馍馍，以备春节祭祖、上供和食用。馍馍形状是圆的，上面挑起七孔，孔里镶入红枣。据当地的老年人说，七孔代表人的眼、耳、口、鼻等。

花饽饽是胶东地区的特色。每年腊月二十三至腊月二十八，家家户户都要蒸馒头、做花饽饽。过年做花饽饽是老一辈人留下来的传统，寓意全家团圆、日子兴旺、年年有余。

聪明、勤劳的牟平农村妇女用面团做出自己喜爱的样式，有“团圆饽饽”“五福临门”“枣饽饽”和“圣虫”等。其中，“圣虫”是过年时存放在馒头缸里的，可保丰收；“枣饽饽”是用来供奉先人的，表达了民众一种向往富裕生活的愿望。花饽饽蒸熟以后显得更加浑厚，在表面点缀上花鸟，看起来色泽亮丽、立体饱满、栩栩如生，既好吃，又好看，又带有祝福，很受人们喜爱。这种家喻户晓的艺术性食品逐渐变成了一件件非常生动的艺术品，既可食用又可供观赏。

百姓们以面为加工对象，用刀、剪、笔等工具进行创作，所做花饽饽的花叶及各种动物等都要是双数，日子也要选双日，以求好事成双之意，具有鲜明的艺术特色。牟平各地流行“鸡随蛤蟆走，小孩活到九十九”，“奶奶送对鸡，姥姥还对鸭，小孩活到九十八”等俗语，反映了牟平人民对幸福生活的美好向往。

花饽饽按其使用功能可分为两类：一类是专用于收藏的花饽饽，通常用精面粉、盐、防腐剂及蜂蜜等制成，其制作流程为“和面—揉面—染色—做型—黏合—风干”；另一类是可以食用的花饽饽，主要用面粉制成，经过“和面—发面—揉面—做型—雕刻—锅蒸—上色”几个步骤制作而成。花饽饽面料有面粉发面、干面（粉）和凉水面三种。色彩处理上有单色点红与彩色点染描绘之分。在技法上，不同地域风格各异。

“小孩剪头（理发）”花饽饽

小孩来到世上，第一次理发比较隆重，一般选在双月的上半月理发，通常情况下是奶奶做一对鸡，姥姥做一对鸭，寓意“奶奶送对鸡，姥姥还对鸭，小孩活到九十八”。

“百岁”花饽饽

百岁花饽饽是为了庆祝小孩来到世上一百天，所做数量为九十九样，形式为鸡、鸭、苹果、凤凰、葫芦、蝙蝠、刺猬等。

“结婚”花饽饽

结婚花饽饽的要求高，做法更讲究。常做的类型有“富贵牡丹”“龙凤呈祥”“喜鹊登梅”“榴花似火”“宝玉葫芦”等，分别寓意喜上眉梢、多子多福、生活红红火火、招财进宝等。还有给新娘手中捧着的脸盆做的盆底花饽饽，一般是莲花底，上面是桃或者鱼。新娘箱子里的花饽饽则是4个大寿桃，一个箱子角上放一对鱼。

"做寿"花饽饽

给老人做寿的花饽饽上面不做花，一般是做4个寿桃，寓意长命百岁，结结实实。

"乔迁"花饽饽

一般做8个大寿桃，蒸糕（糕的大小与锅一样大），还要做支锅饼，一般要做两个、六个或八个等，数量为双数。

"上梁"花饽饽

"上梁"花饽饽是盖新房上大梁时做的花饽饽，一般是8个大寿桃，还有猪头花饽饽等，寓意生活富裕，家业兴旺。

"过年"花饽饽

每年腊月二十三至腊月二十八这段时间，家家户户都开始蒸馒头、做大枣饽饽、"圣虫"花饽饽等。"圣虫"放在装馒头的缸里，可保当年丰收，不会断粮；枣饽饽用来供奉先人，表达民众对美好生活的向往。

过年花饽饽的种类有"团圆饽饽""圣虫""五福临门""连年有余""枣饽饽"等，寓意全家团圆、日子兴旺、年年有余。

"祭祀"花饽饽

"祭祀"花饽饽只做白色的大寿桃。如果家中另一位老人还健在的话就做5个大寿桃，如果两位老人都去世了就做10个大寿桃。

"六月六兔生日"花饽饽

农历六月六俗称兔生日，所做花饽饽类型为兔子。花饽饽做两种模样：一种是蹲兔，一种是卧兔，都是各做一对。

牟平花饽饽所使用的材料虽然很普通，以我们日常食用的面粉为主要原料配制而成，但质朴大方，可塑性强，有很好的表现力，具有深厚的历史价值、艺术价值和实用价值。